Learning Together

Learning Together

The Law, Politics, Economics, Pedagogy, and Neuroscience of Early Childhood Education

Michael J. Kaufman, Sherelyn R. Kaufman
& Elizabeth C. Nelson

ROWMAN & LITTLEFIELD
Lanham • Boulder • New York • London

Published by Rowman & Littlefield
A wholly owned subsidary of The Rowman & Littlefield Publishing Group, Inc.
4501 Forbes Boulevard, Suite 200, Lanham, Maryland 20706
www.rowman.com

Unit A, Whitacre Mews, 26-34 Stannary Street, London SEN 4AB

British Library Cataloguing in Publication Information Available

Library of Congress Cataloging-in-Publication Data

Kaufman, Michael J., 1958-
  Learning together : the law, policy, economics, pedagogy, and neuroscience of early childhood education / Michael J. Kaufman, Sherelyn R. Kaufman, and Elizabeth C. Nelson.
     pages cm
  Includes index.
  ISBN 978-1-4758-0643-4 (hardcover)—ISBN 978-1-4758-0644-1 (pbk.)—ISBN 978-1-4758-0645-8 (e-book)
  1. Early childhood education—United States. 2. Early childhood education—Government policy—United States. 3. Early childhood education—Law and legislation—United States. 4. Educational law and legislation—United States. I. Kaufman, Sherelyn R., 1957–II. Nelson, Elizabeth C. III. Title.
  LB1139.25.K38 2015
  372.21—dc23

                                        2015005394

♾™ The paper used in this publication meets the minimum requirements of American National Standard for Information Sciences—Permanence of Paper for Printed Library Materials, ANSI/NISO Z39.48-1992.

Printed in the United States of America

To the One Hundred

Contents

Preface

Early childhood education is the new frontier of law, politics, pedagogy, economics, and neuroscience. Scholars from across many disciplines have begun to demonstrate its significance, and policy makers from across the political spectrum have begun to appreciate its value.

Yet early childhood education still is not taken seriously. It is often relegated to the arena of "pre" school and analyzed as a public policy question separate and apart from "real" school. Similarly, path-breaking work in the developmental psychology of early learners is not always understood to be relevant to the learning process that takes place once school begins. Attempts to develop early childhood education programs for three- and four-year-olds are sometimes looked at as: "it's just pre-school."

As the world's best educators, scholars, and policy makers know, however, early childhood education is not "just pre-school." In this book, we take early childhood education seriously, very seriously. The social construction of law and policy governing early childhood education (and all education) requires a profound appreciation for the ways in which young children (and all human beings) learn. The manner in which a society chooses to educate its youngest learners reveals a great deal about how it chooses to treat all of its citizens.

We analyze early childhood education therefore not as an isolated, political, or pedagogical concern. Rather, we hope to demonstrate that early childhood education is central to any effort to improve the entire education system in America, and thereby to make the American regime more perfect.

Taking early education seriously requires a comprehensive, interdisciplinary approach. Our approach is comprehensive and interdisciplinary on several levels.

First, we bring together the research from the fields of law, economics, politics, pedagogy, and neuroscience. Second, we bring together insights from educators of children of all grade levels. Third, we recognize the connection between the healthy attachment and integration that takes place within the developing mind of a child and that child's subsequent well-being.

Fourth, we suggest specific strategies for achieving the proven educational, economic, and social benefits of early childhood education that include bringing advocates of different education reform initiatives together to support teaching and learning, bringing the public and private sector together to invest in effective programs, and bringing children from diverse racial and economic backgrounds together within those programs.

Finally, by integrating law, politics, economics, and neuroscience, we seek to present a compelling case that America should invest in early childhood programs that are designed to develop in children the capacity to construct knowledge socially and to build meaningful relationships.

The knowledge that we offer in this book is itself a social construction. We have learned a tremendous amount about early childhood education from the world's foremost educators, legal scholars, jurists, policy makers, economists, and neuroscientists. This book draws on the best practices and the best research performed by leading experts in diverse fields.

Specifically, we build the political argument for investing in early childhood programs from blueprints created by our greatest political philosophers, including Plato, Aristotle, de Tocqueville, Madison, and Jefferson. We construct the legal argument by putting together important work authored by our greatest Supreme Court justices and legal scholars. We develop the economic argument in the book by bringing the research of James Heckman together with the invaluable work of W. Steven Barnett and others at the National Institute for Early Education Research.

We also draw on the neuroscientific research presented by the National Academy of Science, the neurobiology of Dan Siegel, and the cognitive psychology of Daniel Kahneman. Finally, we bring together insights from the world's greatest educators and developmental psychologists, including Lev Vygotsky, John Dewey, Loris Malaguzzi, David Hawkins, and Howard Gardner.

We hope that by integrating and making visible the learning of our foremost thinkers in diverse fields, this book will provide a compelling provocation to educators, policy makers and, indeed, to any adult who has ever been a child. Our provocation is unassailable evidence that one of the most effective investments of resources that a society can make is to develop early childhood programs for all of its children, particularly those programs that are designed to construct in children the capacity to build meaningful relationships. We wonder how educators and policy makers might respond to that provocation.

Acknowledgments

We thank the foremost scholars and practitioners in the field of early childhood education who made invaluable comments and suggestions on prior drafts of this book—Joan Bradbury, Carolyn Edwards, Angela Fowler, Maureen Hager, David Kirp, Diana Rauner, Lella Gandini, Rachel Gubman, Dolores Kohl, and James Ryan.

We also thank the extraordinary educators who inspired this book, particularly Rose Alschuler, Norman Amaker, George Anastaplo, Nina S. Appel, Mary Bell, Cathy Fishbain Brown, Svetlana Budilovsky, James P. Carey, Margie Carter, Patricia F. Carini, Harry Clor, Maureen Condon, Richard Conviser, Margie Cooper, Barbara Cross, Deb Curtis, John Dewey, Meredith Dodd, Amelia Gambetti, Howard Gardner, Diane Geraghty, David Hawkins, Frances Hawkins, James Hayes, Alise Shafer Ivey, Brittny Lissner Johnson, Daniel Kahneman, Judy Kaminsky, Rebekah F. Kaufman, Alfie Kohn, Michelle Korte, Mary Korte, Jody Lapp, Richard Louv, Lisa Makoul, Loris Malaguzzi, Cindy McPherson, Pam Myers, Honi Papernik, Trish Parenti, Francis W. Parker, Ann Pelo, Neil Postman, Alan Raphael, Carlina Rinaldi, Peter Rutkoff, Daniel Siegel, William Shapiro, Ronald Sharp, Cathy Topal, Paul Tough, Vea Vecchi, Merrilee Waldron, Carleton Washburne, Lynn White, and Carolyn Wing.

For the wisdom and guidance with regard to education law and policy, we thank the U.S. Department of Education, Office for Civil Rights, directors and attorneys, especially Kenneth A. Mines and John Fry; elected school board members and public servants—Rebecca Baim, Joan Herczeg, Debbie Hymen, Michael Lipsitz, Jerrold Marks, and Terri Olian; school district administrators—Gregory M. Kurr and Michael Lubelfeld; and school lawyers—Nancy Krent, Mike Loizzi, Bob Kohn, Heather Brickman, John A. Relias, and James C. Franczek, Jr.

Our thanks also goes to the caring and dedicated colleagues we have encountered from early childhood education to law and graduate school: the Ravinia Nursery School staff, including Marilyn Straus, Rosalie Edelstein, Midge Hechtman, Ginger Scott, Ginger Uhlmann, and Roberta Wexler; the elementary school professionals and middle school educators who opened our eyes to what a "good" school could be; the "teachers' teachers" at National-Louis University and Baker Demonstration School in Evanston, Illinois, especially Paula Jorde Bloom, Marge Leon, Kathleen McKenna, Cynthia Mee, Alan Rossman, and Jane Stenson; the students, faculty, and administrators of Erikson Institute, particularly Stephanie Bynum and Rhonda Gillis, the wonderful teachers, board members, and families of Winnetka Public School Nursery, and the visionary early childhood education experts of Family Network and the Community Family Center, particularly Barbara Haley, William S. Kaufman, Ruth Stern, Herbert S. Wander, and Rosalie Weinfeld. Thank you to the extraordinary learning community of Francis W. Parker School, especially Tommy Grogan, Gretchen Kaluzny, Andy Kaplan, Mary Ann Manley, Javier Rivera, and the amazing junior and senior kindergarten teachers. And we extend our sincere gratitude to Linda McLaren at Northwestern University Settlement House Head Start and to Jean Wallace Baker at Highland Park Community Nursery School, for demonstrating what unfailing dedication to young children, their families, and communities looks like.

For their invaluable research, editorial assistance, and feedback on early drafts of the book, we are grateful to an outstanding group of Loyola University of Chicago law students and graduate fellows, including Adam Betzen, Traci Copple, Katherine A. Buchanan, Leah G. Feldhendler, Sarah B. Ferguson, Megan L. Ferkel, Sarah Giauque, Amy S. Hammerman, Anne M. Graber, Elizabeth H. Greer, Anuradha Gupta, Gretchen M. Harris, Meghan Helder, Alison L. Helin, Erin Hickey, Caroline Hosman, Joanne Krol, Nicole Williams Koviak, Alisha J. Massie, Beth Miller-Rosenberg, Shannon Reeves-Rich, Beatriz Rendon, Laura R. Rojas, Sarah Smith, Helaine N. Tiglias, Nicole Torrado, Christina L. Wascher, Pam Witmer, and John Wunderlich.

In addition, we thank the outstanding team at Rowman & Littlefield for the tremendous support and assistance throughout this project, particularly Thomas Koerner and Carlie Wall.

For their incredible support, patience, and talent, we thank Christine Heaton and Elaine Gist.

Finally, we thank Loyola University Chicago and Loyola University Chicago School of Law for providing financial and administrative support for this project.

Introduction

What is our image of the child?

Is the child passive, weak, vulnerable, easily overcome by destructive emotions, and in need of an authoritarian training system designed to punish undesirable behavior? Or is the child instead capable, curious, creative, caring, connected, and led naturally to develop meaningful relationships from which knowledge and well-being are constructed?[1] A nation's fundamental image of the child has important implications for the kind of early education system that it supports and for the kind of regime that it becomes.

This book makes a comprehensive, multi-disciplinary argument for investing in effective early childhood education programs, particularly those that develop in children their proven natural capacity to construct knowledge by building meaningful relationships.

The book brings together the persuasive authority of judicial precedent and legal analysis; the wisdom, coherence, and depth of political and educational philosophy; the foresight of the founders of the American regime; the observations, experiences, and profound understandings of educators; the prudence of policy makers; the data sets and statistical regression analyses of economists; and the experiments and empirical evidence of cognitive psychologists and neuroscientists. These diverse disciplines and perspectives offer different methods of examining an issue and establishing elements of proof.

As demonstrated in this book, recent insights from each of these fields all support the same conclusion: children learn together in meaningful relationships, and therefore an investment in early childhood education programs in which highly respected and skilled professional educators develop in children their capacity to construct knowledge by building those relationships produces particularly robust educational, social, and economic benefits for children and for the country.

As used throughout this book, a meaningful relationship is an emotionally significant interpersonal attachment between a child and the child's family, caregivers, teachers, peers, and surrounding communities. These attachment relationships can first be seen in the wondrous non-verbal communication that occurs when a primary caretaker responds reflectively to an infant's crying, cooing, mimicking, laughing, smiling, and gesturing.

But those profound attachments also develop when children join with their classmates and teachers to explore the materials in their environment and to share their reflections on their evolving understanding of their place in the community. Young children who learn to build or to re-build these meaningful relationships in early learning environments achieve remarkable life-long success and well-being.

Section 1: The Political, Pedagogical, Legal, and Economic Case for Investing in Early Childhood Education

This first section constructs the political, pedagogical, legal, and economic foundations for the development of early childhood education programs in America.

Chapter 1 shows that American education policy supports the development of early childhood education programs designed to encourage children to construct knowledge through meaningful relationships. In particular, the first chapter traces classical, modern, and current philosophies of education, all of which demonstrate that the well-being of the American regime and its citizens depends on an accessible system of early childhood programs that foster those relationships.

Chapter 2 then shows that the Framers of the United States Constitution fully appreciated that knowledge is constructed and spread through meaningful relationships and associations. Although they justified their constitutional structure by suggesting that government was necessary to curtail individual self-interest, the Framers also believed that the diffusion of knowledge through associations was vital to the survival of the nation.

As demonstrated in chapter 3, the foundations of American education law also support the development of early childhood programs that are designed to provide environments in which all children can construct knowledge in meaningful relationships. The liberty of parents and guardians to direct the upbringing of their children would not preclude the states from providing to all three- and four-year-olds access to publicly funded early childhood education programs. Nor is the federal government's limited power to regulate education inconsistent with the creation of those programs.

Chapter 3 describes how Congress may use its spending power to incentivize the states to provide early childhood education for their young learners. That chapter also demonstrates that the legal structure of American education supports the right of all families to have adequate and equitable access to early childhood education programs.

Chapter 4 presents overwhelming evidence answering the question "Do the states in America fail to provide adequate and equitable access to early childhood education?" The combined federal and local sources of revenue do not provide adequate or equitable educational opportunities. The federal educational mandates are unfunded or underfunded. The bulk of revenue available to support education in America derives from local property taxes. The formulas for allocating local property taxes to educational purposes are based at least in part on the property wealth of a school district. Districts with high property wealth thus receive significantly more resources per child than districts with low property wealth.

This educational finance regime creates wide disparities in the resources given to different districts and their children. Because neighborhoods are still generally segregated by race and ethnicity, and most minority children reside in property poor districts, the disparity in educational funding adversely affects minority children. These overall inequities in educational funding are replicated in the disparities in access to early childhood programs. As chapter 4 shows, there are meaningful racial and socioeconomic disparities in access to early childhood programs.

Chapter 4 also demonstrates that the resources needed to remedy those disparities and to provide all young learners access to early childhood education programs are relatively modest. The amount of additional funding required to provide outstanding early childhood education programs for all three- and four-year-olds in America would be at most $52 billion per year, or less than 10 percent of the public funds spent each year on education, and far less than 1 percent of the federal budget.

In addition, chapter 4 shows that the return on the investment from those funds would be robust. More than 100 separate empirical studies have proved that an investment in early childhood education produces substantial educational, social, and economic benefits. No credible study shows otherwise. In fact, the evidence compiled in this chapter makes clear that every dollar invested in early childhood education produces a return on that investment of *at least* $7.00.

Chapter 5 considers other important initiatives designed to reform American education. Those initiatives include the "accountability" movement, which involves reliance on standardized testing to evaluate schools and teachers, the "privatization" or "school choice" movement, which involves vouchers and charter schools, and remedial education and training programs. These movements have generated tremendous debate, particularly about the efficacy of standardized tests, charter schools, and vouchers.

As demonstrated in chapter 5, an investment in early childhood programs can bring together advocates with different perspectives on issues of accountability and school choice. Advocates on all sides of these issues undoubtedly share the goal of ensuring that children receive the remarkable educational, social, and economic benefits of early childhood education. Moreover, a system of effective early childhood programs in which professionally trained educators make learning visible through documentation can serve as a model of genuine accountability, and a system of effective early childhood programs in which government funds are made available to support both public and private providers can serve as a model of genuine school choice.

Together, the book's first five chapters build a compelling case for investing resources in early childhood education programs. That investment is supported by a uniquely American educational philosophy, by the regime envisioned and formed by the Framers of the Constitution, and by the legal and economic structure of American education. Those chapters also show that a relatively modest investment in providing all three- and four-year-olds access to early childhood education programs would produce substantial educational, social, and economic benefits.

Section 2: The Proven Benefits of Early Childhood Education Programs That Encourage Children to Construct Knowledge by Building Meaningful Relationships

Section 2 of the book examines the issue of whether there are particular pedagogical approaches to early childhood education that are best able to produce educational, social, and economic benefits. If the nation is going to invest resources in early childhood programs, it will become increasingly important to consider the efficacy of various kinds of teaching within those programs. Furthermore, as access to early education increases, parents will begin to consider seriously which approach to early education is best suited to their own children.

Chapter 6 provides a continuum of different approaches to early childhood education from programs that are traditionally considered purely academic, to constructivist programs, to social constructivist programs exemplified by the early learning centers in Reggio Emilia, Italy. Although these categories oversimplify the approaches of many exceptional early childhood education programs in which highly skilled educators are given the professional autonomy to employ several different pedagogies, the taxonomy provided in chapter 6 sets forth a range of methods in the field. Each of these methods has strengths, and an investment in programs in which teachers are trained to utilize any of them appropriately would produce benefits for young learners.

This section presents evidence that the most effective early childhood education programs are those that develop in children the capacity to construct knowledge by building meaningful relationships with their families, caregivers, teachers, peers, and surrounding communities.

Chapter 7 explores in detail the social constructivist approach to early childhood education, which is designed to develop in children the capacity to build those meaningful relationships. The chapter presents the strong empirical evidence demonstrating the social constructivist approach's particular efficacy in producing the educational, social, and economic benefits desired from an investment in early childhood education.

Chapter 7 also analyzes the most recent research from neuroscience that reveals precisely how and why an investment of resources in social constructivist early childhood education programs has produced, and will continue to produce, robust educational, social, and economic benefits.

By developing habits of mind and heart that enable children to construct knowledge through meaningful relationships, these programs help to: (1) realize the Framers' vision of a regime that depends for its survival on the capacity of individuals to advance and disseminate knowledge through their associations; and (2) build skills such as inter-subjectivity, cognitive integration, attachment, executive function, self-regulation, discipline, synthesis, creativity, respect, and ethics. Those particular skills bring economic success and well-being and reduce harmful, externalizing behaviors that would otherwise increase the personal and social costs of crime, health care, imprisonment, grade retention, and remedial education programs.

Section 3: Strategies for Expanding, Developing, and Designing Early Childhood Learning Communities That Construct Knowledge Through Meaningful Relationships

In the third section, the book suggests strategies for achieving the proven benefits of expanding access to early childhood education.

Chapter 8 provides legal, political, economic, and comprehensive methods of expanding access to early childhood education programs in America. That chapter delineates viable legal claims that can be used to challenge the current lack of sufficient access to early childhood education programs, suggests national, state, and local policy initiatives that can be used to support legislation expanding access to early childhood education, and sets forth an array of financing mechanisms that can be used to incentivize public and private investments in expanding access to early childhood education.

Because social constructivist early childhood education programs have proven to be particularly able to achieve robust returns on an investment in early childhood education, chapter 9 then provides strategies for developing those programs. This chapter gathers common ingredients and best practices used by the professional educators in those learning communities, including role-playing, shared projects, and the social construction of literacy, mathematics, and science.

Chapter 10 demonstrates the power of documentation to make learning visible to multiple important stakeholders, thereby providing a model of authentic assessment and genuine accountability. The book concludes by making visible through documentation the wonderful learning that can take place in an early education environment in which teachers are afforded the professional judgment to encourage children to construct—even to invent—their own knowledge through meaningful learning relationships.

NOTE

1. See UNESCO Policy Brief on Early Childhood, "What Is Your Image of the Child?" (2010), http://unesdoc.unesco.org/images/0018/001871/187140e.pdf; Loris Malaguzzi, "For an Education Based on Relationships," *Young Children* 49(1) (1993): 10.

Section 1

THE POLITICAL, PEDAGOGICAL, LEGAL, AND ECONOMIC CASE FOR INVESTING IN EARLY CHILDHOOD EDUCATION

This section of the book paints the landscape of early childhood education in America. The chapters that comprise this section demonstrate that the political, pedagogical, legal, and economic foundations of the American regime all support an investment in early childhood programs, particularly those programs that are designed to develop in children the capacity to construct knowledge through meaningful relationships.

Chapter One

The Foundations of American Education Policy

Chapter 1 roots early childhood education in the landscape of American education policy. The chapter chronicles the history of educational thought that informed the nation's founders and traces that history to the current educational policy debates.

Specifically, the Framers of the U.S. Constitution accepted from classical political philosophers, like Plato and Aristotle, the view that early education must be a public concern because it has the power to shape character and support the regime. The Framers also accepted from modern political philosophers like Locke, Montesquieu, and Rousseau the view that education is vital to moral freedom and self-government. Although the Framers justified aspects of their constitutional structure by suggesting that it was necessary to diffuse the natural tendency of human beings to pursue their individual self-interest, they also believed that knowledge is constructed in meaningful social relationships.

This chapter tracks the evolution of the Framers' educational philosophy up to the development of common schools, the democratic educational philosophy of John Dewey, and the authoritarian and progressive movements in American education. The chapter concludes with an effort to reconcile those movements in a manner that fully supports a regime of early childhood education programs designed to develop in children the capacity to construct knowledge through meaningful relationships.

CLASSICAL PHILOSOPHIES OF EDUCATION: EARLY EDUCATION MUST BE A PUBLIC CONCERN BECAUSE IT HAS THE POWER TO SHAPE CHARACTER AND SUPPORT THE PARTICULAR POLITICAL REGIME[1]

Plato's *Republic* is arguably the greatest text regarding the philosophy of education.[2] The regime displayed in the *Republic* is built upon critical assumptions about the educational process. First, the goal of education is to create relatively stagnant and stratified role players for the good of the state; it is a purely public concern. Second, education is extremely powerful; it is capable of altering a person's natural instincts, including the instinct of love of one's own, and of shaping character.

In Book VIII of the *Politics*, Aristotle expressly shares Plato's assumption that "education should be regulated by law and should be an affair of the state."[3] Aristotle declares that the "citizen should be molded to suit the form of government under which he lives"; each type of government has a "peculiar" character, and its education should strive to replicate the character required in its citizens to preserve its peculiar form.[4] Since the whole regime has one end, "it is manifest that education should be one and the same for all, and that it should be public, and not private."[5]

In the *Politics*, Aristotle also concludes that the type of "education of citizens" in a regime must depend on the political structure of that regime. Education in a democracy, for example, must teach all citizens the political skills necessary to participate in both ruling the regime and in being ruled by popular choice.[6] Democratic education must be specifically designed to develop in children the capacity to govern others by appreciating their needs and also the capacity for self-governance. As classical educational theorists, Aristotle and Plato share a belief in the supreme importance of public education for the health of the regime.

MODERN EDUCATIONAL PHILOSOPHY: PUBLIC EDUCATION IS VITAL TO FREEDOM AND SELF-GOVERNMENT

In *Some Thoughts Concerning Education* (1693), John Locke emphasizes the significance of rationality and reason in the education of each child. Most people, Locke writes, are "good or evil, useful or not, by their education."[7] Like the ancients, therefore, Locke understands the power of education. Yet education is designed to teach the child to comprehend reason so that there is no need for external politically or religiously imposed forms of discipline.[8]

Locke believes that reason, if rightly understood and taught, can be the instrument of political freedom and self-governance.

In 1748, in *The Spirit of the Laws*, Montesquieu also argues that public education is particularly necessary in democracies. In a democratic society that values freedom and self-government, public education is critical to social cohesion. Only public education can inspire that civic virtue requisite to democratic government, which includes the "love of the laws" and a preference for community, social, and public life over private life.

Rousseau, as well, shares Locke's emphasis on individual educational development, declaring that the "supreme good is not authority, but freedom."[9] In the *Emile*, he expressly links the development of a free people with a proper education: "This is my fundamental maxim. Apply it to childhood and all the rules of education follow."[10] Rousseau associates freedom with mankind's natural childhood state and authority with mankind's unnatural, social condition. The rules of education, if they are to serve the supreme good of freedom, must be aligned with a child's natural condition.[11]

Rousseau demonstrated that children are by nature competent and curious. Educators must understand the "distinctive genius" of each child, and allow the child "full liberty" to grow.[12] Hence, Rousseau creates the foundation for contemporary arguments against a standardized curriculum and in favor of child-centered education. He suggests that any educational process that fails to "differentiate"—to take into account the unique developmental needs of each child—will fail.

In their distinct calls for an education that promotes freedom and self-government, Rousseau, Locke, and Montesquieu also share a fundamental distrust of direct instruction of dogma or unquestioned presumptions built merely upon faith in the educational process. Locke's belief in the power of reason suggests the subordination of preconceived beliefs to individual examination and rational thought. Slavish adherence to dogma is inimical to self-governance and self-determination. Thus, an education for self-government must develop in children the capacity to construct knowledge by questioning accepted beliefs.

For Montesquieu, public education also was necessary to replace private religious zeal with a uniform national allegiance to law and country. Rousseau, as well, believes that a proper education is the antidote to politically imposed moral doctrines. If allowed to develop their own interests free from such artificial constraints, children will naturally seek to form socially useful alliances and boundaries, and they will naturally avoid socially destructive behavior.

THE FOUNDATION OF AMERICAN EDUCATIONAL POLICY: DEMOCRATIC EDUCATION MUST DEVELOP MEANINGFUL RELATIONSHIPS BETWEEN INDIVIDUALS AND THE COMMUNITY

Private Education Before the Constitution

The history of American education typically begins with the story of the importation of the English educational system to colonial America.[13] Contrary to common understanding, the educational tradition brought by the European settlers who colonized America was not based on a singular New England mode of educational hierarchy and religious conformity.

Rather, education in the colonial period was diffuse, localized, haphazard, and heterogeneous. There were significant differences between the educational practices in the northern, southern, and middle colonies and significant differences within each colony as well.[14] Nonetheless, it is fair to say that American colonists attempted for the most part to recreate the heavily religious educational institutions with which they were most familiar from their European experience.[15]

In 1647, for instance, the Massachusetts General Court enacted the "Old Deluder Satan Act." The Act declared that because Satan was keeping people in the colony from understanding scripture, every town with at least 50 families must provide for reading and writing instruction. If a town had 100 or more families, the town also had to provide grammar schools that would prepare boys for higher education at Harvard. The law threatened the town with a fine if it did not comply.

Despite this somewhat modest initial movement toward community-based education, those families with educated adults continued to rely primarily on the home as the institution of learning. Children who did not have the advantage of a learned adult in the home were sent to other homes occupied by adults who offered to teach groups of children together. These private schools were run by men and women who typically instructed their own children and, for a fee, instructed the neighborhood children as well.

These private schools soon developed a shared curriculum with a strong religious flavor. Children were taught to read by first memorizing the Bible. As was true in England, the lessons were often presented on hornbooks—pieces of parchment placed on a wooden paddle, covered with a strip of clear horn to protect them from being smudged.

The lesson typically included a prayer, Biblical passage, religious maxim, or psalm. The hornbooks were coupled with primers, such that religion and literacy were literally tied together. For example, the *New England Primer* contained the letters of the alphabet arranged so that each letter began a Biblical verse. A series of illustrated rhymes taught children both the alphabet and the doctrine of original sin. The primary goal of these lessons was to teach children to read, but the lessons employed religious doctrine as the setting for language.

A variety of church-affiliated or -sponsored schools sprang up together with the officially established religious institutions. The various religious sects in America developed a variety of private schools. Moreover, splinters that developed in the Protestant church led to competing schools even within the same religion. The various sects soon competed vigorously for the scarce public resources devoted to education.

The Founders' Educational Philosophy: Toward a Common Education

After independence and before the Constitution was drafted, the nation's founders were well aware that the nation was not yet a union. The founders grew to believe that one of the most effective ways to achieve common values was to create a shared system of education. As Urban and Wagoner have observed, "[e]ducation, then, emerged as an essential consideration in the minds of those who faced the momentous task of establishing the new nation."[16] The political structure of the new regime became dependent on the educational structure of the regime, and therefore the "architects of the American nation clearly and deliberately fused educational theory with political theory."[17]

Benjamin Franklin, for example, developed a consistent argument for the education of each individual in practical skills, useful in the world.[18] For Franklin, learned treatises and other established texts were important, but only insofar as they generated ideas that could be put into practice. Ultimately, Franklin wrote *Poor Richard's Almanack* between 1732 and 1757 for the purpose of "conveying instruction among the common people, who bought scarce any other books."[19]

In order to create collections of books that could be used by more than a wealthy few, Franklin and his colleagues created the first colonial library by donating their most precious books to a common collection called the "Library Company of Philadelphia." The collection contained classic works such as *Plutarch's Lives*, as well as history books and maps.

In 1749, in his *Proposals Relating to the Education of Youth in Pennsylvania*, Franklin designed the Philadelphia Academy, whose mission was to create not a generation of select scholars, but a generation of common men able to perform practical skills and community service.[20] Although Franklin's success in implementing his ideas was limited, he did succeed in generating a vital discourse regarding the type of education that would serve the new nation and its people.

Thomas Jefferson attempted to advance the ideal of a public education in his "Bill for the More General Diffusion of Knowledge," which he placed before the Virginia legislature in 1779.[21] Rooted in his philosophy that public education was necessary to support the new republic and its democratic government, Jefferson proposed a system of free elementary-level education administered by separate counties or divisions. Each of these so-called little republics would provide children with basic literacy skills and with knowledge of history.

Jefferson's vision was that American children would have the education necessary to prepare them to participate as citizens in a democracy. He believed that the benefits of education should not be reserved solely for the established aristocracy or for any religious group.[22] The government had a compelling interest in providing sufficient resources to insure that all young Americans gained the skills needed for democratic citizenship.

In fact, Jefferson believed that a public education was vital to the preservation of liberty. He wrote that a publicly supported educational system would raise the "morals" of children to the "high ground of moral respectability necessary to their own safety, and to orderly government.[23] The "most certain and the most legitimate end of government," according to Jefferson, was the provision of a free, public education to its citizens.[24]

Jefferson's system of public education is not hostile to private education; rather, it simply understands private education to be inadequate to accomplish the political objective of educating all citizens for participation in their own government. To the extent that private education depletes resources from the public education system, which is indispensable for the survival of democracy, private education is inimical to the ultimate realization of the democratic ideal.

The Growth of the Founders' Conception of Public Education for Children Through Common Schools

Benjamin Rush, who had signed the Declaration of Independence and served as Surgeon General of the revolutionary army, was instrumental in advancing a free and uniform system of public education.[25]

In particular, Rush argued that a general tax should be used to finance a system of American public education, asserting that such a system would in the long run lessen taxes for all. In arguments that foreshadow contemporary debates about public education, Rush even claimed that all taxpayers benefit from public education because criminal activity and the expenses of the criminal justice system would be reduced in a nation of educated, law-abiding citizens. Moreover, a national system of education for all children would bring diverse people together through a shared patriotic love of country that would allow them to internalize prudential restraints on their own freedom.

The founders' idea of a uniform, free, public, and publicly funded educational system was further realized in the "common school" movement of the early 1800s. Horace Mann, a Massachusetts legislator and Secretary of the Massachusetts Board of Education, was a leading advocate for common schools. Mann believed that the public, common school could bring diverse peoples and cultures into a common bond. Although Mann's own values were aligned with Protestant beliefs, he advocated broad, unifying principles of morality. Division in religion and class could be overcome by a common education in a common morality.

Like Rush, Mann argued that publicly financed education for the masses was good for society as a whole. In particular, he convinced the wealthy property owners that proper education would give to the working class a respect for the property and wealth of others that would help to preserve the existing power structure.[26]

He argued that property landowners had a special obligation to fund public education in proportion to their ownership. Yet Mann also believed that property was a national asset that had been entrusted to individual owners for their use in ways that served the common wealth. Hence, the state had the right to tax personal property for public uses such as the education of all children in an integrated, state-controlled system of common or "normal" schools.[27]

In 1852 Massachusetts became the first state to erect a compulsory attendance law, thereby exercising the type of power Mann argued states should employ in regulating the education of their children.[28] By 1918 every state had passed some form of compulsory school attendance statute.[29] As public school attendance significantly increased in the late 1800s and early 1900s, the illiteracy rate among Americans significantly declined.[30]

John Dewey and American Democratic Education

John Dewey's uniquely American educational philosophy has had a profound impact upon the law and practice of education in America.

Writing in the early 1900s, Dewey creates a comprehensive educational philosophy built upon democratic principles of equality and individuality. In *Democracy and Education*, Dewey argues that because "a democratic society repudiates the principle of external authority, it must find a substitute in voluntary disposition and interest; these can be created only by education." Education serves democratic institutions, where it facilitates the "breaking down of those barriers of class, race, and national territory which kept men from perceiving the full import of their activity."[31]

Dewey then traces the development of educational philosophy from the social constructs of Plato to the individualist ideal of the enlightenment ideals of Locke and Rousseau. He advances a specific "democratic ideal" of education that makes educational resources available in America regardless of class or status and uses those resources to encourage American children to reach beyond their borders and discover things that unite mankind: "The emphasis must be put upon whatever bind people together in cooperative human pursuits and results, apart from geographical limitations."[32] Dewey understands democratic education as a "freeing of individual capacity in a progressive growth directed to social aims."[33]

In *Experience and Education*, Dewey declares that the educator must understand that learning is "a continuous process of reconstruction of experience."[34] Dewey is often credited with the fundamental belief that students learn by "doing." Children actively construct their own knowledge in relationships through their shared experiences.

Dewey also believed that the "scientific method" was "the only authentic means at our command for getting at the significance of our everyday experiences of the world in which we live."[35] Only by having the freedom to explore their environment and to test their interactions with materials and with others can children truly develop the capacity for constructing knowledge.

With the help of the scientific method adapted to various degrees of student maturity students can freely construct for themselves patterns discernible in everyday experience. That method, and the "constructivist" learning process that results, include "the formation of ideas, acting upon ideas, observation of the conditions which result, and the organization of facts and ideas for future use."[36]

Dewey shows that knowledge is not delivered or revealed by an authority figure. To the contrary, children construct knowledge as they explore, experiment, mess about, and question their environment. Educational programs therefore must be designed to encourage children to construct meaning in their lives by interacting with their environment in cooperation with teachers and peers.

THE FOUNDATIONS OF CONTEMPORARY DEBATES ABOUT AMERICAN EDUCATION POLICY

Many of the insights developed by the classical, modern, and American educational philosophers are now the foundation for contemporary ideas about education in the American regime. In the current debates about the proper direction of education in America, the following principles are generally well accepted:

- Plato's view that education is a public, political matter that plays a vital role in shaping the character of children and the nature of a regime;
- Aristotle's understanding that a democratic regime requires for its health a unique democratic form of education that trains all children both to govern and to be governed;
- Locke's view that society must educate its children in the self-restraint necessary for self-government;
- Montesquieu's view that children can be free to govern themselves only if given through education a love of their community;
- Rousseau's perception that education must be attuned to the natural, developmental needs of each child so that each citizen can come to understand their connection with the community;
- The founders' belief that the general diffusion of knowledge to all citizens through a public educational system is vital to creating a unified American regime;
- Mann's insight that such an education should be accomplished by the creation of uniform, comprehensive, state-centralized "common" schools, funded by property owners for the good of society; and
- Dewey's doctrine that American education must be designed to allow children the freedom to "construct" their own experience and to find the common human bonds that link all persons, regardless of race, class, or religion.

Although there may be a philosophic consensus that a public education is particularly important in a liberal democracy, the purported tension between individual freedom and collective authority in such a regime drives the current debates about the proper role of education in America.

In *Democratic Education*,[37] Amy Gutmann argues that America needs a unique type of authoritarian education that "recognizes that educational authority must be shared among parents, citizens and professional educators." According to Gutmann, a "democratic state recognizes the value of professional authority in enabling children to appreciate and to evaluate ways of life other than those favored by their families . . . [and] recognizes the value of political education in predisposing children to accept those ways of life that are consistent with sharing the rights and responsibilities of citizenship in a democratic society."

In *Moral Education and the Democratic Ideal*,[38] however, Israel Scheffler argues that a more *progressive* democratic education is indispensable to the democratic "ideal." He contends that education must create an environment in which children are free to question authority. Democratic education must support "a society that sustains itself not by the indoctrination of myth, but by the reasoned choices of its citizens, who continue to favor it in the light of a critical scrutiny both of it and its alternatives." Scheffler observes that democratic education is much more difficult than filling students with facts; it requires developing a habit of reasonableness that accompanies free inquiry.[39]

In *The Schools Our Children Deserve: Moving Beyond Traditional Classrooms and "Tougher Standards,"*[40] Alfie Kohn explicitly describes the current division in American educational thought as a conflict between the "authoritarian" and "progressive" educational approaches. The desire to inculcate young people with a core set of properly held national beliefs often leads to an "authoritarian" approach to educational institutions and ultimately to the "standards" movement reflected in the No Child Left Behind Act of 2001[41] and the Common Core.[42]

This educational approach is designed to deliver to children the facts and values deemed important by the government. As relatively passive recipients of orthodox wisdom, children can be trained to behave like patriotic citizens and disciplined workers. Proponents of this view of American education may even rely on the Aristotelian notion that democratic citizens must be taught how to be ruled. Education in this form prepares Americans to be consumers.

By this "authoritarian" perspective, learning can be measured by objective standards. If the memorization of accepted facts is the goal of education, then tests can be devised to assess whether or not students have memorized such facts. When students fail to recall facts on these tests, the school has failed in its mission to prepare students to recount such facts on command. Students who fail to demonstrate appropriate external behavior can be made to do so with negative reinforcements like being held back in school. Schools that fail to train their students to perform also will suffer negative reinforcements such as the withdrawal of funds.

This prominent contemporary view of education also has the advantage of the perception that it is cost-effective. If the goal of education is to give the same information to classrooms full of children so that they can all recall that information in a testing environment, then there is little apparent need to spend the money required to foster meaningful teacher-student relationships. The "standards" movement generally accepts the idea that a single teacher can impart a single set of facts to a large number of students at the same time. Consequently, this type of education seems cost-efficient.

The contrary, the "progressive" strand in contemporary American education policy, originates in the educational philosophy of the founders of the Constitution, as well as Rousseau and Dewey. By this perspective, the over-riding goal of a uniquely American education is to prepare American youth to participate in citizenship by allowing them freedom to create the thinking, processing, and communication skills necessary to lead rather than to follow. This "child-centered" or "learner-centered" approach takes children seriously, and understands that each child learns in a different way and at a different developmental rate.

Genuine learning requires "differentiation" in the sense that a teacher must respond to the unique needs and learning styles of each child, one at a time. As such, education cannot be given by an authoritarian figure to many students in the same way and at the same time. Rather, children construct knowledge with the help of meaningful, positive relationships with teachers and peers.

Progressive schools generally reflect a commitment to core educational values, including attending to the whole child, community, collaboration, service to others, intrinsic motivation, emergent curriculum, engaged learning, and deep understanding. Educational systems pursuing this progressive approach may have to hire significantly more adult professionals than those pursuing a more authoritarian approach. The desire to meet each child's unique needs may also lead to additional special education services.

This student-centered approach, therefore, appears to be far more expensive than the authoritarian, standards-based approach. As Benjamin Rush and Horace Mann argued long ago, however, the public funds expended on educational excellence are an invaluable social investment. Proponents of the progressive approach, like Rush and Mann before them, marshal substantial evidence that the cost of genuine educational excellence is far less than the health care, crime, and welfare costs created by its absence.

RECONCILING THE AUTHORITARIAN AND PROGRESSIVE MOVEMENTS: EDUCATING CHILDREN FOR THE FUTURE BY ENCOURAGING THEM TO CONSTRUCT KNOWLEDGE THROUGH MEANINGFUL RELATIONSHIPS

In his book *The End of Education: Redefining the Value of School*, Neil Postman suggests that the current debates between the "authoritarian, standards" movement and the "progressive, child-centered" movement miss the point.[43] These debates disregard the most important question of all: what is the goal of American education and the law that supports it?

Postman declares that "there is no surer way to bring an end to schooling than for it to have no end."[44] In recent decades, the legal and political debates surrounding education have been largely devoted to processes and tests. Ignored in those discussions has been a serious reconsideration of the fundamental *purpose* of education in the American regime. Postman propose redevelopment of a shared vision of the goals of American education. Rely on Jefferson, Mann, and Dewey, Postman observes that in America, "public education does not serve a public. It *creates* a public." What kind of public should the American early childhood education system create?

The Fundamental Purpose: Developing Habits of Mind and Heart in Children That Will Foster Well-Being

In addressing the question regarding the fundamental purpose of education, policy makers and educators must try to predict the kinds of lives that children will lead in the future, and to determine what dispositions and habits of the mind and heart will foster their future well-being.

Professor David Perkins, of the Harvard Graduate School of Education and Project Zero, argues that schools should facilitate "lifeworthyness" education—learning that is likely to matter in the lives that learners are likely to live.[45] He believes that twenty-first-century education should focus upon globalization, digital communication, neuroscience, behavioral economics, the psychology of happiness, bioethics, and conflict resolution.

Howard Gardner—one of the nation's most influential educational psychologists—similarly concludes that education must be directed toward creating habits of mind that will be valuable in the future, not the past. He observes four mega-trends: globalization, neuroscience, virtual realities, and learning from infancy to death.[46] He then shows that in the future, individuals who wish to thrive must develop five different kinds of "minds" or "capacities":

- a disciplined mind—the ability to become an expert in at least one area;
- a synthesizing mind—the ability to gather information from many sources, to organize the information in helpful ways and to communicate the information to others;
- a creating mind—the ability of adults to keep alive in themselves the mind and sensibility of a young child, including an insatiable curiosity about other people and the environment, an openness to untested paths, a willingness to struggle, and a desire and capacity to learn from failure;
- a respectful mind—the ability to understand the perspectives and motivations of others, particularly those who appear to be different; and
- an ethical mind—the ability to appreciate one's social or professional role and to act in accordance with shared standards for that role.

The Proven Pedagogy: Creating Cultures of Thinking and Communities of Learning

Early childhood education for the twenty-first century requires a "culture of thinking" in schools.[47] That culture must respect and value professionally trained educators. In a culture of thinking and a community of learning, teachers are trusted to exercise their professional judgment about the best ways to create meaningful relationships from which children will develop the five mental capacities that they will need for the future. Educators also are given authority to design day-to-day in-school routines and structures that value, promote, and make visible the development of these capacities by individuals and groups.[48]

These practices should give children the message that they are fully capable of co-constructing their own knowledge and co-creating their own learning through meaningful relationships with their teachers, peers, and environments. In particular, the lessons from neuroscience and developmental psychology indicate that genuine learning is purposeful, social, shareable, emotional, and empowering.

While a common core curriculum based on math and language arts development may provide a minimal floor of competence, that curriculum cannot fully support a meaningful twenty-first-century education. Rather, schools must build a curriculum around a culture of respect for teaching that fosters the five indispensable minds for the future. Accordingly, the best early childhood education programs will further the co-creation of knowledge through meaningful relationships in respectful learning communities.

The Authentic Assessments: Making Learning Visible Through Documentation

An educational system designed to foster twenty-first-century habits of mind also will provide authentic assessments of student learning through documentation. As used in this context, documentation is the "practice of observing, recording, interpreting and sharing through a variety of media the processes and products of learning in order to deepen learning and make it visible."[49]

Documentation is vital to the process of individual and group learning. It is an intentional act of reflecting on the process of individual and group growth. It collects and holds up artifacts of shared group learning experiences to assist the group to reflect on its own progress. The documentation informs all subsequent teaching in the classroom and outside the classroom.

Moreover, documentation provides direct evidence of learning that can be shared with the community surrounding the school. In this way, documentation provides an authentic assessment of the learning process. The promise of documentation is that it will augment forms of assessment and accountability based primarily on standardized tests.

AMERICAN EDUCATION POLICY ESTABLISHES A STRONG FOUNDATION FOR EARLY CHILDHOOD EDUCATION PROGRAMS DESIGNED TO CONSTRUCT KNOWLEDGE THROUGH MEANINGFUL RELATIONSHIPS

The fabric of American education policy is woven from the threads of the greatest educational philosophers, from Plato to Howard Gardner. In the American democratic regime, education must prepare citizens for self-government, empower them to construct and diffuse knowledge through experience, and nurture in them love of their community.

To accomplish that political purpose, America must offer all of its youngest learners access to early childhood education programs. But, in keeping with the strongest traditions of American education policy, those early education programs must be designed to develop habits of mind and heart that will foster well-being in communities in which knowledge is constructed through meaningful relationships and is made visible with the support of respected and valued professional educators.

NOTES

1. See Steven M. Cahn, *Classic and Contemporary Readings in the Philosophy of Education* (New York: Oxford University Press, 1997).

2. See Plato, *Republic*, reprinted in Cahn, *Classic and Contemporary Readings*, 39–109.

3. See Aristotle, *Politics, Book VIII,* reprinted in Cahn, *Classic and Contemporary Readings*, 137.

4. Ibid.

5. See Aristotle, *Nicomachean Ethics*, reprinted in Cahn, *Classic and Contemporary Readings*, 111-118.

6. See Aristotle, *Politics, Book VIII,* 134.

7. See Locke, *Some Thoughts Concerning Education*, reprinted in part in Cahn, *Classic and Contemporary Readings*, 145.

8. Ibid., 147 ("Every man must some time or other be trusted to himself.").

9. See Rousseau, *Emile, Book II,* reprinted in Cahn, *Classic and Contemporary Readings*, 167.

10. Ibid.

11. Ibid., 170 ("Let the childhood ripen in children.").

12. Ibid., 171.

13. See, e.g., Kern Alexander and M. David Alexander, *American Public School Law* (Belmont, California: West/Thomson Learning, 2001), 21–23.

14. Urban and Wagoner, *American Education: A History*, 15.

15. Kenneth A. Lockridge, *Literacy in Colonial New England: An Enquiry Into the Social Context of Literacy in the Early Modern West* (New York: W.W. Norton, 1974).

16. Urban and Wagoner, *American Education: A History*, 70.

17. Ibid.

18. See Leonard W. Larabee et al., *The Autobiography of Benjamin Franklin* (New Haven, CT: Yale University Press, 1964); Leonard W. Larabee and Whitfield J. Bell, *The Papers of Benjamin Franklin* (New Haven, CT: Yale University Press, 1959); John Hardin Best, *Benjamin Franklin on Education* (New York: Teachers College Press, 1962).

19. See *Poor Richard's Almanack*, in Larabee and Bell, *The Papers of Benjamin Franklin*.

20. See *Proposals*, in Best, *Benjamin Franklin on Education*.

21. Thomas Jefferson, *Bill for the More General Diffusion of Knowledge, The Educational Work of Thomas Jefferson* (1964), 199–204. See also Thomas Jefferson, *Writings* (Library of America: 1984); John Adams, *The Adams-Jefferson Letters* (New York: Simon & Schuster, 1971).

22. See *Act Establishing Religious Freedom (1779)*, in Adrienne Koch and William Pedren, *The Life and Selected Writings of Thomas Jefferson* (New York: Modern Library, 1998), 289–291.

23. Urban and Wagoner, *American Education: A History*, 73–74 (citing Thomas Jefferson to John Adams, October 28, 1813).

24. Ibid.

25. See Benjamin Rush, *A Plan for the Establishment of Public Schools and the Diffusion of Knowledge in Pennsylvania; to Which Are Added, Thoughts Upon the Mode of Education, Proper in a Republic* (Philadelphia, 1786). See also Urban and Wagoner, *American Education: A History*, 79–85.

26. See Urban and Wagoner, *American Education: A History*, 102–3.

27. See Urban and Wagoner, *American Education: A History*, 108–9. Urban and Wagoner also trace the rise of women in the teaching profession to Mann's "common" or "normal" school movement.

28. See Urban and Wagoner, *American Education: A History*, 173.

29. Ibid., 172.

30. Ibid., 174 (attendance increased at the turn of the century from 49 percent to 64 percent, while illiteracy declined from 20 percent to 13 percent).

31. See John Dewey, *Democracy and Education*, reprinted in Cahn, *Classic and Contemporary Readings*, 288–93.

32. Ibid.

33. Ibid.

34. See John Dewey, *Experience and Education*, reprinted in Cahn, *Classic and Contemporary Readings*, 362.

35. Ibid.

36. Ibid.

37. See Amy Gutmann, *Democratic Education*, reprinted in Cahn, *Classic and Contemporary Readings*, 411–34.

38. See Israel Scheffler, *Moral Education and the Democratic Ideal*, reprinted in Cahn, *Classic and Contemporary Readings*, 436–42.

39. See James Traub, "New York's New Approach," *New York Times,* August 3, 2003, 20–21.

40. Alfie Kohn, *The Schools our Children Deserve: Moving Beyond Traditional Classrooms and "Tougher" Standards* (Boston: Houghton Mifflin, 1999).

41. 20 U.S.C. §6301 et seq.

42. National Governors Association Center for Best Practices & Council of Chief State School Officers, *Common Core State Standards* (2010).

43. Neil Postman, *The End of Education: Redefining the Value of School* (New York: Knopf, 1995), 5, 17.

44. Ibid.

45. See David Perkins, *Educating for the Unknown* (2012).

46. See Howard Gardner, *Five Minds for the Future* (Cambridge: Harvard Business Review Press, 2008).

47. See, e.g., Ron Ritchhart, *Intellectual Character: What It Is, Why It Matters and How to Get It* (San Francisco: Jossey-Bass, 2002).

48. See, e.g., Daniel Wilson, *Making Learning (and Learners) Visible: Reggio-Inspired Practices Pre-School to High School* (2012).

49. See Project Zero and Reggio Children, *Making Learning Visible: Children as Individual and Group Learners* (Reggio Emilia, Italy: Reggio Children, 2001).

Chapter 2

The Pedagogical Foundations of American Early Childhood Education

The structure governing American education is supported by the Framers' particular educational philosophy, which in turn is based on the Framers' particular view of human nature and human development. That view is nuanced. Although the Framers justified their constitutional structure based on a fear that human beings have a natural desire to pursue their self-interest, they also created a regime dependent on the human capacity to construct knowledge through meaningful relationships.

THE FRAMERS' NUANCED UNDERSTANDING OF HUMAN NATURE AND HUMAN DEVELOPMENT

The Framers rationalized their constitutional structure by arguing that it reflects aspects of human nature. There is evidence that the Framers feared that human beings would be overcome by their natural desire to serve their own self-interest, necessitating a constitutional order designed to check that desire. That perception of human nature can be, and has been, employed to justify a pedagogy based on behaviorism. Yet, as demonstrated in this chapter, the Framers actually held a nuanced view of human nature that led them to erect a regime dependent upon the human capacity to construct knowledge in meaningful relationships.

The Incomplete View of Human Nature Mistakenly Ascribed to the Framers

The Federalist Papers are a collection of 85 essays written by James Madison, Alexander Hamilton, and John Jay. Originally published as a series of newspaper columns signed by "Publius" between 1787 and 1788, they provide the fundamental justification for the U.S. Constitution.[1] They also contain important evidence of the Framers' understanding of human nature and development.

In Federalist #51, James Madison wrote: "What is government itself, but the greatest of all reflections on human nature?"[2] The Framers presumed that human nature was flawed. Men are not angels; they are driven by passions that are difficult for them to overcome. In Federalist #55, Madison explicitly declares: "In all numerous assemblies, of whatever characters composed, passion never fails to wrest the scepter from reason."[3] Alexander Hamilton in Federalist #6 similarly presumed the "depravity in mankind": "Has it not . . . invariably been found that momentary passions, and immediate interests, have a more active and imperious control over human conduct than general or remote considerations of policy, utility or justice?"[4] These passions can lead individuals to pursue their own interests at the expense of others.

As Madison declared: "If men were angels, no government would be necessary."[5] Government is necessary to "control" the governed because men are generally incapable of self-control.[6] In fact, the Framers expressed the view that "sown in the nature of men" is a "propensity" to "fall into mutual animosities."[7]

Madison also argued that a regime's "parchment barriers" are not alone adequate to guard against the "encroaching spirit of power."[8] Rather, the only way for civil society to control the natural passions of mankind is to diffuse them. The passions of one person or group can be diffused only when they interact with the passions of another person or group. As Madison writes: "Ambition shall be made to counteract ambition."[9]

As a "reflection on human nature," therefore, the Framers devised a constitutional structure and regime that seems to be based on "animosities." The separation of legislative, executive, and judicial powers, for instance, is designed to diffuse, not to elevate, the passionate pursuit by each branch of government of their own power, ambition, and self-interest. Similarly, the Framers attempted to diffuse, not elevate, the passions by retaining the sovereignty of the states and placing that sovereignty in tension with that of the limited national government.[10]

In addition, the Framers intended the judicial branch to play a critical role in diffusing the passions of mankind. In Federalist #78, Alexander Hamilton argued that the limits on governmental power could be "preserved in practice no other way than through the medium of the courts of justice." The courts must guard the Constitution and the rights of individuals against the natural "ill humours" of mankind pursuing their own powerful self-interests.[11]

The regime that the Framers constructed therefore seems to be justified by their view that humans are driven by their natural instinct to survive and are overcome by their own emotions and desires. Indeed, the Framers cautioned that in the absence of meaningful social relationships, individuals would pursue their own self-preservation and self-interest.

The Use of the Incomplete View of the Framers' Understanding of Human Nature to Justify a Behaviorist Pedagogy and Standardized Assessments

The presumption that individuals are naturally motivated to pursue their own self-interest, which is commonly attributed to liberal democratic principles and to the Framers, can be used to support an educational philosophy built on inter-personal separation and intra-personal dualities. Strangers are threats to survival. The educational success of a neighbor's child is a threat to the educational success of my child. The individual is in conflict with the community. An individual's private life is distinct from his or her public life.

This understanding of human nature also can be used to erect binaries: child v. adult; reason v. passion; intellect v. emotion; and science v. art. The presumption that these animosities are natural, inevitable, and necessary even led the Supreme Court in *San Antonio Indep. School Dist. v. Rodriguez* to justify undisputed inequality in educational funding by contending that there is a "continual struggle between two forces: the desire by members of society to have educational opportunity for all children and the desire of each family to provide the best education it can afford for its own children."[12]

These perceived binaries also could justify a corresponding pedagogy and system of assessments. By this view, children are naturally undisciplined, but as rational actors, their external behavior can be shaped by rewarding positive behavior and punishing negative behavior. Education shapes behavior by focusing on the intellect as separate from emotions, and then rewarding positive expressions of intellect and punishing negative expressions of passion. Positive expressions of "intelligent" behavior are assessed and rewarded through a regime of standardized tests.

The behaviorist approach to psychology can be used to rationalize this approach to education and assessment. Behavioral psychology and behaviorism became an extremely influential educational construct in the twentieth century. The foundation of behaviorism is the belief that learning is defined as a change in observable behavior.

In 1913, John Watson published *The Behavioral Learning Theory*.[13] Based on his review of Pavlov's conclusions regarding conditioned responses by animals and humans to external stimuli, Watson showed that children could be "conditioned" as well. A child could be conditioned to fear an object by repeatedly aligning that object with a painful experience.[14] For example, by pairing a child's observation of a white rabbit with a harsh noise, a child could be conditioned to fear (and to avoid) all similar white objects.[15]

B.F. Skinner then extended Watson's research, finding that animals could be conditioned to perform a particular behavior (such as pushing a lever) when that behavior is repeatedly and immediately rewarded (such as with food).[16] In 1958, Skinner developed a teaching machine based upon his behaviorist approach to education. The machine presented direct instruction of information that was tested in a "carefully prescribed order." Correct answers were rewarded and incorrect ones punished. As described by Skinner:

> In using the device, the student refers to a numbered item in a multiple-choice test. He presses the button corresponding to his first choice of answer. If he is right, the device moves to the next item; if he is wrong, the error is tallied and he must continue to make choices until he is right.[17]

Skinner's work in operant conditioning led naturally to the rewards and punishments offered by a standardized test of rote knowledge. Although Skinner eventually appreciated that individual behavior could not be explained merely by reactions to external stimuli, his approach to learning nonetheless came to be understood as a "reductionist view in which all that can be addressed is the relation between sensory stimuli and the unique corresponding response."[18]

Employing aspects of the behaviorist approach fashioned by Skinner, educators began to contend that children could be conditioned to demonstrate desired behavior on tests through a system of external rewards and punishments.[19] The implementation of a system of routinized tests could be justified as an application of Skinner's model of operant conditioning, in which behavior is shaped by external stimuli. In this construct, the process by which the human mind functions is not particularly important. A person's thoughts, feelings, emotions, intentions, and cognitive processes are irrelevant to behavior and hence irrelevant to learning.

The role of the teacher is to provide direct instruction of information. The school delivers external rewards for behavior that demonstrates acquisition of the information and punishments for behavior that does not. Skinner also argued that his approach was economically efficient: "It is a labor-saving device because it can bring one programmer into contact with an indefinite number of students."[20]

Although behaviorists such as B.F. Skinner came to understand that both internal and external stimuli could influence observable behavior, the focus of behaviorists is upon rewards and punishments.[21] Positive external reinforcement for behavior deemed to be good combined with negative external reinforcement through punishment for behavior deemed to be bad will "teach" individuals to behave in a socially desired manner.[22] Behaviorism depends on separating the human being into distinct and often oppositional pieces. The internal, private core of the individual is virtually irrelevant to the learning process and must be distinguished from the individual's external observable and measurable behaviors.[23]

The goal of education becomes the production of measurable behavior. The next logical step is to create methods of measuring the desired observable behavior. Once it is determined which observable behaviors are desired, the measurements can be standardized to correspond with those desired behaviors. As a consequence, the behaviorist assumptions about human nature and development seem to lead quite easily to the creation of a regime of standardized testing.[24]

Within each classroom, the behaviorist approach leads teachers to use positive and negative reinforcements to reward or punish student conduct. The principle of "operant conditioning" also suggests that teachers should deliver their external rewards and punishments immediately after the student has demonstrated the particular behavior being observed. As a consequence, teachers must present their instruction in a linear way in which one particular desired behavior is observed before the next conditioning takes place.

Only after the student has been conditioned by rewards and punishments to demonstrate one particular desired behavior can that student then proceed to be conditioned to demonstrate the next desired behavior. This method of operant conditioning requires breaking learning into small bits so that the student recognizes which precise behavior he or she is being rewarded or punished for. The teacher therefore breaks lesson plans into small bits as well, which must proceed in a predetermined linear fashion.

As one of the nation's foremost education experts, Linda Darling-Hammond has observed:

> Behaviorist learning theory has had substantial influence in education, guiding the development of highly-sequenced and structured curricula, programmed instructional approaches, workbooks and other tools. It has proved useful for the development of some types of skills—especially those that can be learned substantially by rote through reinforcement and practice. However, evidence has accrued that tasks requiring more complex thinking and higher mental processes are not generally well-learned through behaviorist methods and require more attention to how people perceive, process, and make sense of what they are experiencing.[25]

The teacher who follows the behaviorist approach will rely primarily on direct instruction to transmit information to students. Direct instruction is teacher-dominated communication to students of information, primarily through lecture. Such instruction is an efficient way to provide students with isolated pieces of information, the acquisition of which can be observed and measured by standardized tests.

The behaviorist method of operative conditioning also has been applied across schools and states. School administrators attempt to condition teacher behavior by rewarding and punishing them depending on the performance of their students on standardized tests. Under the federal regimes created by the No Child Left Behind Act and the Race to the Top, states are conditioned to change school performance through a system of monetary rewards and punishments. Accordingly, the behaviorist approach still dominates much of education pedagogy and policy.

The Framers Actually Formed a Regime That Depends on the Natural Human Capacity to Construct Knowledge in Meaningful Relationships

The behaviorist approach to education, however, is actually inconsistent with a proper understanding of the democratic regime established by the Constitution and its Framers. Although the Framers justified their constitutional structure by claiming that their government was necessary to diffuse the otherwise unbridled human passions, they also understood that human nature had a positive, hopeful side as well. They erected a regime of self-government that "presupposes" the existence of other qualities in human nature that justify a certain portion of "esteem and confidence."[26] Specifically, the Framers built into their regime legal structures that presume the natural human capacity to construct and disseminate knowledge through meaningful relationships.

The Framers fully appreciated that the choices made by citizens in a democracy are not merely the product of subjective utility. The Framers relied on the overriding human capacity for empathy as the check on the passionate pursuit of self-interest and the abuse of power. The quality of empathy empowers individuals to put themselves in someone else's shoes, to understand someone else's feelings and intentions.

The Framers presumed that human beings have a natural instinct to associate with others. Those associations are protected in the Constitution by structures of shared power, by the First Amendment, by intellectual property provisions, and by limitations on the reach of the government into the life of the mind and the community.

The Constitution's limitation on the term of appointment of representatives is based on the presumption that even those prone to share power are self-regulated by empathy. Those who govern will always consider the interests of the governed. According to the Framers, elected representatives will "anticipate the moment" when they are not in power, and will naturally put themselves in the shoes of the governed.

The Framers believed that: "There is in every heart a sensibility to marks of honor, of favor, of esteem . . . which, apart from all considerations of interest, is some pledge for grateful and benevolent returns."[27] There is disposition toward gratitude in human nature, by which representatives "will be bound to fidelity and sympathy with the great mass of people."[28]

The structure of the American regime, fully appreciated, also presumes that the construction of knowledge requires collaboration. The First Amendment's free speech and press clauses depend on the belief that human interactions—in dialogue, in the marketplace of ideas, and in myriad forms of "expression"—are vital to human progress. Knowledge is constructed and spread in the common, public sphere.

Indeed, the Supreme Court has recognized that the First Amendment's protections of the freedom to construct knowledge, form beliefs, and express oneself are dependent on the freedom to develop meaningful associations in which knowledge is constructed, belief is formed, and expression is respected:

> It is beyond debate that freedom to engage in association for the advancement of beliefs and ideas is an inseparable aspect of the "liberty" assured by the Due Process Clause of the Fourteenth Amendment, which embraces freedom of speech. . . . Of course, it is immaterial whether the beliefs sought to be advanced by association pertain to political, economic, religious or cultural matters, and state action which may have the effect of curtailing the freedom to associate is subject to the closest scrutiny.[29]

In Article 1, Section 8, Clause 8, the U.S. Constitution further reflects the Framers' appreciation of the importance of meaningful associations to the construction and dissemination of knowledge. That section grants to Congress the power to promote "the progress of science and the useful arts." One method by which Congress is empowered to promote such "progress" is by giving to "Authors and Inventors the exclusive right to their respective writings and discoveries."[30]

The Constitution recognizes that human discovery requires the ingenuity of individual inventors. Yet the Constitution does not grant to Congress the power to give such inventors unlimited exclusive control over their inventions; rather, it provides such control only for "limited times."[31] As James Madison wrote in the Federalist Papers, the "public good fully coincides in both cases with the claims of individuals."[32]

The intellectual property protections in the Constitution can be traced to the political philosophy of John Locke. In his *Second Treatise of Civil Government*, Locke wrote that human beings have a natural right to property in their own bodies.[33] That natural right leads to the natural instinct and therefore the natural right to self-preservation.[34] The right of individuals to their own bodies also gives them a property right to the "labors" of their bodies and the fruits of those labors.[35] A person has a natural right to own that which his labor has created. Locke's understanding of a natural right to property which pre-dates civil society undoubtedly influenced the drafters of the Constitution.[36]

Yet, as the Framers understood, Locke's conception of the development of human knowledge was not limited to the work of solitary individuals. Even as he proposed a natural right to property, Locke cautioned against its excesses. Because the right to property is an extension of the right to self-preservation, it cannot be used to justify the appropriation of tangible and intangible material that is not necessary for self-preservation.[37] There is no natural right to the acquisition of property that is not necessary for self-preservation.[38]

On the contrary, Locke believed that individuals who appropriated to themselves more property than they could efficiently use to sustain themselves acted in a way contrary to their true natures, particularly where there is not enough left in common for others.[39] While there is a natural law basis for an individual's property right to the fruits of his own intellectual labors, that law also includes its own natural limits. There is no natural right to appropriate that which is not useful for the improvement of knowledge, the progress of civilization, and the advancement of human happiness.

The Framers not only understood the natural limits on individual work-product, they also grasped the collaborative nature of human discovery. Their temporal limit on Congress's power to protect the individual creator's exclusivity was designed to ensure that knowledge will enter the public domain.[40] By ensuring that a discovery will enter the public domain at some point, the Framers also recognized the value of collaboration in constructing human knowledge.[41]

The Framers' understanding of the social nature of the construction of knowledge is captured by Thomas Jefferson's thoughtful analysis of the nature of ideas: "If nature has made one thing less susceptible than all others of exclusive property, it is the action of thinking power called an idea."[42] Jefferson understood that the moment a person divulges an idea, "it forces itself into the possession of every one, and the receiver cannot dispossess himself of it."[43] He appreciated that the acquisition of any private property is necessarily limited by time. No individual, he argued, "has, of natural right, a separate property in an area of land. . . . By an universal law . . . indeed, whatever, whether fixed or movable, belongs to all men equally and in common is the property for the moment of him who occupies it; but when he relinquishes the occupation, the property goes with it."[44]

Jefferson concluded that "[s]table ownership is the gift of social law, and is given late in the progress of society."[45] In light of Jefferson's perspective and the limiting language of the Constitution, it is clear that the American regime is founded on the principle that intellectual property joins the public domain. The government must affirmatively act to enable individuals to own it, and may do so only for "limited times."[46]

According to Jefferson, it is the social construction of knowledge that is natural, not the individual's property interest in any particular discovery: "That ideas should freely spread from one to another over the globe, for the moral and mutual instruction of man, and improvement of his condition, seems to have been peculiarly and benevolently designed by nature."[47]

Jefferson employs the image of a flame emanating from a candle to demonstrate the inherently social nature of knowledge: "He who receives an idea from me, receives instruction himself without lessening mine; as he who lights his taper at mine, receives light without darkening me."[48] An individual's ideas are like fire. They "spread from one to another," they illuminate all without "lessening their density in any point," and thus they are "incapable of confinement or exclusive appropriation."[49]

Jefferson's candle metaphor describes very well the fundamental tenets of social constructivism. Like Jefferson, the social-constructivists appreciate that knowledge cannot be delivered or captured by any particular individual or group. Rather, knowledge is constructed when ideas are "spread from one to another" through meaningful relationships. To the extent that the Constitution's unique "limit" on the appropriation of intellectual property reifies Jefferson's understanding of human knowledge, therefore, it supports the development of an educational system based on a view that knowledge is socially constructed through those relationships.

In "The United States as a Regime and the Sources of the American Way of Life," Joseph Cropsey also brilliantly demonstrates that the U.S. Constitutional structure depends upon and facilitates collective self-knowledge:

> the United States is the microcosm of modernity, repeating in its regime, on the level of popular consciousness, the major noetic events of the modern world. Our national self-dissatisfaction is the mirror of modernity's self-criticism. In our own way, we are mankind.[50]

He concludes that the "genius of the American regime assigns [the] highest task of statesmanship to the people themselves, and in so doing brings the nation to the outer limit of self-government rightly understood."[51]

The founding documents encourage an evolving definition of the United States regime. The regime consists of the "Constitution, laws, judicial opinions and the speeches of public men," but it also includes the evolution of all "decisive influences" on daily life, including "ongoing, changing thought."[52] The structure of the government itself invites self-reflection, and that self-reflection is influenced by the ongoing progress of political philosophy and science.

To the extent that the Constitution erects a government based on Locke's view of human nature and civil society, therefore, it also facilitates the critical examination of that view by subsequent generations. Cropsey recognizes that although the founding documents may have constructed a government rationalized by the natural desires of mankind to preserve their life, liberty, and property against others, the "currents of thought" since the founding questioning that rationale have become a vital part of the regime. In fact, the founding documents are the "premise of a gigantic argument" about the nature of human development.

As the regime becomes "more perfect" with advances in thought, it also becomes inseparable from a more perfect understanding of human development. Contemporary thought, which must be included within the American "regime," now gives to Americans a natural, moral imperative to form associations that together view the "world as an opportunity for greatness" rather than as a justification for isolated, subjective desires to satisfy "privately-felt predilections."[53]

In *Democracy in America*, Alexis de Tocqueville also writes beautifully about the propensity of Americans to join associations:

> Americans of all ages, all minds constantly unite. . . . As soon as several of the inhabitants of the United States have conceived of a sentiment or an idea that they want to produce in the world, they seek each other out; and when they have found each other, they unite.[54]

In a democratic regime like the United States, de Tocqueville argues, "the art of associating must be developed."[55] Associations are indispensable to human progress: "In democratic countries, the science of associations is the mother science; the progress of all the others depends on the progress of that one."[56]

Associations of all varieties are particularly necessary to the American people because of their yearning for freedom and equality. In fact, de Tocqueville concludes that the "art of associating must be developed and perfected" among Americans in order that they "remain civilized."[57]

The natural inclination of people in America to unite with their neighbors into associations large and small must be cultivated and celebrated. According to de Tocqueville, of all "the laws that rule human societies," the law requiring the act of associating is the most "precise" and "clear."[58] As de Tocqueville and Cropsey fully recognized, therefore, the United States regime depends upon a view of human nature that drives individuals to develop meaningful relationships through which they achieve well-being and find joy in the social construction of knowledge.

THE PEDAGOGICAL CONSEQUENCES OF THE FRAMERS' NUANCED VIEW OF HUMAN NATURE AND HUMAN DEVELOPMENT

In his essay, "Human Nature and the Scope of Education," David Hawkins develops a theory of education based on profound understanding of the view of human nature that informed the Constitution's drafters.[59] Hawkins recognizes that the Framers' conception of the "state of nature," adopted from the influential political philosophy of Thomas Hobbes and John Locke, was a fictional construct designed to persuade policy makers of the value of equality, freedom, and rationality.[60]

According to the "state of nature" "thought experiment," human beings are born into a natural state of freedom and equality. In the absence of civil society, they become "competitive" and "dangerous to each other" because they are "determined by self-preservation to be enemies."[61] But human beings are also given the gift of reason, which leads them to develop social bonds that lead them out of their natural "nasty, brutish and short" lives.[62]

As Hawkins recognizes:

> In this model all men being equal and rational, realize the source of their misery and create by rational consent a sovereign person or group to whom they surrender their power as far as possible.[63]

In order to advance their desire for self-preservation, individuals choose rationally to forfeit to a sovereign the freedoms they would have in a natural state in return for the sovereign's equal protection of their lives, liberty, and property.

As Hawkins astutely demonstrates, the concepts of equality, liberty, and rationality that seem to support the founding of the American democracy are incomplete, particularly as they apply to children. Although the premise that humans are born "equal" has tremendous political, social, and even spiritual meaning, it also masks the actual differences in children.

All children are equal in their capacity to learn, but they learn in different ways and at different rates. Moreover, there are material differences in the neo-natal and early childhood resources afforded children. The principle of equality requires that "like cases be treated in a like manner." Yet, if children are not alike in their resources or their learning, an educational regime that treats them as if they were alike violates the essence of equality.

Similarly, the essence of "freedom" is not merely the liberty to pursue self-interest and self-preservation at the expense of others. Rather, the "innate" core of freedom is the "capacity for using knowledge in deliberate choice."[64] That human capacity "expands with experience and knowledge, so that it is not possible to draw a sharp distinction between self-preservation and self-development."[65]

Finally, the concept of rationality includes more than static, self-interested, utility-maximizing, cost-benefit decision making that is devoid of emotion and intuition. Instead, "rational capacity" is a fluid concept that is "manifest from early infancy," is formed through an "association with others," and requires the "interplay of perception, imagination and understanding."[66] This view of rationality, like Hawkins's view of freedom and equality, is far more authentic and nuanced than the superficial view often ascribed to the Framers' understanding of the state of nature.

In fact, the Framers of the Constitution actually promulgated a subtle conception of human nature and development not inconsistent with that suggested by Hawkins. Human beings are equal in their capacity to govern and to be governed. They have the innate ability to understand another person's perspectives, feelings, and intentions. Freedom is natural as well, but it is the freedom to construct and to use knowledge to make deliberate choices. The Constitutional structure of self-governance depends on the belief that individuals have a natural desire for the freedom to construct knowledge, to act on their knowledge to question authority, and to make informed decisions.

As Hawkins shows, the human being envisioned by the Framers suggests a uniquely American early childhood pedagogy. He concludes that the "'poetic' process of choice—the experimentation with new ways of thinking and behaving—is the root of the dynamics of learning.[67] The best teacher in a democracy will respect the natural instinct in every child to construct knowledge through associations, will provide an environment that gives the child the freedom to construct knowledge through experimentation, and will value the collective choices made by associations of children.

In particular, Hawkins recommends that the teacher facilitate the discovery by children of "cognitive knots"—questions naturally embraced by children that do not have readily ascertainable answers. The teacher will be tempted to untie the knot for the child. The education system will be tempted to assess whether or not the child mimics the teacher's instructions.

But that would be inimical to learning. Rather, the teacher should "try to provide from many sources that which will enrich the empirical matrix of a child's thought or will suggest analogies or connections from previous experiences which are, at that moment, un-retrievable by the child himself."[68] In other words, the teacher should insure that the educational environment fosters the child's natural curiosity, inquisitiveness, perseverance, and experimentation.

Such an environment allows children to develop the capacity to construct their own knowledge through their meaningful associations. It is that educational environment that is truly consistent with the American democratic regime envisioned by the Framers.

THE POLITICAL CONSEQUENCES OF THE FRAMERS' NUANCED VIEW OF HUMAN NATURE AND HUMAN DEVELOPMENT

B.F. Skinner himself recognized that behaviorism could be misappropriated to frustrate the growth of a genuine democracy. Even as he was proposing his teaching machines, Skinner was rejecting any calls for "aversive" educational practices. Aversive educational practices included punishing students and schools for "failure, the frequency of which is to be increased by 'raising standards.'"[69]

Skinner cautioned that the "discipline of the birch rod" or the threat of failure may "facilitate learning," but it also "breeds followers of dictators and revolutionists."[70] Skinner applauded the progressive educational practices advocated by John Dewey and the rejection of aversive learning strategies. Skinner claimed only that his behaviorist approach could help replace those aversive practices based on the negative reinforcement of failure. He understood that such aversive educational practices threatened "democratic principles" and hoped that his insights could be used to support teachers in their efforts to reach all of their students.[71]

Roberto Mangabeira Unger also has shown how a complete understanding of the Framers' vision can support the growth of a genuine democracy in which all members of a community are encouraged to construct their knowledge through meaningful relationships and to exercise their power to perform different leadership roles. As Unger has suggested, there is nothing in human nature or in true democratic regimes that requires an adversarial relationship between the individual and the community.

On the contrary, the notion that there that must be a continual "struggle" between the educational best interests of the child and those of the community is a "false necessity."[72] That false necessity may help to legitimate a particular form of political order, but it ultimately stands in the way of the development of a genuine democracy.

Political structures justified by the belief that individuals are naturally governed by their subjective desires "undermine the conception of a shared humanity."[73] The belief that individuals should overcome their passions through reason, however, ultimately leads to an effort to negate or dissolve the individuality of the person.

The legal and political dimension of the artificial antinomy between reason and desire is the "contrast between public and private existence."[74] The "public" sphere is characterized by the necessity of being governed by common standards and laws. In the "private" sphere, by contrast, individuals are free to follow our own individual and natural desires. As a consequence, people are compelled to negate their full identities in the public realm of law and the market place, while they also are compelled to pursue their own desires only in isolation from the community.

The presumption that human desire is natural and negative while reason is acquired and positive makes difficult both individual well-being and community. The "antinomy" of reason and desire undermines the formation of a complete human being in which reason and desire act in harmony, just as it undermines the formation of a community in which individuals and others can act in harmony.

In *Law and Modern Society: Toward a Criticism of Social Theory*,[75] Unger shows how the emergence of the conception of the individual who is in opposition to society corresponds with the disintegration of community. In a community, there is a "closely held communion of reciprocal expectations, based on a shared view of right and wrong."[76] The standards of behavior are not established primarily through formal rules or positive law. Rather, there is an organic "allegiance to common moral understandings."

Individual members of a community are not in opposition to the commonwealth. They have internalized the desire to remain faithful to the group's customs and they may rely comfortably on their belief that their neighbors will do the same. In the community, desire is not in opposition to reason. The individual has already internalized the group's expectations so that the individual will instinctively desire what is expected by the group. At the same time, the group's expectations are fully informed by the collective desires of its members, so that those expectations are not imposed by some external force of "reason."[77]

Unger suggests that in a genuine democracy, the artificial tension between the individual and the community would dissolve because power would be rotated and shared in meaningful associations. All members of the community would play multiple roles.

In fact, teaching children the habits of mind and heart that are required for "role-playing" is essential to the development of a true democracy. Although their concerns about self-interest have been used to justify a political and educational regime based on the supposed struggle between the individual and the community, the Framers also fully appreciated that the development of such a democracy depends on the natural capacity of children to learn to share roles, to construct meaning, and to spread knowledge through meaningful associations.

Empathy

NOTES

1. Charles Kesler and Clinton Rossiter, *The Federalist Papers* (New York: Penguin Putnam, 1999) ("*The Federalist* is the most important work of political science that has ever been written . . . in the United States.").

2. James Madison, *The Federalist Papers*, #51 (New York: New American Library, 1961), 322.

3. Madison, *The Federalist Papers*, #55, 340.

4. Alexander Hamilton, *The Federalist Papers*, #6, 51–53.

5. Madison, *The Federalist Papers*, #51, 322.

6. Ibid.

7. Madison, *The Federalist Papers*, #10, 78.

8. Madison, *The Federalist Papers*, #48, 308.

9. Ibid., 309.

10. Madison, *The Federalist Papers*, #39, 241.

11. Madison, *The Federalist Papers*, #51, 343.

12. 411 U.S. 1, 49 (1973).

13. John B. Watson, *The Behavioral Learning Theory* (1917).

14. John B. Watson and Rosalie Rayner, Conditioned Emotional Responses, *Journal of Experimental Psychology* 3(1) (1920): 1–14.

15. Ibid.

16. B.F. Skinner, "Teaching Machines," *Science* 128(3330) (October 1958): 970.

17. Ibid., 971.

18. James Webb, "Pragmatisms (Plural) Part I: Classical Pragmatism and Some Implications for Empirical Inquiry," *Journal of Economic Issues* 41(4) (2007): 1086.

19. T.H. Leahey, "Control: A History of Behavioral Psychology," *Journal of American History* 87(2) (2000): 686-687.

20. Skinner, "Teaching Machines," 971.

21. Ibid.

22. Robert E. Slavin, *Education Psychology: Theory Into Practice* (Boston: Allyn & Bacon, 2012).

23. M.R. Lepper, D. Greene, and R.E. Nisbett, "Undermining Children's Intrinsic Interest with Extrinsic Reward," *Journal of Personality and Social Psychology* 28 (1973).

24. Phillip Harris, Bruce M. Smith, and Joan Harris, *The Myths of Standardized Test: Why They Don't Tell You What You Think They Do* (New York: Rowman & Littlefield, 2011), 73-75.

25. Linda Darling-Hammond, "How People Learn: Introduction to Learning Theories," Stanford University School of Education, 2001, 6, http://web.stanford.edu/class/ed269/hplintrochapter.pdf.

26. Ibid.

27. Madison, *The Federalist Papers*, #57.

28. Ibid.

29. *NAACP v. Alabama ex rel. Patterson*, 357 U.S. 449, 460-61 (1958). See also *NAACP v. Alabama ex rel. Patterson*, 357 U.S. 449, 461, 463 (1958); *NAACP v. Button*, 371 U.S. 415, 429–30 (1963); *Cousins v. Wigoda*, 419 U.S. 477, 487 (1975); *In re Primus*, 436 U.S. 412, 426 (1978); *Democratic Party v. Wisconsin*, 450 U.S. 107, 121 (1981).

30. U.S. Constitution, Art. 1, Section 8, Clause 8.

31. Ibid.

32. Madison, *The Federalist Papers*, #43.

33. John Locke, *Two Treatises of Government, the Second Treatise of Civil Government* (1698), sections 27–28.

34. Ibid.

35. Ibid.

36. *Note: Textualism as Fair Notice*, 123 Harv. L. Rev. 542, 544, n. 10 (2009). *See also* Alfred Yen, *Restoring the Natural Law: Copyright as Labor and Possession*, 51 Ohio St. L. J. 517, 523 (1990).

37. Locke, *Second Treatise*, section 25.

38. Ibid., section 31.

39. Ibid., sections 27 and 31.

40. Tzen Wong, "Intellectual Property Through the Lens of Human Development," *Intellectual Property and Human Development* (Public Interest Intellectual Property Advisors 2011): 18.

41. Ibid., 18–19.

42. Thomas Jefferson, Letter to Isaac McPherson (August 13, 1813).

43. Ibid.

44. Ibid.

45. Ibid.

46. U.S. Constitution, Article 1, Section 8, Clause 8.

47. Jefferson, Letter to Isaac McPherson.

48. Ibid.

49. Ibid.

50. Joseph Cropsey, *Political Philosophy and the Issue of Politics* (Chicago: University of Chicago Press, 1977), 12.

51. Ibid., 15.

52. Ibid.

53. Ibid., 6.

54. Alexis de Tocqueville, *Democracy in America*, ed. and trans. H. Mansfield and D. Winthrop (Chicago: University of Chicago Press, 2000), 489–92.

55. Ibid., 489–92.

56. Ibid.

57. Ibid.

58. Ibid.

59. David Hawkins, *The Informed Vision: Essays on Learning and Human Nature* (New York: Agathon Press, 2002), 205–42.

60. Ibid., 211–13.

61. Ibid., 212.

62. Ibid., 213.

63. Ibid., 212.

64. Ibid., 224.

65. Ibid., 224–25.

66. Ibid., 229–40.

67. Ibid., 242.

68. Ibid., 241.

69. Skinner, "Teaching Machines," 977.

70. Ibid.

71. Ibid.

72. See Roberto Mangabeira Unger, *False Necessity: Anti-Necessitarian Social Theory in the Service of Radical Democracy* (Boston: Cambridge University Press, 1987).

73. Ibid., 57.

74. Ibid., 59.

75. Roberto Mangabeira Unger, *Law and Modern Society: Toward a Criticism of Social Theory* (New York: Free Press, 1976).

76. Unger, *Law and Modern Society*, 61.

77. Ibid.

Chapter Three

The Legal Foundations of American Early Childhood Education

This chapter describes the structure of American education law. It demonstrates that the U.S. Constitution generally prohibits the federal government from directly regulating America's schools, and usually protects the power of the local community to govern education.

Although parents and guardians have a constitutional liberty interest in directing the upbringing of their children, the state has tremendous power to establish public schools, and to require that all children be educated according to its curricular standards—even in private school or homeschooling. The state also has the authority to determine the age at which formal education must begin and thus has the power to proscribe early childhood education.

As this chapter indicates, the state's power over education is influenced by federal legislation passed primarily under the Constitution's Spending Clause and is limited by principles of liberty and equality protected by the Constitution's amendments. The right of the government to mandate education for children must be balanced against these federal directives.

Nonetheless, there is no doubt that the state could establish early childhood education programs, could develop the particular pedagogy employed in those programs, and could even mandate attendance at those programs. Nor is there any doubt that the lack of equal access to existing programs could present significant state and federal constitutional concerns. Moreover, acting pursuant to its constitutional spending power, Congress could incentivize states to provide all of their children access to early childhood education programs that implement a particularly effective pedagogical approach.

THE FUNDAMENTAL RELATIONSHIP BETWEEN FEDERAL AND STATE CONTROL OVER EDUCATION

The Constitution does not grant to the federal government any direct power to regulate education. It does not even mention "education." In the absence of an express delegation to the federal government of constitutional power to regulate schools, therefore, that power is reserved to the states.

The Tenth Amendment to the Constitution reserves to the states all powers that are not expressly delegated to the federal government. That reservation of non-delegated powers to the states insures that the state and local governments generally retain sovereignty over affairs such as the education of their own citizens. As such, education law in America is primarily a matter of state and local concern. As long as they do not run afoul of constitutional or federal statutory prohibitions, state and local governments have virtually unlimited power to regulate the education of their children.

Local Control of Education

The states have virtually unlimited power to regulate education. The state has the power to pass legislation mandating attendance at school, punishing the failure of children at specific ages to attend school without legitimate justification, and imposing reasonable regulations on basic education, including: (1) required and elective curriculum, (2) instructional practices, (3) facilities, (4) attendance zones, (5) transportation, (6) security, (7) teacher qualifications, (8) policies and procedures, and (9) assessments. The states' power to mandate education and to regulate instructional practices extends to all private schools, and even to home schooling.

The states' interests in compulsory education and reasonable school regulations include: standardizing children; preparing citizens for political life; preparing citizens to be self-sufficient; instilling a love of country; facilitating the diffusion of knowledge; preventing children from prematurely entering the workforce; shaping character; developing critical thinking skills; developing intellectual autonomy; preparing students to interact in a culturally, ethnically, religiously and racially diverse community; and developing habits of mental and physical wellness.

In exerting their control over education, the states typically delegate their power to local educational agencies or school boards. School boards set policies that incorporate legal requirements for the school district. Boards also establish specific rules governing district administration, personnel, community relations, student rights, dispute resolution, curriculum, and instructional practices.

The school board also is empowered to establish a school district's mission, belief statement, strategic objectives, and annual goals. School boards typically are composed of elected, volunteer public servants. The locally elected public officials, in turn, often delegate their managerial authority to an educational professional such as a chief administrator or superintendent.

The theme of "local control" is a recurring one throughout education law. In his dissent in *Board of Education of the Westside Community Schools v. Mergens,*[1] Justice Stevens explored the "pedagogical, political, and ethical" arguments supporting local control of education:

> As a matter of pedagogy, delicate decisions about immersing young students in ideological cross-currents ought to be made by educators familiar with the experience and needs of the particular children affected, and with the culture of community in which they are likely to live as adults. . . . As a matter of politics, public schools are often dependent for financial support upon local communities. The schools may be better able to retain local favor if they are free to shape their policies in response to local preferences.[2] As a matter of ethics, it is sensible to respect the desire of parents to guide the education of their children without surrendering control to distant politicians.[3]

Federal Congressional Power to Influence Education

Although state and local governments have significant direct control over education, the U.S. Constitution does give Congress the power to wield indirect power to influence educational practices pursuant to its authority to regulate interstate commerce and its authority under the Spending Clause.

The Commerce Clause gives Congress the power to regulate the channels of interstate commerce, persons, or instrumentalities of interstate commerce and activities that substantially affect interstate commerce. Congress's power to regulate education under the Commerce Clause, however, is limited. For example, the Supreme Court has held that Congress has no power to pass a statute criminalizing gun possession in a "school zone" because such possession alone does not "substantially affect" interstate commerce.[4]

The federal government therefore regulates education primarily through the Spending Clause which permits Congress to attach conditions to the states' receipt of federal funds, so long as: the expenditures are used by the states for the general welfare, as opposed to a purely local concern; the conditions imposed by Congress on funding are clear and unambiguous; the conditions imposed by Congress on funding are reasonably related to the purpose of the expenditures; and the conditions imposed by Congress do not violate any independent constitutional prohibition. In addition, the Supreme Court also has made clear that the conditions that Congress attaches to its funding must not be coercive, and must afford the states a genuine choice of whether to forego the funding stream.[5]

Acting primarily pursuant to its "spending" power, Congress has passed an array of federal statutes that regulate school affairs, including the employment of teachers[6]; the treatment of female students[7]; the education of children with learning disabilities[8]; the privacy rights of teachers and students[9]; the rights of teachers to take family and medical leave[10]; the access of public and private groups to educational facilities[11]; and even the qualifications of teachers, the content of curriculum, and the standards for student achievement.[12]

The No Child Left Behind Act of 2002 is a prime example of Congress's use of its spending power to influence education. The Act requires the states, as a condition to their receipt of federal funds, to ensure that students are taught by "highly qualified" teachers; that students are assessed on a periodic basis; that assessment data is disaggregated by categories such as race, gender and special needs; and that schools make "adequate yearly progress" with respect to the assessment scores of students in each category.

The "Race to the Top"—a United States Department of Education program funded by the American Recovery and Reinvestment Act of 2009—is another example of the way in which Congress has influenced school affairs pursuant to its spending power. The initial round of Race to the Top funding dedicated over $4 billion to 19 states that participated in a competitive process to receive funding. These states serve 22 million students and employ 1.5 million teachers in 42,000 schools, representing 45 percent of all K-12 students and 42 percent of all low-income students nationwide.

To be eligible for these competitive federal Race to the Top grants, states are required to adopt "internationally benchmarked standards and assessments that prepare students for success in college and the workplace."[13] States are awarded points for satisfying certain criteria such as turning around the lowest-achieving schools, implementing and using data systems to support instruction, and developing and adopting common standards and assessments.

The Race to the Top program also has incentivized the states to adopt the Common Core Standards.[14] States were given extra points on their applications if they adopted those Common Core Standards by August 2, 2010.[15] While state education standards were first implemented in the early 1990s[16]—and, by the early 2000s, every state had developed and adopted some standards—the standards were not uniform. It was this lack of uniformity and the ability to obtain significantly increased funding that led the states to develop national standards known as the Common Core State Standards.[17]

The Common Core Standards, in contrast to the education standards that were implemented in previous decades, are uniform and specify what "proficiency" should look like at each grade level and at graduation. They were informed by state standards already in existence, and to some extent by the experience of teachers, experts, and states, and feedback from the public.[18]

Due in large part to the funding they would receive if they obtained the Race to the Top grants, state leaders from 48 states, two territories, and the District of Columbia began adopting these standards in 2009.[19] During two public comment periods, the National Governor's Association and the Council of Chief State School Officers received nearly 10,000 comments on the standards from teachers, parents, school administrators, and concerned citizens.[20]

After the development process ended, states began voluntarily adopting the Common Core State Standards based on their own processes for education standard adoption.[21] While 19 states received funding initially, 34 states modified state education laws or policies, and 48 states took part in the efforts to create the Common Core Standards. Presently, 43 states, the District of Columbia, 4 territories, and the Department of Defense Education Activity have adopted the Common Core and are implementing the standards.[22]

This state-level Race to the Top program was followed by a second Race to the Top competition aimed at providing incentives for innovative district-level programs designed to personalize learning to meet student needs. These grants were awarded to 16 applicants representing 55 school districts across 11 states and the District of Columbia. These districts will share nearly $400 million to support locally developed plans to personalize and deepen student learning, directly improve student achievement and educator effectiveness, close achievement gaps, and prepare every student to succeed in college and their careers.[23] The federal government is using a similar competitive grant process to encourage innovation in the areas of early learning and assessment.

As such, the Common Core and the Race to the Top represent attempts to mediate the relationship between federal and state governance of education. The Common Core invites each state to adopt standards, with the hope that the collective decision of the states ultimately will result in the development of common, nationwide educational objectives. The Race to the Top is a federal Department of Education program, but it does not require the states to adopt any standards. Rather, the federal program incentivizes state compliance by awarding states funds for their innovation efforts. Both programs demonstrate the strength of Congress's ability to influence local education through its spending power.

Constitutional Limits on Local Control

The Constitution also places important limits on state and local control of education. For example, the Fifth and Fourteenth Amendments' Due Process

Clauses prohibit the state and federal governments from enacting educational programs that deprive parents and guardians of the "liberty" to direct the upbringing of their children. Moreover, although the Fourteenth Amendment's Equal Protection Clause generally does not prevent the states from employing education-financing systems that produce dramatic disparities in the funds available in different school districts, that Clause does preclude them from absolutely depriving children of a minimally adequate level of education. State constitutional provisions may also limit inadequate and inequitable education funding systems.

THE RELATIONSHIP BETWEEN THE STATE'S POWER TO REGULATE EDUCATION AND THE CONSTITUTIONAL RIGHTS OF PARENTS AND GUARDIANS TO DIRECT THE UPBRINGING OF THEIR CHILDREN

In the seminal cases of *Meyer v. Nebraska*[24] and *Pierce v. Society of Sisters*,[25] the Supreme Court found in the "liberty" guaranteed by the Due Process Clause of the Fourteenth Amendment a constitutional right of "parents and guardians to direct the upbringing and education of children under their control." In *Meyer*, that right precluded the state of Nebraska from criminalizing the practice of teaching in languages other than English and in *Pierce* that right precluded Oregon from requiring all of its children to attend only public school.

In both cases, the Court emphasized that a child in America is not "the mere creature of the state."[26] Accordingly, the state's power to "standardize" its children cannot interfere with the right of parents and guardians to direct the upbringing and education of their own children. Nonetheless, even as it recognized that the state has no power to "submerge the individual," the Supreme Court made clear that the state has tremendous authority over the education of its children.

The Supreme Court also has recognized that parents and guardians have a right to "direct the upbringing of their children" in a manner consistent with the "fundamental mode of life mandated" by their "deep religious convictions." State programs violate that right if they place a substantial burden on the free exercise of religion. In *Wisconsin v. Yoder*,[27] the Supreme Court held that Wisconsin's compulsory school attendance law violated the constitutional rights of Amish parents to direct the upbringing of their children in a manner consistent with the fundamental mode of life mandated by their deep religious convictions.

Since *Yoder*, however, parents challenging compulsory school attendance and state regulation of the education of their children in public school, private school, and at home have rarely been able to meet the test for demonstrating a violation of their right to free exercise of religion. They cannot show, as they must, that their fundamental mode of life is inseparable from their deep religious convictions; that the state's compulsory education regime or its regulation of education sharply conflicts with, or unduly burdens, the free exercise of their religious convictions; and that the state's interest is either not compelling, or the state's interest is compelling, but its method of achieving its interest is not the least restrictive of religious exercise.

Accordingly, the state has virtually unlimited power to govern the education of its citizens. The state may establish the age of which schooling must begin; may require all children of that age to be schooled; may establish the curriculum and assessment to be administered to all of its school age children, and may even dictate the way in which education is provided and assessed for children who are homeschooled.

THE RELATIONSHIP BETWEEN THE STATE'S POWER TO REGULATE EDUCATION AND FEDERAL AND STATE CONSTITUTIONAL RIGHTS TO EQUITABLE AND ADEQUATE EDUCATION FUNDING

The Federal Constitutional Right to a Minimally Adequate Education

In *San Antonio Indep. School Dist. v. Rodriguez*,[28] Mexican-American parents of children in elementary and secondary schools challenged the Texas system of funding public schools largely through local property taxes. The Texas educational funding regime at issue in this case is typical of state and local educational finance systems throughout the nation. Under the Texas funding scheme, poor areas were taxed at a high rate relative to the value of individual property, but had little to spend on education; wealthier areas could tax at low rates, but still had much more to spend on education. Although the Texas Minimum Foundation School Program guaranteed a minimum level of funding for each child, that foundation level undisputedly failed to compensate for the dramatic disparities in educational funding among schools in the school district and throughout the state.

Plaintiffs challenged the funding scheme, arguing that it violated the Fourteenth Amendment, which precludes states from denying to any person within their jurisdiction the "equal protection of the laws." The Supreme Court however rejected the challenge.

The Court first addressed the issue of the level of judicial scrutiny that should be applied to assess the constitutionality of the funding regime. In order to determine whether any state or federal legislation violates the equal protection clause, the Supreme Court has established different levels of judicial scrutiny. The Court analyzes most legislation by determining only whether the law is rationally related to a legitimate state interest. Under that deferential "rational basis" standard of review, legislation enjoys a strong presumption of constitutionality.

If, however, legislation impinges upon a fundamental constitutional right of a "discrete and insular minority," the Court will "strictly scrutinize" the statute. Under that exacting standard, a statute will be declared unconstitutional unless it is narrowly tailored to achieve a compelling governmental interest.[29] In *San Antonio*, the Supreme Court did not apply strict scrutiny because it determined that the educational funding system did not discriminate against a suspect class of discrete and insular minorities and did not impinge upon any fundamental constitutional right.

First, the court reasoned that the plaintiffs could not show that the funding regime worked to the particular disadvantage of a discrete and insular minority. Rather, the regime adversely affected a "large, diverse, and amorphous class, unified only by the common factor of residence in districts that happen to have less taxable wealth than other districts." According to the Court, the plaintiffs did not have traditional indicia of a suspect class: an immutable characteristic, a history of purposeful unequal treatment, or political powerlessness. Moreover, there was no basis in the record to assume that the poorest people all live in the same school district. Nor did Texas' policies result in an absolute deprivation of a minimally adequate education.

Second, the Court reasoned that there is no right to education explicitly or implicitly guaranteed by the U.S. Constitution. The Court refused to create substantive constitutional rights in the name of guaranteeing equal protection of the laws. Although education is linked to the exercise of other constitutional rights such as free speech and voting, the Court also declined to find an implicit right to education in the Constitution. The Court recognized that although its past cases had expressed an abiding respect for the vital role of education in a free society, it concluded that the importance of a service does not determine whether it must be regarded as fundamental for purposes of examination under the Equal Protection Clause.

Having determined that strict scrutiny should not be used to analyze the constitutionality of Texas's funding regime, the Court concluded that the regime meets the rational basis test. Under that minimal level of scrutiny, the Court found that Texas's educational regime is rational because it reflects local control over funding for education.

In reaching its conclusion regarding the constitutionality of Texas's educational finance system, the Court also declared that "the history of education since the industrial revolution shows a continual struggle between two forces: the desire by members of society to have educational opportunity for all children, and the desire of each family to provide the best education it can afford for its own children."[30] In this telling declaration, the Supreme Court presumes that there is a natural "struggle" between what is best for the family and what is best for the community.

That "struggle" presents a "myriad of intractable economic, social, and even philosophical problems."[31] These "problems" are then used by the Court as a justification for its decision to refrain from entering an arena traditionally relegated to local control. The Court also stressed that although the Texas regime created disparities in funding, its "foundation" level insured that no student would be absolutely deprived of a minimally adequate education.[32]

In *Plyler v. Doe*,[33] however, the Supreme Court declared unconstitutional a law that completely denied to undocumented school-age children the free public education that it provides to children who are citizens of the United States or who are legally admitted aliens. Although the Court did not find a fundamental constitutional right to education, it did recognize "the importance of education in maintaining our basic institutions" and "the lasting impact of [education] deprivation on the life of a child."

The Court also declared that: "Education has a fundamental role in maintaining the fabric of our society." Accordingly, in *Plyler*, the Court affirmed that the Equal Protection Clause prohibits the state or federal government from absolutely depriving persons of a minimal level of education. In *Papasan v. Allain*,[34] the Supreme Court also indicated that there may well be a constitutional right to receive a "minimally adequate education."

In the wake of *San Antonio* and its progeny, therefore, the Equal Protection Clause in the federal constitution prohibits legislation that absolutely deprives persons of a minimally adequate level of education. In addition, any legislation that discriminates against a discrete and insular minority in its provision of educational benefits or burdens could be subjected to strict judicial scrutiny under the equal protection clause. Nonetheless, in the wake of the Supreme Court's deferential approach to disparities in education funding, and in light of the unmistakable reality of such disparities in virtually every state, the focus of legal challenges to educational funding regimes has shifted from the federal constitution to state constitutions.

The State Constitutional Right to an Adequate and Equitable Education

All state constitutions contain their own "equal protection" clause, as well as language that requires the establishment of public schools. Nearly half of the states also have constitutional language declaring education to be a fundamental value or goal. A strong minority of states has constitutional language requiring an "efficient" or "thorough" educational system. Under these provisions of the state constitutions, a majority of the state courts have found education to be a fundamental right that could invalidate disparities in educational funding.

In *DeRolph v. Ohio*,[35] for instance, the Ohio Supreme Court found disparities in educational funding within the state to violate that state's constitutional guarantee of a "thorough and efficient" educational system. The Court reasoned that the harm presented by inadequate and inequitable funding should not be left for the General Assembly to remedy. A massive amount of evidence was presented showing that the schools at issue were "starved for funds, lacked teachers, buildings, and equipment, and had inferior educational programs, and that their pupils were being deprived of educational opportunity."

The Court concluded that Ohio's elementary and secondary public schools are neither thorough nor efficient. The reasoning of the Ohio Supreme Court generally has carried the day as a majority of the state courts have interpreted similar language in their own constitutions to require equitable or adequate funding of education.[36]

In *Edgewood Independent School District v. Kirby*,[37] in fact, the Texas Supreme Court explicitly reconsidered the Edgewood School District at issue in *Rodriguez*. The court concluded that Texas's statewide system for funding education based on local property taxes, which produced a disparity of resources per student of 700 to 1, was contrary to the constitutional requirement that the legislature support and maintain an "efficient system of public free schools."[38]

Similarly, in *Campaign for Fiscal Equity, Inc. v. State of New York*,[39] the New York Court of Appeals concluded that the New York City schools failed to satisfy the state constitution's requirement of a "system of free common schools, wherein all the children of the state may be educated."[40]

After defining a "sound basic education" as one that affords students the skills and knowledge for "meaningful participation in contemporary society," the court found a "systematic failure" to provide New York City high school students with that constitutionally mandated standard of education. In fact, the court concluded that there was a "mismatch" between the disproportionately higher needs of the city's students and the disproportionately lower level of statewide funding allocated to meet those needs.[41] The court ordered the governor and the legislature to "ascertain the actual cost" of constitutional compliance and then to revise the state's funding formula to insure necessary resources to provide a "sound basic education" for all public school students in New York City.[42]

In *Serrano II*,[43] the California Supreme Court similarly declared that under the equal protection clause in the California state constitution, education is a fundamental right that precludes the state from providing dramatic disparities in education funding. In Wyoming,[44] Connecticut,[45] and North Dakota[46] as well, the courts invalidated inequitable educational funding regimes under the Equal Protection Clause in the state constitution.

Since *Rodriguez,* litigants have challenged school finance systems in 45 states, claiming primarily that those systems fail to meet the state's constitutional requirement to provide a minimally adequate level of educational resources for all students. They have been successful in a majority of the cases.[47]

Their success is based in part on unassailable data demonstrating the remarkable disparities in educational funding throughout the country. The *median* disparity in per-pupil spending between the wealthiest and poorest school districts throughout the United States is nearly $12,000 per student.[48]

This economic gap correlates to a racial gap. The Education Trust reported that "[s]chool districts that educate the greatest number of low-income and minority students receive substantially less state and local money per student than districts with the fewest such students."[49]

THE RELATIONSHIP BETWEEN THE STATE'S POWER TO REGULATE EDUCATION AND FEDERAL STATUTORY RIGHTS AND PROTECTIONS FOR YOUNG CHILDREN WITH EDUCATIONAL DISABILITIES

Special education legislation, including the Individuals with Disabilities in Education Act, requires the states, as a condition to the receipt of federal funds, to ensure that their young children with educational disabilities receive free and appropriate special education and related services in the least restrictive educational environment.

In *P.A.R.C. v. Commonwealth of Pennsylvania*,[50] the federal district court addressed the then-systemic practice of excluding students with educational disabilities from regular public school classrooms. The court declared that there must be a presumption that, among the alternative programs of education and training required by statute to be available, placement in a regular public school class is preferable to placement in a special public school class and placement in a special public school class is preferable to placement in any other type of program of education and training.

In *Mills v. Board of Education of District of Columbia*,[51] the court also adopted a presumption that among the alternative programs of education, placement in a regular public school class with appropriate ancillary services is preferable to placement in a special school class.

These two cases and a national political campaign for better educational services, spurred Congress to pass three major federal statutes: The Rehabilitation Act of 1973 (RHA), the Individuals with Disabilities Education Act (IDEA) (originally passed in 1975 under the name Education for all Handicapped Children Act), and the Americans with Disabilities Act of 1990 (ADA).

Section 504 of the Rehabilitation Act states "No otherwise qualified individual with disabilities in the United States . . . , shall solely by reason of his disabilities, be excluded from participation in, be denied the benefits of, or be subjected to discrimination under any program, or activity received Federal financial assistance."

The four purposes of the Individuals with Disabilities Education Act are: (1) to provide all children with disabilities a free appropriate public education that emphasizes special education and related services designed to meet their unique needs; (2) to assist states in implementing a system of early intervention services for infants and toddlers with disabilities; (3) to ensure that educators and parents have the necessary tools to improve educational results for children with disabilities; and (4) to assess and ensure the effectiveness of efforts to educate children with disabilities.[52]

The Individuals with Disabilities Education Act states that children with disabilities are to be educated to the maximum extent with children who do not have disabilities. This statutory regime gives to public school districts an obligation to provide or to find special education services to children, beginning at three years old.

Congress requires that all such children receive Individual Education Plans (IEP) that include a statement describing how the child's disability affects his or her involvement and progress in the general curriculum and a statement of goals and objectives that is related to enabling the child to achieve progress in the general curriculum. The statement of services in the IEP must also include a statement of the supplemental aids and services that will be provided for the child and a statement of the program modifications and supports for school personnel that will be provided for the child to progress in the general curriculum and to participate in extracurricular and nonacademic activities.

The Americans with Disabilities Act (ADA) extended civil rights similar to those of the Civil Rights Act of 1964 to people with disabilities. That Act prohibits discrimination on the basis of disability in: private sector employment; services rendered by state and local governments; places of public accommodations; transportation; and telecommunications systems.

The Duty to Make Reasonable Accommodations

The ADA and RHA both require educational institutions to make reasonable accommodations for students with educational disabilities. The Supreme Court in *Southeastern Comm. College v. Davis*,[53] however, held that the duty does not rise to requiring a substantial modification, "of an existing program, nor or schools required to create an undue financial or administrative burden."

In *Davis*, the Supreme Court concluded that an "otherwise qualified" person is one who meets all requirements for licensure in spite of his handicap, not except for his handicap. Davis, who had a serious hearing disability, wished to enter a registered nurse educational program. The Court agreed with the trial court that Davis's handicap prevented her from safely performing in both her training program and her desired profession. The Court determined that in such circumstances, the Rehabilitation Act does not impose an obligation to lower or substantially modify an educational institution's standards to accommodate a disabled person.

The Duty to Provide a Free Appropriate Public Education

The Individuals with Disabilities Education Act (IDEA) requires public schools to provide a Free, Appropriate Public Education (FAPE) to students with disabilities. In *Board of Ed. v. Rowley*,[54] the Court held that FAPE requires services that provide students with "some educational benefit." This standard permeates nearly every aspect of special education because it is the standard against which services are measured.

In *Rowley*, the Court held that the requirements of IDEA to provide a free appropriate public education were satisfied when a school district provided "personalized instruction with sufficient support services to permit the child to benefit educationally from that instruction." The Court further stated that the IEP (Individualized Education Plan) must be formulated in accordance with the requirements of IDEA. The standard for assessing the IEP is: reasonably calculated to achieve some benefit—no guarantee the child will achieve the goals. Since the student involved was performing better than average and was receiving personalized instruction that was reasonably calculated to meet her educational needs, the Court held that a sign-language interpreter was not required.

The Duty to Provide Special Education and Related Services

A free and appropriate public education includes special education and related services. While *Rowley* defined an appropriate education, it did not define the requirements under the "related services" requirements of IDEA and the Rehabilitation Act of 1973. In *Irving Indpt. Sch. Dist. v. Tatro*,[55] the Supreme Court recognized that a free appropriate public education includes supplemental and medical services that enable a child to remain at school during the day. In *Cedar Rapids Cmty. Sch. Dist. v. Garret F.*,[56] the Supreme Court held that a student who needs assistance with his ventilator throughout the school day is entitled to nursing services under the related services requirement of the IDEA.

The Duty to Educate Students in the Least Restrictive Environment

The IDEA provides that states, and thus districts, "must assure that to the maximum extent appropriate that children with disabilities are educated with children that are not disabled, and that special classes, separate schooling or any other removal of children with disabilities from the regular education environment occurs only when the nature or severity of the disability is such that education in regular classes with the use of supplementary aids and services cannot be achieved satisfactorily." This is commonly referred to as educating a child with disabilities in the least restrictive environment (LRE).

The federal courts are split on the proper test for determining the school district's obligations, but all of the courts consider the following factors: (1) the educational benefits of a "mainstream" placement; (2) the non-academic benefits of a "mainstream" placement; (3) the effect the disabled student would have on the teacher and students in the regular education environment; and (4) the cost of the "mainstream" placement, including supplemental services.

The Duty to Provide Appropriate Alternative Placements

When a public school district is unable to provide a disabled student with an appropriate education within its own facilities, the district is required to locate and pay for an appropriate alternative placement. In analyzing the issue of alternative placements, the Supreme Court in a combination of two cases, *Burlington v. Dept. of Ed. Massachusetts*,[57] and *Florence County School*

Dist. v. Carter,[58] requires school districts to develop an appropriate IEP and to provide an alternative placement if necessary to meet the IEP's objectives. Districts must fund private placements if the school itself is not able to provide the appropriate education for the disabled student.

The Duty to Provide Process Protections

In addition, there are procedural protections, such as the right to "stay put." In *Honig, California Superintendent of Public Instruction v. Doe,*[59] the Supreme Court held that school districts may not remove students with disabilities from their educational placement during the process of reviewing those placements. The Court rejected the district's attempts to create a "dangerousness" exception to the statute's presumption that students "stay put" in their placements, noting that districts may use their normal discipline procedures for dealing with dangerous children, including suspension from their placement for up to 10 days.

An additional procedural protection is the right to due process hearing. Under IDEA, if parents believe that the school district's IEP for their child is not "appropriate," they have the right to request an "impartial due process hearing." Lastly, there is the protection of the burden of proof. In *Shaffer v. Weast,*[60] the Supreme Court held that the burden of proof at the due process hearing rests with the party seeking relief, which in most cases will be the parents challenging the district's plan.

The Duty to Provide Special Education and Related Services to Children Beginning at Age Three

The IDEA generally requires public school districts, and private schools that contract with public schools, to provide special education services to children beginning at age three. In particular, free and appropriate pre-K programs must be given to children between the ages of three and five, if those children have one or more of the disabilities identified in IDEA.[61] School districts may also use pre-K funds to provide special education services to two-year-olds who will become three during the school year.[62]

The disabilities identified in the IDEA include physical, educational, learning, or cognitive disabilities that necessitate special education and/or related services.[63] Specifically, school districts have an obligation to provide or to contract with a third party to provide special education and related services to all three- to five-year-old children who reside within the district who have: "intellectual disabilities, hearing impairments (including deafness), speech or language impairments, visual impairments (including blindness), serious emotional disturbance (referred to as "emotional disturbance"), orthopedic impairments, autism, traumatic brain injury, other health impairments, or specific learning disabilities; and who, by reason thereof, needs special education and related services."

In addition, states have discretion to provide a free appropriate public education to all pre-K children who have "developmental delays." These include delays in physical, cognitive, communication, social, emotional, and adaptive development. If a state decides to serve children with such developmental delays, it must provide to them the full range of services and protections otherwise required by IDEA. Accordingly, these children must receive a free and appropriate special education and related services in the least restrictive environment.

The local school district must provide special education and related services to all children protected by IDEA by including them in one of their own district-run pre-K programs, or by financing the child's education in an appropriate local Head Start program, community-based program, or private program.

The IDEA also requires early intervention services for children from birth to age three.[64] These children must be served by multiple public and private agencies that coordinate services pursuant to the dictates of a mandatory "individualized family service plan." To the maximum extent appropriate, these children must be served in their "natural environment" such as in their homes, or in community programs for typically developing children of their age. Moreover, states and school districts must establish procedures for ensuring that such children are identified and will make a smooth transition from the early intervention programs to pre-K services and ultimately to elementary school.

In enacting and consistently reauthorizing legislation that encourages states to provide special education services to all eligible three- and four-year-olds, Congress expressly recognized that there was an "urgent and substantial need" for early childhood education for these children. Congress specifically found that early childhood education not only enhanced the "development of infants and toddlers with disabilities," it also reduced "the educational costs to our society, including our Nation's schools, by minimizing the need for special education and related services after infants and toddlers with disabilities reach school age."[65]

Children with disabilities who attend appropriate pre-K programs in fact make dramatic and lasting advances in their educational, social, and emotional development. The evidence also is clear that children with disabilities who are included in educational environments with their typically developing peers significantly outperform such children who are not included in all domains of development, particularly social skills, executive function, language, and cognition.[66]

With appropriate supportive services, the inclusion of children with disabilities in the regular pre-K environment significantly increases the educational and social development of all children in that environment.[67] Despite these proven benefits and the IDEA requirement that three- to five-year-old children with disabilities to be placed in the least restrictive environments, only one-third of these children throughout the country are included in educational environments with their typically developing peers.[68]

THE FOUNDATIONS OF AMERICAN EDUCATION LAW SUPPORT COMPELLING LEGAL ARGUMENTS FOR PROVIDING ACCESS TO EARLY CHILDHOOD EDUCATION PROGRAMS

In light of the structure of American law, there are four types of legal arguments that can be made to support access to early childhood education programs: (1) federal constitutional arguments; (2) state constitutional arguments based on equity, adequacy, thoroughness, or efficiency; (3) state constitutional arguments based on proper judicial remedies for constitutional violations; and (4) state statutory arguments based on a violation of a state's Civil Rights or Human Rights Act.

Federal Constitutional Arguments Based on an Absolute Deprivation of a Minimally Adequate Education

Although the United States Supreme Court has definitively held that the United States Constitution does not include a right to education, the Court in *San Antonio v. Rodriguez*, however, recognized a federal constitutional right to be free from an absolute deprivation of a minimally adequate education. Moreover, in *Plyler* and *Paspasan*, the Supreme Court reaffirmed the existence of such a constitutional right to be free from an absolute denial by the government of access to a minimally adequate level of education.

Accordingly, in circumstances where the lack of access to early childhood education constitutes an absolute deprivation of a minimally adequate education, the U.S. Constitution supports a right to such access. A claim that the failure to provide sufficient access to early childhood programs infringes upon the federal constitution's right to be free from the absolute deprivation of a minimally adequate education is thus a viable legal argument that can support increased access to early childhood programs.

State Constitutional Arguments Based on Equity and Adequacy

Additionally, litigants can continue to turn to state courts to achieve increased access to early childhood education programs by relying on the education clauses in state constitutions. A majority of state courts have recognized state constitutional rights to equity and adequacy in educational opportunities. These decisions—some expressly, and others implicitly—create a state constitutional right to access to early childhood education programs.

All state constitutions guarantee children a right to education by requiring that legislatures create and maintain a system of free, public schools.[69] Most state constitutions are silent about who is entitled to an education.[70] Only seven states specify age limits.[71] Most legislatures allow states to decide what the initial age of compulsory education should be, usually ages five or six, which falls under kindergarten or first grades.[72] This later changed as plaintiffs continued to focus on the needs of low-income students and showed evidence of the positive impact of early childhood development and early childhood education.

A few states suggest that public school begins with kindergarten, while others indicate that it might begin earlier.[73] Seven states require that a free education be provided to "all children" of the state or "at all stages of human development," while two other states require that education be available to "all children of school age" without specifying the age.[74] Even in those states that specify the age at which mandatory education begins, however, a strong argument can still be made that the failure to provide adequate or equitable early childhood education programs constitutes a violation of the state's constitution.

The plaintiffs in *Abbott v. Burke*, for example, successfully argued for early childhood education for New Jersey's most disadvantaged children. In that case, the New Jersey Supreme Court created a "quasi-constitutional" right to early childhood education for some three- and four-year-old children, despite the fact that the education clause limited the right of public education to children ages five and older.[75] North Carolina's case also led to increased funding for early childhood funding.[76]

In 2005, South Carolina's circuit court found that in *Abbeville County School District v. State,* the state failed its constitutional responsibility to provide for a minimally adequate education by failing to provide and fund early childhood intervention programs.[77] Though a Massachusetts trial court found that high-quality early childhood education programs offer the "only realistic chance" for the state's at-risk three- and four-year-olds to be successful in school, the state's Supreme Judicial Court failed to come to the same conclusion, and held that it was up to the Legislature to decide whether to provide early childhood education to at-risk children.[78]

Similar setbacks played out in Massachusetts and Arkansas. In 2002, an Arkansas court found in *Lake View v. Huckabee (Lake View III)*, that the state's constitution specifically grants the legislature the power to implement educational programs for children under the age of six, so the court could not determine a pre-kindergarten remedy. In 2005, Massachusetts' Supreme Court in *Hanock v. Driscoll* found the state's funding formula to be constitutional, therefore refusing to consider any of the plaintiffs' remedies, including providing pre-kindergarten education.[79]

Additionally, legislatures in forty states have already provided access to publicly funded early childhood education programs to at least some children, thereby demonstrating tacit acceptance that children are entitled to educational services.[80]

The Unconstitutional Denial of Access to Adequate Early Childhood Education

A majority of state courts have interpreted the education clauses in their own constitutions to guarantee students the right to an adequate education, and to guarantee the funding necessary to provide that adequate education.[81] The state constitutional right to an adequate education thus could support a claim that the state's failure to provide access to early childhood education is a denial of the right to an adequate education.[82] In the school finance area, adequacy cases generally involve: (1) defining the goals of an adequate education, and (2) determining the resources necessary to reach those goals.[83]

These cases require the articulation of a concrete outcome goal or goals and some demonstration that a particular input would assist in reaching those goals.[84] The data indicate that one indispensable input is early childhood education. Pre-kindergarten education has proven short- and long-term benefits that are strongly related to outcomes included in any definition of an adequate education.[85]

Early childhood education contributes to school readiness, avoiding special education placements and grade retention, and high school graduate rates. School readiness is critical to school success because those who begin behind tend to stay there or fall further behind.[86] Avoiding special education placements and grade retention is critical because an adequate education must prepare students to advance from grade to grade within the regular curriculum.[87] High school graduation is critical because a school system that fails to enable students to graduate from high school is not adequate.[88]

Many of these outcomes have already been incorporated in court definitions of adequacy, and none is controversial or requires expanding the adequacy concept.[89] As long as some or all of these goals are considered part of the "adequacy" definition, there is a compelling argument that early childhood education programs ought to be included within a student's right to an adequate education—because early childhood education helps students achieve each of these goals.[90]

Furthermore, research indicates that early childhood education programs offer equal or greater benefits than many interventions ordered as part of adequacy cases, such as increased funding, smaller class sizes, or improved facilities.[91] Therefore, a strong legal case can be made for including such programs for all children in any definition of an adequate education.[92]

Early childhood education provides benefits for all children.[93] Litigants do, however, have the option of pursuing a more targeted intervention focused on disadvantaged students.[94] This approach may be advantageous where courts and advocates are worried about costs and political plausibility of ordering universal access to these programs.[95]

Relying on a version of this targeted adequacy theory, four state courts have recognized a right to early childhood education.[96] In New Jersey, the Supreme Court granted a right to early childhood education programs to three- and four-year-olds in poor, urban districts.[97] In Arkansas, North Carolina, and Massachusetts, trial courts determined that the state should provide free access to early childhood education programs for at least some three- or four-year-olds in the state.[98] Though these three decisions have been overturned, the four favorable rulings together are instructive as all employed similar reasoning.[99] Each court reasoned in the following manner:

- An adequate education entails achieving certain academic goals (such as reading), advancing from one grade to the next, and graduating from high school;
- "At-risk" children begin school behind their more affluent peers, and that gap often grows larger as schooling continues; and
- Poor children who have attended high-quality early childhood education programs start school on more of a level playing field and are therefore more likely to achieve the academic milestones that constitute an adequate education.[100]

Therefore, to ensure all children have a reasonable opportunity to obtain an adequate education, these courts concluded that "at-risk" children must be provided at least one year of pre-K.[101]

The Unconstitutional Denial of Equitable Access to Early Childhood Education

Like the right to adequacy, the right to equitable educational opportunity can support both a universal claim and an even stronger claim for a right to pre-K for disadvantaged children.[102]

To determine whether or not to recognize a right to equal educational opportunity, courts first determine whether education is a fundamental right or whether a school funding system discriminates on the basis of wealth.[103] If the court concludes that education is a fundamental right and/or that a suspect class is implemented, it applies strict scrutiny.[104] Then, the relevant inquiry is whether existing inequalities in funding or programs are necessary to satisfy a compelling state interest.[105] If strict scrutiny is not triggered, courts apply the rational basis test. Generally speaking, strict scrutiny leads to a finding of unconstitutionality and rational basis does not.[106]

Though forty states and the District of Columbia provide early childhood education programs, not all disadvantaged children are served.[107] Simultaneously, nine states recognize the right to equal educational opportunity.[108] Therefore, a state that recognizes a right to equal educational opportunities and does not provide early childhood education programs to all children should have to demonstrate either (1) a compelling state interest or (2) a truly rational basis for failing to do so.[109]

Because early childhood education programs are as beneficial as other programs or services that are explicitly or implicitly required to be available to all children, these claims should fare well in states that recognize a constitutional right to equal educational opportunity.[110] They could also succeed in states that have tentatively recognized this right but have rejected claims for equal funding.[111]

State Constitutional Arguments Based on Developing a Proper Judicial Remedy for a Constitutional Violation

States can also be obligated to provide access to early childhood programs in order to remedy a constitutional violation. Some state courts have ordered access to early childhood education programs for three- and four-year-olds as a remedy for a state's constitutional failure to prepare its children to learn.

These remedies have arisen in public education finance cases. In this litigation, a majority of state courts have concluded that the state's failure to provide an adequate or equitable level of funding for its schools violates the state's own constitution. The New Jersey Supreme Court in *Abbott V*,[112] for example, concluded that the state's method for financing public education primarily through local property taxes was a violation of the state constitution's guarantee of a thorough and efficient system of public education. The North Carolina Supreme Court also found that a similar property-tax regime for funding public schools violated that state's constitutional right to a "sound basic education."[113]

In both of these cases, the issue of pre-K arose in the context of the judicial creation as a remedy for a state's unconstitutional denial of a minimum level of public education to some students.

New Jersey

In *Abbott V*, the New Jersey Supreme Court ordered the state to provide full-day kindergarten and half-day early childhood education programs to three- and four-year-olds as a remedy for the state's failure to provide school-age children in the Abbott districts with a thorough and efficient education. Significantly, the New Jersey Constitution only mandates a thorough and efficient system of free public education to children when they reach five years old.[114]

Nonetheless, the New Jersey Supreme Court ordered pre-K education for three- and four-year-olds because it was necessary to ensure that those children will receive the education guaranteed to them when they reach five. In other words, the Court recognized that in the absence of early childhood education, five-year-old children would be deprived of their constitutional right to a thorough and efficient public education.[115]

The *Abbott V* pre-K decision was the culmination of decades of litigation challenging the state's method of financing public education. In *Robinson v. Cahill*, 62 N.J. 473 (1973), the New Jersey Supreme Court first addressed challenges by the state's low-income school districts to the state's use of property taxes to fund public education, which resulted in inadequate and inequitable resources in those districts. In 1990, the New Jersey Supreme Court in *Abbott v. Burke*, 119 N.J. 287 (1990) (*Abbott II*), held unconstitutional the state's maintenance of inadequate educational opportunities for children in those low-income districts. The court specifically found that "[m]any poor children start school with an approximately two-year disadvantage compared to many suburban youngsters."[116]

The court further declared that "an intensive pre-school and all day kindergarten enrichment program [would help] to reverse the educational disadvantage these children start out with."[117] In *Burke v. Abbott*, 136 N.J. 444 (1994) (*Abbott III*), the New Jersey Supreme Court again declared the state's educational funding regime unconstitutional and indicated that the state should employ pre-K as a supplemental program to remedy its constitutional violations. In response to that court decision, the New Jersey legislature then enacted the Comprehensive Education Improvement and Financing Act

(CEIFA), N.J.S.A. §18A:7F-16. The CEIFA created a foundation level for funding a basic education and also provided additional funds for early childhood education programs and full-day kindergarten programs for low-income three- and four-year-olds.

In *Abbott IV*, 149 N.J. 145 (1997), however, the New Jersey Supreme Court found that the legislation had not allocated sufficient funds to meet the actual needs of low-income children. In the absence of sufficient legislative action, the Court remanded the remedial matter for an evidentiary hearing to determine the funding and programmatic steps required to satisfy the educational needs of those children.

At the hearing, Dr. W. Steven Barrett of the National Institute for Early Education Research (NIEER) offered comprehensive expert testimony regarding the benefits of high-quality early childhood education programs. Based on the evidence at the hearing, the court recommended that the state provide funding for a full-day early childhood education program for all three- and four-year-olds in low-income districts. Finally, in *Abbott V,* the New Jersey Supreme Court ordered the state to provide "high quality" half-day pre-K programs for all of those three- and four-year-olds.

By any measure, the court-mandated *Abbott* early childhood education programs have been a great success. By the 2009 school year, 43,775 three- and four-year-olds were enrolled in the program through public schools, private providers, and Head Start centers. In 2007 NIEER published the *Abbott Preschool Program Longitudinal Effects Study.* That initial study measured the effects of the learning gains attributable to the early childhood education programs for children as they enter kindergarten. According to the study, there is:

> clear evidence of the following: (1) classroom quality in the Abbott Preschool Program continues, on the whole, to improve; (2) . . . children who attend the program, whether in public schools, private settings or Head Start, are improving in language, literacy, and math at least through the end of their kindergarten year; and (3) . . . children who attend preschool for two years at both age 3 and 4 significantly out-perform those who attend for only one year at 4 years of age or do not attend at all.[118]

NIEER then followed up its study by measuring the performance of these children through second grade. In *The Apples Blossom: Abbott Preschool Program Longitudinal Effects Study (APPLES) Preliminary Effects through 2nd Grade*, NIEER finds that the significant pre-K gains in oral language, early literacy, mathematics, and grade retention either increased or persisted through second grade. The latest study concludes:

These gains in learning and ability are large enough to be practically mean-ingful and are already beginning to result in savings for taxpayers who do not have to pay for extra years of schooling. The results of this study add to the considerable body of evidence indicating that quality preschool education can make a significant contribution to improve children's learning and development. . . . This study extends the evidence that such effects can be produced for to-day's children on a large scale by public programs administered through public schools by demonstrating persistent and not just initial effects on children's cognitive abilities.[119]

North Carolina

Similarly, the North Carolina Supreme Court concluded that the issue of whether children are entitled to early childhood education did not depend upon the legislature's judgment about the age at which children should or must enter school.[120] Although the North Carolina legislature only mandated school attendance at age seven, the North Carolina Supreme Court deter-mined that the state still had a constitutional responsibility to "prepare those students who enter the schools to avail themselves of an opportunity to obtain a sound basic education."[121]

In *Hoke*, however, the Court initially found a judicially imposed remedy to be premature because the trial court lacked an evidentiary foundation for such a remedy, and the legislature had not had an initial opportunity to develop an early childhood education program. The Supreme Court in *Hoke* left it to the executive and legislative branches to design services for at-risk pre-K chil-dren. In the wake of North Carolina's education finance litigation, the state legislature established a program called "More at Four" (MAF) to provide pre-K services to at-risk children.

In 2011, the North Carolina legislature directed that the number of "at-risk" children served by the state's program could be no more than 20 percent of the total number of pre-K children served. The Hoke County Board of Educa-tion successfully sued to enjoin this artificial cap on the provision of pre-K services to at-risk children.

In *Hoke County Bd. of Educ. v. State of North Carolina,* No. COA 11-1545 (Aug. 21, 2012), the North Carolina Court of Appeals affirmed the trial court's decision to order the state to admit all "at-risk" four-year-olds throughout the state into its pre-K program:

Now, it has been approximately eight years since the Supreme Court's ruling in *Leandro II*. During this time, the State has had ample opportunity to develop a program that would meet the needs of "at-risk" students approaching and/or attaining school-age eligibility. The only program, evidenced in the record, that was developed by the State since *Leandro II* to address the needs of those students was MAF, a pre-kindergarten program. Thus, unlike the Supreme Court in *Leandro II*, we are not faced with the decision of selecting for the State which method would best satisfy their duty to help prepare those students who enter the schools to avail themselves of an opportunity to obtain a sound basic education. Rather, the State made that determination for itself when in 2001 it developed the pre-kindergarten program, MAF.

Thus, we do not deem it inappropriate or premature at this time to uphold an order mandating the State to not deny any eligible "at-risk" four year old admission to the North Carolina Pre-Kindergarten Program. Under *Leandro II*, the State has a duty to prepare all "at-risk" students to avail themselves of an opportunity to obtain a sound basic education. Pre-kindergarten is the method in which the State has decided to effectuate its duty, and the State has not produced or developed any alternative plan or method. Accordingly, we affirm the trial court's order . . .

Simply put, it is the duty of the State of North Carolina to protect each and every one of these at-risk and defenseless children, and to provide them their lawful opportunity, through a quality pre-kindergarten program, to take advantage of their equal opportunity to obtain a sound basic education as guaranteed by the North Carolina constitution.

State Statutory Arguments Based on a Violation of a State's Civil Rights or Human Rights Act

States can use their Civil Rights or Human Rights Acts to argue that a lack of access to early childhood education programs has a disparate impact on minority children. For example, in August of 2008, the Chicago Urban League filed a lawsuit against the State of Illinois and the Illinois State Board of Education to have the State of Illinois' current public school funding scheme declared unconstitutional and in violation of the Illinois Civil Rights Act of 2003.

The complaint alleges that the State of Illinois has deprived African American, Latino, and other minority children of a high-quality education by discriminating against families based on race, that the State of Illinois' funding scheme has a discriminatory impact on minority students, and that the funding scheme creates inadequate educational opportunity for thousands of public school children.

Specifically, the Chicago Urban League asserts that the State's public school funding scheme: (1) disparately impacts racial and ethnic minority students who attend Majority-Minority Districts in violation of the Illinois Civil Rights Act of 2003; (2) violates the Uniformity of Taxation provision of the Illinois Constitution; (3) violates Plaintiffs' right to attend "high-quality educational institutions" guaranteed by the Education Article under the Illinois Constitution; and (4) violates Plaintiffs' right to equal protection under the Illinois Constitution.[122] The court rejected these arguments except for the claim under the Illinois Civil Rights Act of 2003.

The foundation for plaintiffs' viable claim under the Illinois Civil Rights Act of 2003 is that Illinois is specifically charged with the obligation to provide for the establishment of high-quality educational institutions and services under the Illinois Constitution, Article X, Section 1.[123] The Education Committee of the Sixth Illinois Constitutional Convention's report on the proposed Education Article of the Illinois Constitution states that "[t]he opportunity for an education where the state has undertaken to provide it, is a right which must be made available to all on equal terms."[124]

The plaintiffs alleged, however, that Illinois' funding scheme has a discriminatory disparate impact on minority students who attend school in poor districts.[125] The plaintiffs pled facts showing that the school funding system has the effect of subjecting minority students to discrimination because they attend schools in "Majority Minority Districts."[126]

The plaintiffs further alleged that, because defendants' system rests too heavily on local property taxes, students who attend schools in property-poor communities do not receive an equal educational opportunity.[127] Thus, defendants' conduct has the effect of subjecting minority students to discrimination because of their race.[128] The court found that the complaint provided a straightforward challenge of the alleged disparate impact produced by defendants' adoption, implementation, enactment, and enforcement of the school funding system and was therefore viable.[129]

Accordingly, the legal structure of American education can be used to support the expansion of access to early childhood education programs. Congress already has used its Spending Power to incentivize states to provide educational services to three- and four-year-old children who have educational disabilities. Similar legislative and administrative structures can be used to create financial incentives that encourage states to extend those programs to all three- and four-year-olds. In addition, where lawmakers fail to appreciate the benefits of investing in early childhood education programs, viable legal claims can be filed in state and federal court seeking the expansion of access to those programs.

NOTES

1. 496 U.S. 226 (1990).
2. See *San Antonio Independent School Dist. v. Rodriguez*, 411 U.S. 1, 49–53 (1973).
3. See *Meyer v. Nebraska*, 262 U.S. 390, 399–403 (1923).
4. *United States v. Lopez*, 514 U.S. 549 (1995).
5. *National Federation of Indep. Bus. V. Sebelvis*, 132 S. Ct. 2566 (2012).

6. See, e.g., 42 U.S.C. §2000e-2 et seq. (Title VII); 29 U.S.C. §206 (Equal Pay Act).

7. See, e.g., 20 U.S.C. §§1681–1688 (Title IX).

8. See, e.g., the Individuals with Disabilities Education Act Amendments of 1997, 20 U.S.C. §§1400–1405.

9. See, e.g., Family Educational Rights and Privacy Act, 20 U.S.C. §1232.

10. See, e.g., the Family and Medical Leave Act, 29 U.S.C. §§2601, 2611, 2612.

11. See, e.g., Equal Access Act, 20 U.S.C. §§4071–4072.

12. See, e.g., the No Child Left Behind Act (NCLB), 20 U.S.C. §6301 et seq.

13. U.S. Department of Education Press Release, "President Obama, U.S. Secretary of Education Duncan Announce National Competition to Advance School Reform," July 24, 2009, http://www2.ed.gov/news/pressreleases/2009/07/07242009.html.

14. The White House, "Race to the Top," http://www.whitehouse.gov/issues/education/k-12/race-to-the-top.

15. Catherine Gewertz, "Ed Dept to States: In Race to Top, Only Common Core Will Do," Education Week Blog, March 18, 2010, http://blogs.edweek.org/edweek/curriculum/2010/03/ed_dept_to_states_for_race_to.html; Tamar Lewin, "Many States Adopt National Standards for Their Schools," *New York Times*, July 21, 2010, http://www.nytimes.com/2010/07/21/education/21standards.html.

16. Common Core State Standards Initiative, "About the Standards: Development Process," http://www.corestandards.org/about-the-standards/development-process/.

17. Ibid.

18. Ibid.

19. Ibid.

20. Ibid.

21. Ibid.

22. Ibid.

23. U.S. Dept. of Education Press Release, "Education Department Announces 16 Winners of the Race to the Top District Competition," December 11, 2012, http://www.ed.gov/news/press-releases.

24. 262 U.S. 390 (1923).

25. 260 U.S. 510 (1925).

26. *Pierce*, 260 U.S. at 535.

27. 406 U.S. 205 (1972).

28. 411 U.S. 1 (1973).

29. See *United States v. Carolene Products Company*, 304 U.S. 144, 152 n4 (1930).

30. 411 U.S. at 49.

31. 411 U.S. at 42.

32. The American Constitution, as interpreted in *Rodriguez*, is inconsistent with the overwhelming international consensus that education is a fundamental right.

33. 457 U.S. 202 (1982).

34. 478 U.S. 265 (1986).

35. 540 U.S. 966 (2003).

36. See e.g., *Roosevelt Elementary Sch. Dist. No. 66 v. Bishop*, 877 P.2d 806, 814 (Ariz. 1994) (interpreting "general and uniform" to require a finance system that "provide[s] sufficient funds to educate children on substantially equal terms"); *Idaho Sch. for Equal Educ. Opportunity v. Evans*, 850 P.2d 724, 734 (Idaho 1993) (interpreting "thorough" in light of the legislature's educational standards and concluding that the standards' requirements of school facilities, instructional programs, and textbooks are "consistent with our view of thoroughness"); *Abbott v. Burke*, 693 A.2d 417, 425 (N.J. 1997) (interpreting

"thorough and efficient" in light of the legislature's education standards); *Robinson v. Cahill*, 287 A.2d 187, 211 (N.J. Super. Ct. Law Div. 1972) (interpreting "thorough" to mean "more than simply adequate or minimal"); *DeRolph v. State*, 677 N.E.2d 733, 741 (Ohio 1997) (interpreting a "thorough and efficient" system as one in which no school district is "starved for funds" or "lack[s] teachers, buildings, or equipment"); *Pauley v. Kelly*, 255 S.E.2d 859, 877 (W. Va. 1979) (defining "thorough and efficient" to require, "as best the state of education expertise allows," a system that prepares students for "useful and happy occupations" and "recreation and citizenship"); *Campbell Cnty. Sch. Dist. v. State*, 907 P.2d 1238, 1258–59 (Wyo. 1995) (defining a "thorough and efficient" system of public schools as one marked by completeness and productivity without waste and that is "reasonably sufficient for the appropriate or suitable teaching/education/learning of the state's school age children"); *Lujan v. Colorado State Board of Educ.*, 649P.2d 1005, 1028 (Colo. 1982) (quoting *Northshore Sch. Dist. No. 417 v. Kinnear*, 530 P.2d 178, 202 (Wash. 1974)). ("A general and uniform system [is] one in which every child in the state has free access to certain minimum and reasonably standardized educational and instructional facilities and opportunities to at least the 12th grade.").

37. 777 S.W.2d 391 (Tex. 1989).

38. 777 S.W.2d at 394.

39. 801 N.E.2d 326 (N.Y. Ct. App. 2003).

40. N.Y. Const., Art. XI, §1.

41. See also *Leandro v. State*, 346 N.C. 336, 488 S.E. 2d 249 (1997) (State failed to meet its obligations under the North Carolina Constitution to provide adequate funding to provide students with a "sound basic education").

42. See also *Rose v. The Council for Better Education, Inc.*, 790 S.W.2d 186 (Ky. 1989) (finding that Kentucky's constitutional requirement of an "efficient system of common schools" was violated by maintenance of an underfunded and unequally funded system).

43. 18 Cal. 3d 728, 764, 557 P.2d 929, 950 (Cal. 1976).

44. See *Washakie County School District No. v. Herschler*, 606 P.2d 310 (Wy. 1980).

45. See *Horton v. Meskill*, 376 A.2d 359 (Conn. 1977).

46. See *In the Interest of G.H.*, 218 N.W. 2d 441 (N.D. 1974).

47. See Michael Rebell, *Courts and Kids: Pursuing Educational Equity through the State Courts* (Chicago: University of Chicago Press, 2009).

48. See also Quality Counts '98, "Resources Data Table: Comparisons of Per Pupil Expenditures," http://www.edcounts.org/archive/sreports/qc98/states/indicators/res-t3.htm; Common Core of Data (CCD), School District Finance Survey (Washington, DC: U.S. Department of Education National Center for Education Statistics, FY 2009), (F-33); Kevin Carey, "The Funding Gap: Low-Income and Minority Students Still Receive Fewer Dollars in Many States," Education Trust, 2003. See also Jonathan Kozol, *Savage Inequalities* (New York: HarperCollins, 1991).

49. See "School Board News," Natl. Assn. School Bds., November 11, 2003, 7. See also Carey, "The Funding Gap," 6 ("The troubling pattern of funding shortfalls repeats itself for school districts educating large numbers of minority students.").

50. 334 F.Supp. 1257 (E.D. Pa. 1971).

51. 348 F.Supp. 866 (D.C. 1972).

52. Individuals with Disabilities Education Act, Section 601(d)(1)(A)-(4).

53. 442 U.S. 397 (1979).

54. 458 US 176 (1982).

55. 468 U.S. 883 (1984).

56. 526 U.S. 66 (1999).

57. 471 U.S. 359 (1984).

58. 510 U.S. 7 (1993).

59. 484 U.S. 305 (1988).

60. 546 U.S. 49 (2005).

61. 20 U.S.C. § 1401(3) (A) (i).

62. 34 CFR § 300.323(b).

63. 20 U.S.C. § 1401(3).

64. 20 U.S.C. § 1431, et seq.

65. Individuals with Disabilities Education Act, Section 631(a)(1)-(2).

66. Annette Holahan and Virginia Costenbader, "A Comparison of Developmental Gains for Preschool Children with Disabilities Inclusive and Self-Contained Classrooms," *Topics in Early Childhood Special Education* 20(4) (2000): 224–25; Samuel L. Odom, "Preschool Inclusion: What We Know and Where We Go From Here," *Topics in Early Childhood Special Education* 20(1) (2000): 20–27.

67. Education Law Center, "Pre-K Policy Brief Series: Including Children with Disabilities in State Pre-K Programs," February 2010, 3n.19.

68. U.S. Dep't of Education, Office of Special Education Programs: "Part B, Individuals with Disabilities Education Act, Implementation of FAPE Requirements," July 30, 2005.

69. James E. Ryan, "A Constitutional Right to Preschool," *California Law Review* 94(1) (2006), 69.

70. Ryan, "A Constitutional Right to Preschool," 70.

71. Ibid.

72. Michael A. Rebell and Molly A. Hunter, "The Right to Preschool in Education Adequacy Litigations," National Access Network, Teachers College, Columbia University, October 2006, http://www.schoolfunding.info/resource_center/issuebriefs/preschool.pdf.

73. Ryan, "A Constitutional Right to Preschool," 70.

74. Ibid., 70–71, citing Alaska's Constitution, art. VII, § 1; Louisiana's Constitution, art. VIII, § 1; Missouri's Constitution, art. LX, § l(a); Oklahoma's Constitution, art. XIII, § 1; South Carolina's Constitution, art. XI, § 3; Utah's Constitution, art. X, § 1; Washington's Constitution, art. LX, § 1; New Mexico's Constitution, art. XII, § 1; Virginia's Constitution, art. VIII, § 1.

75. Ryan, "A Constitutional Right to Preschool," 71, citing *Abbott v. Burke*, 710 A.2d 450, 461–62 (N.J. 1998).

76. *Hoke Cty. Bd. of Educ. v. State*, 95 CVS 1158 (Superior Court Oct. 2000), 36, 43–45.

77. *Abbeville Cty. Sch. Dist. v. State*, No. 31-0169 (S.C. Ct. Comm. Pl. Dec. 29, 2005), 157.

78. *Hancock v. Commissioner of Education*, 2004 Mass. Super. LEXIS 118 (Mass. Superior Court 2004), 9; *Hancock v. Commissioner of Education*, 822 N.E.2d 1134 (Mass. 2005).

79. *Lake View Sch. Dist. No. 25 v. Huckabee*, 91 S.W.3d 472, 502 (Ark. 2002); *Hancock v. Driscoll*, 822 N.E.2d 1134, 1136–37 (Mass. 2005).

80. Ryan, "A Constitutional Right to Preschool," 73.

81. Ibid., 69 and 52, citing Molly S. McUsic, "The Future of Brown v. Board of Education: Economic Integration of Public Schools," 117 Harv. L. Rev. 1334 (2004): 1345–46 and n.72.

82. Ryan, "A Constitutional Right to Preschool," 75.

83. Ibid.

84. Ryan, "A Constitutional Right to Preschool," 76.

85. Ibid., citing, e.g., Lynn A. Karoly, RAND, *Investing in Our Children* xi (1998), 35; Lawrence J. Schweinhart, *Lifetime Effects: The High/Scope Perry Preschool Study Through Age 40* 1 (2002).

86. Ryan, "A Constitutional Right to Preschool," 76.

87. Ibid.

88. Ibid.

89. Ibid., referencing *Hoke County Bd. of Educ. v. State*, 599 S.E.2d 365, 386 (N.C. 2004).

90. Ryan, "A Constitutional Right to Preschool," 77.

91. Ibid., citing, e.g., *Abbott*, 710 A.2d 450 (considering funding levels, class sizes, and facilities in determining whether school finance system is constitutional); *State v. Campbell County Sch. Dist.*, 19 P.3d 518 (Wyo. 2001) (same).

92. Ryan, "A Constitutional Right to Preschool," 77.

93. Ibid.

94. Ibid.

95. Ibid.

96. Ibid., 78.

97. Ibid., citing *Abbott*, 710 A.2d, 461–62.

98. Ryan, "A Constitutional Right to Preschool," 78.

99. Ibid., 79.

100. Ibid., 78.

101. Ibid. 79, citing *Lake View Sch. Dist. No. 25 v. Huckabee*, 91 S.W.3d 472, 500-02; *Hancock v. Driscoll*, No. 02-2978, 2004 WL 877984, 136–46 and n.221; *Abbott*, 710 A.2d 450, 461-62; *Hoke County Bd. of Educ. V. State*, No. CVS1158, 2000 WL 1639686, 112–13.

102. Ryan, "A Constitutional Right to Preschool," 81.

103. Ibid.

104. Ibid.

105. Ibid., 81–82, citing e.g., *Serrano v. Priest*, 557 P.2d 929, 951 (Cal. 1977); *Horton v. Meskill*, 376 A.2d 359, 372 (Conn. 1977); *Pendleton Citizens for Comm. Schs. v. Marockie*, 507 S.E.2d 673, 680-81 (W.Va. 1998); *Campbell County Sch. Dist. v. State*, 907 P.2d 1238 (Wyo. 1995).

106. Ryan, "A Constitutional Right to Preschool," 82, citing *Shofstall v. Hollins*, 515 P.2d 590, 592–93 (Ariz. 1973); *Lujan v. Bd. of Educ.*, 649 P.2d 1005, 1023 (Colo. 1982); *Hombeck v. Somerset County Bd. of Educ.*, 458 A.2d 758, 789 (Md. 1983) for decisions applying the rational basis test and upholding the challenged funding scheme.

107. Ryan, "A Constitutional Right to Preschool," 82, citing Barnett et al., *The State of Preschool: 2003 State Preschool Yearbook* (New Brunswick, NJ: National Institute for Early Education Research, 2003), 8, http://nieer.org/sites/nieer/files/2003yearbook.pdf, 140; Nat'l Ctr. For Educ. Stat., U.S. Dep't. of Educ., Digest of Education Statistics 2002, 59 tbl.43 (2003).

108. Ryan, "A Constitutional Right to Preschool," 82, citing William S. Koski, *Of Fuzzy Standards and Institutional Constraints: A Re-Examination of the Jurisprudential History of Educational Finance Reform Litigation*, 43 Santa Clara L. Rev. 1185, 1189n.9, 1191n.14 (2003); Molly S. McUsic, *The Future of* Brown v. Board of Education: *Economic Integration of Public Schools*, 117 Harv. L. Rev. 1334, 1345–46 and n.72 (2004); James E. Ryan, *Schools, Race, and Money*, 109 Yale L.J. 249, 284–307 (1999).

109. Ryan, "A Constitutional Right to Preschool," 82.

110. Ibid., 84.

111. Ibid.

112. *Raymond Abbott et al. v. Burke*, 153 N.J. 400 (1990).

113. *Leandro v. State*, 346 N.C. 336, 400S.E.2d 249 (1997).

114. N.J. Const. Art. V.

115. *Abbott v. Burke,* 149 N.J. 145 (1997) (*Abbott IV*).

116. *Abbott v. Burke,* 149 N.J. at 179.

117. 119 N.J. at 373.

118. Ellen Frede, Kwanghee Jung, W. Steven Barnett, Cynthia Esposito Lamy, and Alecandra Figueras, "The Abbott Preschool Program Longitudinal Effects Study (APPLES)," National Institute for Early Education Research, June 2007, 3.

119. Ellen Frede, Kwanghee Jung, W. Steven Barnett, and Alecandra Figueras, "The APPLES Blossom: Abbott Preschool Program Longitudinal Effects Study (APPLES) Preliminary Results through 2nd Grade," National Institute for Early Education Research, June 2009, 25.

120. *Hoke County Bd. v. State of North Carolina*, 599 S.E. 365 (M.C. 2004).

121. *Hoke*, 599 S.E.2d at 365.

122. Chicago Urban League News Release, "Urban League Achieves Major Milestone in Education Funding Lawsuit," April 16, 2009, http://www.thechicagourbanleague.org/site/default.aspx?PageID=342.

123. Chicago Urban League and Quad County Urban League v. State of Illinois and Illinois State Board of Education Verified Complaint, No. 08 CH 30490, 26.

124. Ibid.

125. Ibid.

126. Chicago Urban League, et al. v. State of Illinois, et al. Memorandum Opinion, No. 08 CH 30490, 4, http://www.scribd.com/doc/21445238/Chicago-Urban-League-et-al-v-Illinois-State-Board-of-Education-4-15-09.

127. Ibid.

128. Chicago Urban League Verified Complaint, 27.

129. Chicago Urban League Memorandum Opinion, 5.

Chapter Four

The Economic Foundations of American Early Childhood Education

This chapter describes the financial structure of American early childhood education. After providing evidence showing that American education is inadequately and inequitably funded, the chapter identifies the sources of revenue for educating America's youngest learners and the national and local costs of doing so. The chapter concludes by demonstrating that a relatively modest investment in early childhood education would produce robust educational, social, and economic returns for children and for the country.

AMERICA'S SCHOOLS AND THEIR STUDENTS[1]

In the United States, slightly more than 50 million students attend public elementary and secondary schools, about 5.2 million students attend private schools, and approximately 1.5 million school-aged children are home-schooled.[2]

There are about 13,600 public school districts in America, and about 99,000 public schools.[3] Of these public schools, about 5,300 are charter schools.[4] In addition, there are approximately 30,900 private schools in the country.[5] Sixty-eight percent of these private schools have a religious orientation.[6] Parochial institutions educate eighty percent of the private school students in America.[7]

Slightly more than 70 percent of all students enrolled in private school are white,[8] 9 percent are African American, 10 percent are Hispanic or Latino, and 5 percent are Asian.[9] The racial composition of America's public schools is as follows: 52 percent white, 16 percent black, and 24 percent Latino or Hispanic.[10] In the past decade, the number of white children enrolled in public schools decreased from 28.7 million to 25.6 million, and the percentage of white children in public schools declined from 60 to 52 percent. During the same period, the percentage of African American students has remained flat, while the percentage of Latino or Hispanic children has increased from 17 to 24 percent.[11] The National Center for Education Statistics projects that by 2023, the percentage of white students in public school will decrease to 45, while the percentage of Hispanic students will grow to 30.[12]

AMERICA'S EARLY CHILDHOOD EDUCATION PROGRAMS AND THEIR STUDENTS

The landscape of early childhood education in America is difficult to describe with precision. The data available regarding the number and composition of children who attend various early childhood programs is notoriously imperfect. The most reliable sources of data employ different definitions of early childhood programs and attendance figures in their programs are extremely fluid.

Nonetheless, this chapter presents the best available data based on a meta-analysis of the United States Census Bureau, American Community Survey (2011); the National Center for Education Statistics, The Condition of Education 2013 Report (2013) and Preprimary Education Enrollment, Table 202.10 (2014); Kids Count Data Center, Annie E. Casey Foundation (2013); Status and Trends in the Education of Racial and Ethnic Groups (NCES 2010-15);

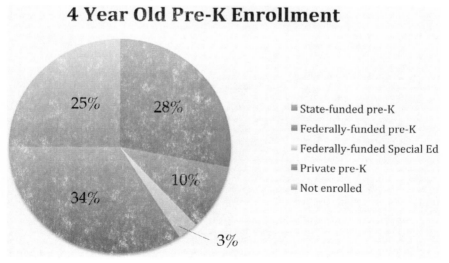

4 Year Old Pre-K Enrollment

- State-funded pre-K
- Federally-funded pre-K
- Federally-funded Special Ed
- Private pre-K
- Not enrolled

25% 28% 34% 10% 3%

Figure 4.1.

and the National Institute for Early Education Research, The State of Preschool 2013 (2013).

There are approximately 4 million four-year-olds in America, and a similar number of three-year-olds. The data indicate that approximately 28 percent (1.12 million) of those four-year-olds are enrolled in state-funded pre-K programs, 10 percent are in federally funded Head Start (400,000), 3 percent are in federally funded special education programs (120,000), 34 percent are in private pre-K programs (1.36 million), and 25 percent are not enrolled in any pre-K program (1 million).[13] Among four-year-olds, the preschool participation rate was 59 percent for children below the federal poverty level and 72 percent for other children.[14]

Among three-year-olds, approximately 4 percent (160,000) are served in state-funded programs, 3 percent (120,000) are served in federally funded special education programs, 7 percent (280,000) are educated in federal Head Start programs, 18 percent (730,000) are in private settings, and 60 percent (2.72 million) do not receive any organized early childhood education services.[15]

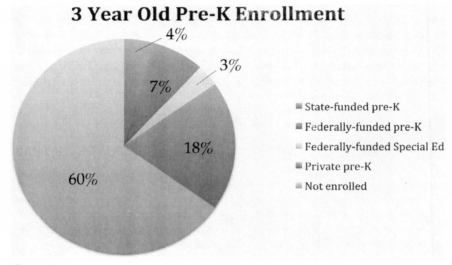

3 Year Old Pre-K Enrollment

- State-funded pre-K
- Federally-funded pre-K
- Federally-funded Special Ed
- Private pre-K
- Not enrolled

Figure 4.2.

The U.S. Department of Education found that, between 1970 and 2011, the enrollment rate for three- and four-year-olds increased from 20 to 52 percent.[16] Most of the growth occurred from 1980 to 2000, when the percentage of children in early childhood education programs increased from 27 to 39 percent for three-year-olds and from 46 to 65 percent for four-year-olds.[17]

From 2000 to 2011, however, the U.S. Department of Education noted that there were no measurable differences in the enrollment rates for children ages three and four or for children ages five and six.[18]

Table 4.1.

	Total	No Program	Private Programs	State Programs	Head Start	Special Ed
Four-Year-Olds	4 million	25% (1 million)	34% (1.36 million)	20% (1.12 million)	10% (400,000)	3% (120,000)
Three-Year-Olds	4 million	68% (2.72 million)	18% (730,000)	4% (160,000)	7% (280,000)	3% (120,000)

About 1.12 million of four-year-olds attend public programs[19] and about 200,000 three-year-olds are enrolled in public programs.[20] These children attend one of the 52 state-funded early childhood education programs in 40 states.[21] Hawaii, Idaho, Indiana, Mississippi, Montana, New Hampshire, North Dakota, South Dakota, Utah, and Wyoming do not have state-funded early childhood education programs.[22]

Most of the children who attend private early childhood education programs are white, while 11 percent are African American and 10 percent are Hispanic or Latino.[23] In fact, 559,000 African American three- and four-year-olds were not enrolled in any early childhood education programs and 1,145,000 Hispanic three- and four-year-olds were not enrolled in any early childhood education programs in 2012.[24]

Publicly funded programs "substantially increase access to children in families with the lowest income."[25] Yet, the enrollment of children from low-income families in which parents have not completed high school is far below average, while the enrollment of children from upper-income households in which parents have graduate degrees is far above average.[26] In fact, 87 percent of four-year-old children whose mothers had a college degree were enrolled in a preschool program, compared with 63 percent of children whose mothers had only a high school degree.[27] Middle-income families have relatively low participation rates in pre-K programs.[28] Moreover, Latino and Hispanic children tend to have very low enrollment rates, and African American children have high enrollment rates, but the least access to programs deemed to be of high quality.[29]

In the 2011–2012 school year, 28 percent of four-year-olds and 4 percent of three-year-olds were served in state-funded pre-K, the same as in the previous year.[30] Combining general and special education enrollments, 31 percent of four-year-olds and 7 percent of three-year-olds are served by public pre-K.[31] When including Head Start programs in addition to this, 41 percent of four-year-olds and 14 percent of three-year-olds are served in these publicly funded programs.[32]

This statistic increases substantially when one considers the percentage of students enrolled in private early childhood education programs. In 2011, almost two-thirds of three- to five-year-olds were enrolled in some sort of early childhood education program, and nearly 60 percent of these children were in full-day programs.[33] Ten years before, in 2001, 25 percent of all three- and four-year-olds attended publicly funded early childhood education programs and a bit more than 25 percent attended private early childhood education programs.[34]

The millions of children left out tend to be from relatively poor and less-educated families.[35] In 2011, higher percentages of three- to five-year-olds whose parents had either a graduate or professional degree (75 percent) or a bachelor's degree (71 percent) were enrolled in early childhood education programs than children of parents with any other levels of educational attainment.[36] Fifty-three percent of children whose parents had less than a high school degree and 58 percent of children whose parents completed high school were enrolled in early childhood education programs.[37]

THE SOURCES OF REVENUE TO SUPPORT AMERICAN EDUCATION

The United States spends a total of about $590 billion per year to educate its students, or about $11,000 per student.[38] That figure is projected to increase to $665 billion by 2021, or about $12,500 per student.[39]

Federal Funding

Of the $590 billion spent on education in America, about $141 billion comes from the federal government.[40]

As itemized in the following chart, that annual federal expenditure includes an annual appropriation for the U.S. Department of Education's discretionary spending, appropriations to the U.S. Department of Education for mandatory spending, school meal programs administered by the U.S. Department of Agriculture, the Head Start program directed by the U.S. Department of Health and Human Services, education tax benefits, and military and veterans education benefits:

Table 4.2.   Federal Education Spending, FY 2014 ($ billions)

Department of Education: Appropriation	67.3
Department of Education: Mandatory (excludes student loans)	9.9
School Nutrition Programs	14.8
Head Start Programs	8.6
Education Tax Expenditures for Individuals	21.3
American Opportunity Tax Credit (Refundable)	6.2
Service Members Education Benefits	.6
Veterans Education Benefits	12.2
TOTAL	**140.9**

The Department of Education's appropriation of $67.3 billion in discretionary spending has been used primarily to fund three programs: the Elementary and Secondary Education Act Title I Grants to local school districts to support low income students; the Individuals with Disabilities Education Act state grants to support children with special education needs; and the Pell grants to support college education. The Department of Education also has utilized its discretionary Title I appropriation to fund approximately $550 million in Race to the Top funds. The administration also has requested $750 million in early childhood education development grants, which are offset in part by a significant reduction in impact aid for schools.[41] The federal government's total expenditures of education comprise approximately 4 percent of the total federal budget.[42]

State and Local Funding

State and local taxes generally make up more than 90 percent of a school district's revenue.[43] Most states produce that local revenue through property taxes, while some states employ income taxes, sales taxes, "sin" taxes, or a combination of taxes.

Property taxes are usually based primarily on a percentage of the assessed valuation of the residential property in a district. Some states redistribute property taxes from property-rich districts to property-poor districts, spread property tax revenue throughout the state, or create a "foundation" level for all districts.

In theory, the foundation level represents a legislative judgment about the amount of money that must be allocated to each student for that student to receive a minimal education. In practice, however, the foundation level often is determined based on the availability of residual funds. Where a district's local taxes do not reach that foundation level, some states will allocate state-wide funds to make up the difference.

THE SOURCES OF REVENUE TO SUPPORT EARLY CHILDHOOD EDUCATION

As is true of education funding generally, the great bulk of money to support early childhood education programs comes from state and local governments. Public financial support for early childhood education derives from federal Head Start funds, federal special education funds from the Individuals with Disabilities Education Act, Part B, Section 619, and state and local educational funds. On average, the states contribute $4,026 toward the overall cost of $4,629 to educate each child enrolled in one of their publicly funded programs.[44] The federal Head Start program on average spends $7,764 per child.

Head Start Funding

In 2014, the federal government spent $6.4 billion on Head Start, and 813,000 three- to five-year-old children were enrolled in Head Start programs.[45]

The federal Head Start program provides early learning programs for children in impoverished families. To be eligible for Head Start, families generally must have income at or below the federal poverty level, which is about $23,550 for a family of four.[46] The median annual income of Head Start families is $22,714.[47]

Head Start also serves a diverse group of children—29 percent identified themselves as African American and 40 percent identified themselves as Hispanic or Latino.[48] Thirty percent of participants are from families in which English is not the primary language, and 25 percent of participants are from homes in which Spanish is the primary language spoken at home.[49] The diversity of the Head Start program can be a source of great strength, enhancing the learning of all students.[50]

Head Start programs are operated by local school districts, other local governmental agencies, or private organizations that receive a five-year renewable grant from the federal government.[51] In 2014, 1,622 organizations received Head Start grants to provide early childhood education, 1,016 of which were local school districts.[52] The federal government spends about $7,900 per student to provide early childhood education in Head Start programs.[53]

In 1995, Congress extended the Head Start program to include Early Head Start. The Early Head Start program is designed to support poor mothers and their children from birth to age three. The program provides home visits and center-based services, including pre- and post-natal counseling, nutritional advice, and support for early childhood health and development.[54] Approximately 115,000 children are served by Early Head Start, with a federal funding stream of $1.37 billion.[55] This amounts to just four percent of those whose families are economically eligible (compared to Head Start programs, which serve 42 percent of eligible three- and four-year-olds).[56]

Special Education Funding

Under the Individuals with Disabilities Education Improvement Act, about 750,000 children between the ages of three and five receive special education and related services.[57] Pursuant to its power under the Spending Clause, Congress appropriates the funds through state grant programs to those states that demonstrate compliance with federal requirements. In Part B, the statute authorizes grants to states and local educational agencies to fund special education for children aged three to five.[58] In fiscal year 2014, $11.47 billion was allocated to provide funding for all special education programs for children between the ages of 3 to 21.[59]

The level of funding provided to each state is based on an elaborate formula. The federal government guarantees to each state at least the same amount of funds that the state received for fiscal year 1999. The 1999 Part B appropriation was $5 billion.[60] The federal funds that are appropriated above the 1999 level are distributed to the states based on their relative share of children within the age range served by IDEA (85 percent of the remainder) and their relative share of children within that age range who are living in poverty (15 percent of the remainder).

States may keep up to 10 percent of the allocated funds for administrative and other state level expenses before distributing the rest to local school districts. Congress also has established a maximum contribution to any particular state of 40 percent of that state's average per pupil expenses.

School districts spend about 1.9 times more to educate a child with special needs than they do to educate other children.[61] Yet, in 2014, the average per student federal dollars distributed for special education services to all children with disabilities was only $1,743, and the average per pupil federal dollars distributed for three- to five-year-olds receiving special education services was only $471. Even if most school districts combine those funds to serve particular children, the total amount of funds falls short of providing adequate funding.

The total average amount per pupil distributed by the federal government is about $2,200. The total cost of providing services to a child receiving special

, 1.9 times the average per student expenditure of $10,034 or ap-
y $20,585. The federal contribution of 40 percent of that amount
about $8,234. The federal allocation of $2,200 per student, therefore, provides only a small fraction of the amount of funding that Congress
itself requires under its IDEA funding regime.

The extent to which the early childhood mandates of IDEA are underfunded also is demonstrated by the aggregate funding gap. If IDEA were
fully funded, the states would receive from the federal government at least 40
percent of the overall cost of educating all of its children with disabilities. In
fiscal year 2014, however, federal funding only covered 16 percent of those
costs.[62] Under Part B, full funding would have required $28.65 billion to the
states. Yet the states only received $11.48 billion. The $17.17 billion shortfall
must then be absorbed by the states and local school districts. Indeed, since
2010, the annual Part B appropriation for special education services has been
consistently less than half of even the amount of funds that Congress requires
of itself to provide full funding.

THE INADEQUATE AND INEQUITABLE FUNDING OF AMERICAN EDUCATION

In most states, school districts receive local revenue in direct proportion to
the value of the residential property in the district. As a result, significant
disparities occur in the per-pupil revenue allotted to different school districts
within the same state. The *median* disparity in per-pupil spending between
the wealthiest and poorest school districts throughout the United States is
nearly $12,000 per student.[63]

Wide disparities also exist in the average per-pupil expenditures between
different states. For example, while the national average per-pupil expenditure is $10,834, New Jersey spends $18,485 per student, and Utah spends
only $6,849 per student.[64] This disparity in revenue is exacerbated because
districts also rely on interest earned on their revenue for additional funds.
Districts and states that attract less revenue, of course, also garner less interest
income from that source of revenue.

These disparities have a racial component as well; districts with mostly
white students spend on average approximately $900 more per student than
do other districts. The Education Trust reported that "[s]chool districts that
educate the greatest number of low-income and minority students receive
substantially less state and local money per student than districts with the
fewest such students."[65]

Some states have enacted property tax extension limitation laws, commonly referred to as "tax caps." Under such a law, a school district is barred from increasing its property tax extension by an amount greater than the consumer price index or a predetermined statutory amount (e.g., 5 percent). Because tax caps are independent of a school district's real expenses, those caps typically reduce the amount of a district's real revenues that are required to keep up with its expenses.

School districts and local educational agencies incur educational expenses, operational and maintenance expenses, transportation expenses, life-safety expenses, and construction expenses. Many of the district's expenses are mandated by law, leaving school district administrators with little discretion in their use of scarce resources.[66]

Some federal statutes require school districts to allocate funds to maintain a safe and healthy environment for students. The federal Occupational Safety and Health Administration (OSHA), for example, regulates the school environment and requires districts to rid their schools of, inter alia, blood-borne pathogens, asbestos, unclean air, lead paint, hazardous waste, and radon.[67] While such requirements are crucial to the creation of a safe environment for children, they also create a series of fixed costs for a school district.

The resources that a school must devote to "educational" purposes also are largely mandated by law. Educational expenditures include teacher salaries and teacher benefits (i.e., health, dental, life insurance, and retirement), special education services (i.e., assistive technology, teaching assistants, therapists, related services, transportation, and alternative placements), purchased services (i.e., liability insurance and workers' compensation insurance), supplies (i.e., textbooks), and equipment (i.e., computers).

In the typical school district, more than 90 percent of these expenses are dictated by law. Teacher salaries and benefits, which often constitute 75 percent of an education fund budget, are usually established by a multiyear collective bargaining agreement. Absent extraordinary circumstances, the terms of that agreement bind the district to make the required expenditures, regardless of evolving economic conditions or other pressing needs for the money.

Federal law also has created a web of mandates requiring districts to fund needed services to students with educational disabilities without regard to cost.[68] The provision of effective special education services typically requires a district to allocate far more than its average per-pupil amount for a special-needs student. Although Congress appropriates federal funding for services required by IDEA, it has failed to provide full funding for these services.[69]

The No Child Left Behind Act itself establishes minimum funding levels that are not sufficient to allow the full implementation of its requirements. Yet not even those minimum funding levels have been achieved. From 2002 to 2006, for example, the amounts budgeted to meet NCLB mandates fell more than $30 billion short of even the minimum amounts established by the statute.[70] These underfunded mandates necessarily tax a school district's non-federal revenue, and require districts to make up the inherent shortfall by reducing other educational programs and expenses, or by creatively finding external revenue sources.

THE CHANGING ECONOMIC LANDSCAPE

State funding for early childhood education programs decreased by over half a billion dollars in 2011–2012, which, when adjusted for inflation, is the largest one year drop ever.[71] This was due to both unprecedented budget cuts and the loss of at least $127 million in American Recovery and Reinvestment Act funds from the previous year that were no longer available.[72]

As a result of this, pre-K has, after a decade of growth, stalled—it is the first time that there has been no increase in the percentage of children served in state early childhood education programs.[73] State funding per child fell by more than $400 compared to the previous year; state spending per child has decreased by more than $1,100 since 2001–2002.[74] Current state spending per child is $3,841.[75] The adverse consequences of less funding were also evident in what NIEER calls a "disastrous" year for meeting quality standards.[76]

Despite the recent contradictions, NIEER concludes that "state-funded pre-K has been one of education's biggest success stories."[77] Enrollment remained at a historic high in 2011–2012: state programs serve more children than ever, putting them on track for success.[78] "[T]he research is clear that only high-quality pre-K has produced substantial gains in school readiness, achievement and educational attainment, higher productivity in the labor force, and decreases in social problems like crime and delinquency. The promised high economic returns associated with these positive outcomes have only been found for programs that were adequately funded and met or exceeded the benchmarks for quality set out in our report."[79] Appropriations for 2012–2013 were up modestly, and reports on 2013–2014 budgets are hopeful.[80]

INVESTING IN EARLY CHILDHOOD EDUCATION

The National Institute for Early Education calculates that it would cost $8,387 per child to provide an early childhood education program that meets every single one of its benchmarks for structural quality.[81] Assuming that it would cost approximately $8,400 per child to provide an outstanding early childhood education, the total annual cost would be about $33.6 billion to educate every four-year-old in America and $67.2 billion to educate every four- and three-year-old in America.

But the country currently spends approximately $9 billion to educate 41 percent of the four-year-olds in state and federal programs. In particular, 1.12 million four-year-olds are currently served in state-funded pre-K programs, at about $4,629 per child or a total of $5.5 billion. The federal government also already spends at least $3.5 billion to educate four-year-olds in its programs. In addition, the federal government spends about $353 million on early childhood special education.

Moreover, 34 percent of the nation's four-year-olds currently are enrolled in private early childhood education programs. Some of them would undoubtedly remain in those programs and would not require any allocation of public funds. Yet, even assuming that every four-year-old in America would enroll in a publicly funded pre-K program, full funding of these programs would require an additional annual public expenditure of approximately $24 billion. Because fewer three-year-olds than four-year-olds are currently served in publicly funded programs, full funding of programs to serve all three-year-olds would require an additional annual allocation of approximately $28 billion.

Therefore, full funding for outstanding pre-K programs for all four-year-olds would require an additional annual expense of $24 billion, full funding for outstanding pre-K programs for all three-year-olds would require an additional $28 billion, and full funding to provide outstanding pre-K programs for all of the country's three- and four-year-olds would require a total additional annual expenditure of public funds of $52 billion.

That amount comprises about 8 percent of the total amount of the approximately $600 billion of public funds spent each year on the education of all elementary and secondary school children.[82] The amount required to educate all three- and four-year-olds in America also is far less than one percent of the entire federal budget.[83]

The expenditure of these funds would benefit all children, and particularly children of color. Access to early childhood education programs in America varies significantly by race and ethnicity. Slightly more than half of African American four-year-olds are not enrolled in any pre-K program, and 63 percent of Latino or Hispanic children do not attend any such program.[84]

The participation rate of Latino or Hispanic children in early childhood education programs is thus particularly low.[85] Of the approximately 960,000 Latino or Hispanic four-year-olds in America, about 600,000 do not receive any organized early education before entering elementary school. So too, about 280,000 of the 560,000 African American four-year-olds do not have access to such early education programs.[86]

Moreover, the percentage of African American or Latino or Hispanic four-year-olds who are enrolled in any private or other early childhood education program is negligible relative to white students in those programs. Expanding early childhood education programs to all four-year-olds would provide access to about 900,000 African American and Latino children every year who would not otherwise receive any pre-K education.[87]

Table 4.3.

Four-Year-Olds*	White	Black	Hispanic	Asian	Native American
Center-Based	53%	37%	31%	55%	29%
Head Start	7%	25%	19%	6%	31%

* *Jodi Jacobson Chernoff et al., Preschool: First Findings From the Third Follow-Up of the Early Childhood Longitudinal Study, Birth Cohort (ECLS-B) (Washington, DC: U.S. Department of Education National Center for Education Statistics, 2007), http://nces.ed.gov/pubs2008/2008025.pdf.*

The payoff is great. As the next section shows, there is unassailable evidence that return on the investment from these relatively modest state and federal funds would be dramatic.

THE ROBUST ECONOMIC RETURNS FROM AN INVESTMENT IN EARLY CHILDHOOD EDUCATION

The Importance of Early Learning Environments

Professor James J. Heckman of the University of Chicago's Department of Economics, who won the Nobel Prize in Economics in 2000, has performed path-breaking research regarding the economic returns from investments in early childhood education programs. In his 2008 paper "School, Skills and Synapses," Professor Heckman documents the wealth of research demonstrating that early learning environments have a dramatic impact on adult success and well-being. In particular, Heckman finds sound empirical research indicating the following:

1. Many major economic and social problems such as crime, teenage pregnancy, dropping out of high school, and adverse health conditions are linked to low levels of skill and ability in society.
2. In analyzing policies that foster skills and abilities, society should recognize the multiplicity of human abilities.

3. Currently, public policy in the United States focuses on promoting and measuring cognitive ability through IQ and achievement tests. The accountability standards in the No Child Left Behind Act concentrate attention on achievement test scores and do not evaluate important non-cognitive factors that promote success in school and life.

4. Cognitive abilities are important determinants of socioeconomic success.

5. Socio-emotional skills, physical and mental health, perseverance, attention, motivation, and self-confidence are also important determinants of socioeconomic success. They contribute to performance in society at large and even help determine scores on the very tests that are commonly used to measure cognitive achievement.

6. Ability gaps between the advantaged and disadvantaged open up early in the lives of children.

7. The family environments of young children are major predictors of cognitive and socio-emotional abilities, as well as a variety of outcomes such as crime and health.

8. Family environments in the United States and many other countries around the world have deteriorated over the past 40 years.

9. Experimental evidence on the positive effects of early interventions on children in disadvantaged families is consistent with a large body of non-experimental evidence showing that the absence of supportive family environments harms child outcomes.

10. If society intervenes early enough, it can improve cognitive and socio-emotional abilities and the health of disadvantaged children.

11. Early interventions promote schooling, reduce crime, foster workforce productivity, and reduce teenage pregnancy.

12. These interventions are estimated to have high benefit-cost ratios and rates of return.

13. As programs are currently configured, interventions early in the life cycle of disadvantaged children have much higher economic returns than later interventions such as reduced pupil/teacher ratios, public job training, convict rehabilitation programs, adult literacy programs, tuition subsidies, or expenditures on police.

14. Life cycle skill formation is dynamic in nature. Skill begets skill; motivation begets motivation. Motivation cross-fosters skill and skill cross-fosters motivation. If a child is not motivated to learn and engage early on in life, the more likely it is that when the child becomes an adult, he or she will fail in social and economic life. The longer society waits to intervene in the life cycle of a disadvantaged child, the more costly it is to remediate the disadvantage.

15. A major refocus of policy is required to capitalize on knowledge about the life cycle of skill and health formation and the importance of the early years in creating inequality in America, and in producing skills for the workforce.

The evidence assembled by Professor Heckman about the importance of early learning environments undercuts the controversial research presented in *The Bell Curve,* written by Hernstein and Murray in 1994. That book suggested that genetics locked into place differences in cognitive ability that could be measured by achievement test scores and that predetermined adult socioeconomic success. Heckman's work demonstrates that "personality factors are also powerfully predictive of socioeconomic success and are as powerful as cognitive abilities in producing many adult outcomes."[88] He concludes:

> Recent research . . . establishes the power of socio-emotional abilities and an important role for environment and intervention in creating abilities . . . [G]enetic expression is strongly influenced by environmental influences and . . . environmental effects on gene expression can be inherited. . . . [H]igh quality early childhood interventions foster abilities and that inequality can be attacked at its source. Early interventions also boost the productivity of the economy.[89]

The Proven Educational, Social, and Economic Benefits of Investing in Early Childhood Education Programs

In his essay "Promoting Social Mobility," Heckman describes the precise early childhood interventions that have been proven to produce substantial educational and economic benefits. He presents compelling evidence that early intervention in the form of early childhood education programs can have positive and lasting effects on the lives of children, particularly those from disadvantaged families. Such early interventions can improve cognitive and socio-emotional skills. They also foster learning, reduce crime, promote workforce productivity, and reduce teenage pregnancy.

Moreover, Professor Heckman calculates that investments in high-quality early childhood education programs pay a dramatic economic return of between $7.00 and $16.00 for every dollar invested, and ultimately concludes that the return actually would be $10.00 for every dollar invested.[90] The high returns on investments in early childhood programs include the significant reduction in health care costs, crime costs, special education costs, and other educational remediation costs. The rate of return also represents additional revenue generated from the income received by, and the taxes paid from, those who have had the advantages of a pre-K education.

Heckman relies in part on two longitudinal studies that he finds to be methodologically sound and statistically significant. The HighScope Perry Preschool Project in Ypsilanti, Michigan, followed 123 impoverished African American children. Between 1962 and 1967, 50 of these three- and four-year-old children were blindly divided into a treatment group and a control group. The "treatment" group received a co-constructivist, play-based, child-centered and emergent curriculum that emphasized social and emotional development. The program included 2.5 hours of classroom education daily and 90-minute home visits weekly over a 30-week school year. The control group of children did not receive this program.

Researchers have followed the control group and the treatment group through age 40. The results are dramatic. The Perry treatment group performed significantly better on achievement tests, attained higher levels of education, required less special education, earned higher wages, were more likely to own a home, were less likely to require public assistance, were less likely to be arrested as juveniles or adults, and were less likely to be imprisoned. The incomes of the treatment group were also materially higher than those of the control group.

In their examination and reexamination of the data, which corrected for every conceivable methodological bias, Heckman and his colleagues concluded that the differences between the treatment and the control group were statistically significant and scientifically reliable.[91] In particular, those children who received the high-quality preschool program dramatically out-performed those who did not:

1. High school completion: Seventy-seven percent received a high school diploma or general education development (GED) diploma, compared to 60 percent.
2. Employment: Sixty-nine percent were employed at age 27, compared to 56 percent; 76 percent were employed at age 40, compared to 62 percent.
3. Income: Those treatment group students who were employed at age 27 had higher earnings (by $2,000 each) than those control group students who were employed; those treatment group students who were employed at age 40 had higher earnings (by $5,500 each) than those control group students who were employed.
4. Home ownership: Twenty-seven percent owned their homes at age 22, compared to 5 percent; 37 percent owned their homes at age 40, compared to 28 percent.
5. Arrest and prison record: Thirty-six percent were arrested five or more times, compared to 55 percent; 28 percent were imprisoned, compared to 52 percent.

6. School readiness: Sixty-seven percent were prepared for elementary school, compared to 28 percent.
7. Educational achievement: Forty-nine percent were achieving at grade level at age 14, compared to 15 percent.[92]

The net economic return from the program to taxpayers also has been remarkable. The program invested a total of $15,166 per student over the course of their entire preschool years. The economic return on that investment has been $244,812 per student.[93] That return is produced from significant reductions in crime costs and general and special education costs. In addition, the economic return includes the increased revenue generated from higher taxable income. Accordingly, each dollar invested yielded a return of $16.14.[94]

The evidence adduced from the Perry School Project is consistent with the data collected from the Abecedarian Project. That North Carolina study involved children born between 1972 and 1977 into high-risk families. Children from four months to eight years old experienced an intensive full-day, year-round program of early childhood education. The treatment group also received home care and parental support. The researchers followed the children through age 30.

As with the Perry School Project, the Abecedarian treatment group significantly outperformed their control group peers in academic achievement, social stability, and economic success. As Professor Heckman concludes, "[T]hese longitudinal studies demonstrate positive effects of early childhood environmental enrichment on a range of cognitive and non-cognitive skills, schooling achievement, job performance, and social behaviors."[95]

The results of the Perry and Abecedarian studies have been replicated in a much larger study of Texas's pre-K program. In *The Effects of Texas's Pre-kindergarten Program on Academic Performance* (2012), the Center for Analysis of Longitudinal Data in Educational Research analyzed evidence compiled from cohorts of over 680,000 racially and economically diverse students who were eligible to attend a Texas state-funded pre-K program. The results were significant:

> We find that having participated in Texas's targeted pre-K program is associated with increased scores on the math and reading sections of the Texas Assessment of Academic Skills (TAAS), and reductions in the probability of receiving special education services. We also find that participating [in] pre-K increases mathematics scores for students who take the Spanish version of the TAAS tests. Those results show that even modest pre-K program[s] implemented at scale can have important effects on students' educational achievements.[96]

In fact, over 123 studies now have been conducted. These studies have been examined and re-examined, analyzed and meta-analyzed. The irrefutable evidence from all of those studies demonstrates that an investment in early childhood education produces substantial educational, social, and economic benefits.[97]

In fact, the only real open question is the size of the return on an investment in early childhood education programs. The evidence indicates that each dollar invested in early childhood education programs will produce from between $7.00 to $16.00 in return.[98] Accordingly, the assumption that the return on an investment in early childhood education will be 7:1 is conservative. The investment returns are likely to be significantly greater, particularly if the programs are designed to develop in children the capacity to construct knowledge through meaningful relationships.

Moreover, the returns on an investment in early childhood education benefit all children: middle-class children as well as disadvantaged children; typically developing children as well as children with special needs; and dual language learners as well as native speakers. But the positive effects of early childhood education are particularly significant for children of poor socio-economic status.

NIEER has found clear evidence that middle-class children can benefit substantially from early childhood education programs and that the benefits outweigh the costs for children from middle-income as well as those from low-income families. But "children from low-income backgrounds benefit more."[99] If early childhood education programs are publicly provided for these children, "it will have many economic benefits: It will increase social mobility, it will reduce income inequality, it will improve college enrollment rate, it will improve community or criminal behavior, and it will also bring higher tax revenues because more workers will be earning higher wages."[100]

Furthermore, because of the positive intergenerational effects of a commitment to early childhood education programs, a clear policy of providing public early childhood education programs to all economically disadvantaged children by taxing all parents actually improves the positive impacts on intergenerational earnings mobility, college mobility, college completion rate, and long-term per capita income.[101] Professor W. Steven Barnett of the National Institute for Early Education Research at Rutgers has noted that, even if early childhood education programs only deliver one-tenth of their proven outcomes, they are still a worthwhile investment.[102]

NIEER cautions, however, that the extent the benefits received from any early childhood program are dependent upon the nature and quality of that program. As a result, NIEER has created ten benchmarks of "quality" that include such ingredients as small class sizes and well-trained and supported educational professionals. NIEER recognizes, and the chapters that follow demonstrate, that: "in order to produce positive effects on children's behavior and later reductions in crime and delinquency, [early childhood education programs] should be designed to develop the whole child, including social and emotional development and self-regulation."[103]

The most authentic markers of quality in an early learning environment are "stimulating and supportive interactions between teachers and children and effective use of curricula" because "[c]hildren benefit most when teachers engage in stimulating interactions that support learning *and* are emotionally supportive. Interactions that help children acquire new knowledge and skills provide input to children, elicit verbal responses and reactions from them, and foster engagement in and enjoyment of learning."[104] In particular, the most effective early childhood education programs are those in which highly trained, skilled, and valued professional educators create an learning environment that encourages children to construct their own knowledge by building meaningful relationships.

NOTES

1. Data regarding America's schools and students (their enrollment numbers, costs, etc.) vary depending on the source because of underreporting, definitional problems, and the fact that this field is constantly evolving. Because of that, data cited in this book are accurate but approximate.

2. William J. Hussar and Tabitha M. Bailey, *Projections of Education Statistics to 2021* (Washington, DC: U.S. Department of Education National Center for Education Statistics, January 2013), http://nces.ed.gov/pubs2013/2013008.pdf; Thomas D. Snyder and Sally A. Dillow, *Digest of Education Statistics 2012* (Washington, DC: U.S. Department of Education National Center for Education Statistics, December 2013), Table 40, http://nces.ed.gov/pubs2014/2014015.pdf. The actual number of homeschooled children is difficult to quantify, and some estimates place the number at close to 2 million. www.hslda.org.

3. Hussar and Bailey, *Digest of Education Statistics 2012*, Table 100.

4. Ibid., Table 108.

5. Stephen P. Broughman and Nancy L. Swaim, *Characteristics of Private Schools in the United States: Results From the 2011–12 Private School Universe Survey* (Washington, DC: U.S. Department of Education National Center for Education Statistics, July 2013), http://nces.ed.gov/pubs2013/2013316.pdf.

6. Ibid., W.S. Barnett et al., *The State of Preschool 2012: State Preschool Yearbook* (New Brunswick, NJ: National Institute for Early Education Research, 2012), http://nieer.org/sites/nieer/files/yearbook2012.pdf.

7. Broughman and Swaim, *Characteristics of Private Schools in the United States*.

8. Ibid.

9. Ibid.

10. *Racial/Ethnic Enrollment in Public Schools*, (Washington, DC: U.S. Department of Education National Center for Education Statistics, April 2014), http://nces.ed.gov/programs/coe/indicator_cge.asp.

11. Ibid.

12. Ibid.

13. W.S. Barnett et al., *The State of Preschool 2013: State Preschool Yearbook* (New Brunswick, NJ: National Institute for Early Education Research, 2013). See also *Enrollment of 3-, 4-, and 5-year-old Children in Primary Programs, by Level of Program, Control of Program, and Attendance Status: Selected Years, 1965 through 2012* (Washington, DC: U.S. Department of Education National Center for Education Statistics Education Preprimary Education Enrollment, May 2013), Table 202.10, http://nces.ed.gov/programs/digest/d13/tables/dt13_202.10.asp.

14. W.S. Barnett and Donald J. Yarosz, "Who Goes to Preschool and Why Does It Matter?," *National Institute for Early Education Research* 15 (November 2007), http://nieer.org/resources/policybriefs/15.pdf.

15. Barnett et al., *The State of Preschool 2013*, 7.

16. Susan Aud et al., *The Condition of Education 2013 Report*, ed. Thomas Nachazel and Allison Dziuba (Washington, DC: U.S. Department of Education National Center for Education Statistics, May 2013), 42, http://nces.ed.gov/pubs2013/2013037.pdf.

17. Ibid., 44.

18. Ibid., 42.

19. Ibid.

20. Ibid.

21. Barnett et al., *The State of Preschool 2012*, 6–7.

22. Ibid., 8.

23. Ibid.

24. *Current Population Survey, Table 3: Nursery and Primary School Enrollment of People 3 to 6 Years Old, by Control of School, Attendance Status, Age, Race, Hispanic Origin, Mother's Labor Force Status and Education, and Family Income* (U.S. Census Bureau, October 2012), https://www.census.gov/hhes/school/data/cps/2012/tables.html.

25. Barnett et al., *The State of Preschool 2013*.

26. Ibid., 9.

27. Barnett and Yarosz, "Who Goes to Preschool."

28. Ibid.

29. Ibid.

30. Barnett et al., *The State of Preschool 2012*, 6.

31. Ibid.

32. Ibid.

33. Aud et al., *The Condition of Education 2013*, iii.

34. John Wirt et al., *The Condition of Education 2002*, ed. Barbara Kridl and Andrea Livingston (Washington, DC: U.S. Department of Education National Center for Education Statistics, June 2002), 43 and 59, Table 43, http://nces.ed.gov/pubs2002/2002025.pdf (indicating that 56 percent of children ages three to five who were not in kindergarten were in an early childhood education program in 2001); Barnett et al., *The State of Preschool* 2003, 8.

35. Aud et al., *The Condition of Education 2013*, 1–2; see also Committee for Economic Development, "Early Education—Preschool for All: Investing in a Productive and Just Society," (2002), 17.

36. Aud et al., *The Condition of Education 2013*, 45.

37. Ibid., 42.

38. Hussar and Bailey, *Projections of Education Statistics to 2021*.

39. Ibid.

40. New America Foundation, U.S. Departments of Education, Health & Human Services, Agriculture, Defense, and Veterans Affairs, White House Office of Management and Budget, and Congressional Budget Office, *The Federal Education Budget* (New America Foundation Federal Budget Project, 2014), http://febp.newamerica.net/background-analysis/education-federal-budget.

41. Ibid.

42. In fiscal year 2013, the federal government spent $3.5 trillion, making its expenditures of $141 billion on education about 4 percent of the total budget. U.S. Department. of Education Budget Tables.

43. See Common Core of Data (CCD), "National Public Education Financial Survey: 2000–01 through 2010–11," *Digest of Education Statistics 2013* (Washington, DC: U.S. Department of Education, National Center for Education Statistics), Table 235.10, http://nces.ed.gov/programs/coe/indicator_cma.asp (calculating that most school districts rely on federal funding for less than 10 percent of their revenue).

44. Barnett et al., *The State of Preschool 2013*, 7.

45. *Justification of Estimates for Appropriations Committees* (U.S. Department of Health and Human Services, Fiscal Year 2002–2015), http://www.hhs.gov/budget/fy2014/secretary-congressional-justification.pdf.

46. See 2013 Poverty Guidelines (U.S. Department of Health & Human Services, 2013), http://aspe.hhs.gov/poverty/13poverty.cfm.

47. See Head Start Family and Child Experiences Survey (FACES) (U.S. Department of Health & Human Services Office of Planning, Research & Evaluation, 2011), http://www.acf.hhs.gov/programs/opre/research/project/head-start-family-and-child-experiences-survey-faces.

48. Head Start Program Facts, Fiscal Year 2012 (U.S. Department of Health & Human Services, 2012), https://eclkc.ohs.acf.hhs.gov/hslc/data/factsheets/docs/hs-program-factsheet-2012.pdf.

49. Ibid.

50. See David L. Kirp, *Improbable Scholars: The Rebirth of a Great American School System and a Strategy for America's Schools* (New York: Oxford University Press, 2013); David L. Kirp, "The Secret to Fixing Bad Schools," *New York Times*, February 9, 2013, http://www.nytimes.com/2013/02/10/opinion/sunday/the-secret-to-fixing-bad-schools.html?pagewanted=all&_r=0 ("There's abundant evidence showing the lifetime benefits of early education.").

51. See 2013 Poverty Guidelines.

52. New America Foundation, The Federal Education Budget.

53. Ibid.

54. Ibid.

55. Ibid.

56. Sara Neufeld, "The Power of Pre-K: Model Early Ed Program in Chicago Lifts Entire Family," in *In Plain Sight: Poverty in America*, November 23, 2013, http://www.nbcnews.com/_news/2013/11/23/21537069-the-power-of-pre-k-model-early-ed-program-in-chicago-lifts-entire-family.

57. Ibid.

58. See §619, Part B.

59. New America Foundation, The Federal Education Budget.

60. Ibid.

61. Ibid.

62. New America Foundation, The Federal Education Budget.

63. See also Quality Counts '98, "Resources Data Table"; Common Core of Data (CCD), School District Finance Survey, F-33; Carey, "The Funding Gap"; Kozol, *Savage Inequalities*.

64. Ranking of the States 2012 and Estimates of School Statistics 2013 (National Education Association, December 2012), http://www.nea.org/home/54597.htm.

65. See "School Board News," National Association of School Boards, 7. See also Carey, "The Funding Gap," 6 ("The troubling pattern of funding shortfalls repeats itself for school districts educating large numbers of minority students.").

66. See "Unfunded Mandates Frustrate Superintendents and Principals," *National School Boards Association School Board News*, November 25, 2003, 3.

67. See, e.g., 29 C.F.R. §1910 et seq.

68. See, e.g., IDEA, 20 U.S.C. §§1400–1405.

69. See Center for Special Education Finance Report, http://csef.air.org (calculating that full funding of IDEA would require an additional $25 billion).

70. See Budget of the United States Government, Fiscal Years 2002, 2003, 2004, http://www.gpo.gov/fdsys/browse/collectionGPO.action?collectionCode=BUDGET. See also "Unfunded Mandates Frustrate," National Association of School Boards ("Eighty-nine percent of superintendents . . . call NCLB an 'unfunded mandate.'").

71. Barnett et al., *The State of Preschool 2012*, 5.

72. Ibid.

73. Ibid.

74. Ibid.

75. Ibid., 7.

76. Ibid., 5.

77. Ibid.

78. Ibid.

79. Ibid.

80. Ibid.

81. Barnett et al., *The State of Preschool 2013*, 18.

82. *Digest of Education Statistics* (Washington, DC: U.S. Department of Education National Center for Education Statistics, 2013), Table 205 http://nces.ed.gov/programs/digest/d12/tables/dt12_205.asp.

83. *Fast Facts* (Washington, DC: U.S. Department of Education National Center for Education Statistics, 2014), http://nces.ed.gov/fastfacts/display.asp?id=372.

84. 2013 Kids Count Data Book, "National Key Indicators by Race and Hispanic Origin," (2013), 15, http://datacenter.kidscount.org/files/2013kidscountdatabook.pdf; 2013 Kids Count Data Book, "Child Population by Race" (2013). See also National Center for Education Statistics, Preschool: First Findings Early Childhood Longitudinal Study, Birth Cohort (2007). This data is consistent with the data cited in the August 2014 Voices for Illinois Children "Disparities in Access to Preschool in Illinois" Report that states that 43 percent of Latino children between the ages of three and five were enrolled in any pre-K program compared with 54 percent of African American children of the same age and 56 percent of white children. Voices for Illinois Children "Disparities in Access to Preschool in Illinois" Report, August 2014, citing Child Trends Databank, "Indicators on Children and Youth: Preschool and Prekindergarten" (2014).

85. See Milagros Nores, "The Economics of Early Childhood Education Programs: Lasting Benefits and Large Returns" (presentation at Loyola University Chicago School of Law Early Childhood Education Symposium, Chicago, Illinois, March 15, 2013), http://www.luc.edu/law/centers/childlaw/institutes/child_education/symposium.html.

86. Ibid.

87. See United States Census, State and County Quick Facts (2014); "Child Population by Race" (The U.S. population is approximately 316 million, 14 percent are African American and 24 percent are Hispanic or Latino.).

88. J. Heckman et al., *School, Skills and Synapses,* 46 Econ. Inquiry, 289–324 (2008).

89. Ibid., 312.

90. See James J. Heckman, "School, Skills and Synapses" (working paper, National Bureau of Economic Research, June 2008): 21, http://www.nber.org/papers/w14064.pdf; James J. Heckman et al., "The Rate of Return to the HighScope Perry Preschool Program," *Journal of Public Economics* 94 (2010): 114–128; F. Campbell et al., "Adult Outcomes as a Function of an Early Childhood Education Program: Abecedarian Project Follow Up," *Developmental Psychology* 48(4) (July 2012): 1033–1043, doi: 10.1037/a0026644; James J. Heckman, Rodrigo Pinto, and Peter Savelyev, "Understanding the Mechanisms Through Which an Influential Early Childhood Program Boosted Adult Outcomes," *American Economic Review* 103(6) (2013), 2052–86.

91. James J. Heckman et al., "Reanalysis of the Perry Preschool Program: Multiple-Hypothesis and Permutation Tests Applied to a Quasi-randomized Experiment," *Qualitative Economics* 1 (2010): 1–49; James J. Heckman, "The Rate of Return to the HighScope Perry Preschool Program," *Journal of Public Economics* 94 (2010): 114–128.

92. See also Lawrence J. Schweinhart et al., *Lifetime Effects: The HighScope Perry Preschool Study Through Age 40* (Ypsilanti: HighScope Press, 2005); Lawrence J. Schweinhart and David P. Weikart, "The HighScope Model of Early Childhood Education," in *Approaches to Early Childhood Education,* ed. Jaipaul L. Roopnarine and James E. Johnson (Boston: Pearson, 2013), 226–28.

93. See Schweinhart et al., *Lifetime Effects,* xvii, Figure 10-2.

94. Ibid., vvii, Fig. 10-21.

95. Heckman, "School, Skills and Synapses," 19cn20.

96. See Schweinhart et al., *Lifetime Effects,* iii, 20; See also Sara Mead, "Texas Pre-K Programs Improve Kids' Elementary Achievement," *Education Week,* November 26, 2012, http://blogs.edweek.org/sarameads_policy_notebook/2012/11/researchers_find_texas_pre-k_programs_improving_kids_elementary_achievement.html (finding the results for the large, diverse Texas programs to be consistent with other large-scale studies such as the Chicago Child Parent Center and Oklahoma's Universal Pre-K Program).

97. See, e.g., W.S. Barnett, "Effectiveness of Early Educational Intervention," *Science* 333 (2011): 975-978, http://leadershiplinc.illinoisstate.edu/researchcompendium/documents/EffectivenessofEarlyEducationalIntervention.pdf; W.S. Barnett and L.N. Masse, "Early Childhood Program Design and Economic Returns: Comparative Benefit-Cost Analysis of the Abecedarian Program and Its Policy Complications," *Economics of Education Review* 26 (2007): 113–25, http://nieer.org/sites/nieer/files/BenefitCostAbecedarian.pdf; J.R. Behrman, Y. Cheng, and P.E. Todd, "Evaluating Preschool Programs When Length of Exposure to the Program Varies: A Nonparametric Approach," *Review of Economics and Statistics* 86(1) (2004): 108–32; S. Berlinski, S. Galiani, and P. Gertler, "The Effect of Pre-Primary Education on Primary School Performance," *Journal of Public Economics* 93 (2009): 219–34; S. Berlinski, S. Galiani, and M. Manacorda, "Giving Children a Better Start: Preschool Attendance and School Age Profiles," *Journal of*

Public Economics 92 (2008): 1416–40; G. Camilli et al., "Meta-Analysis of the Effects of Early Education Interventions on Cognitive and Social Development," *Teachers College Record* 112(3) (2010): 579–620; A. Diamond and K. Lee, "Interventions Shown to Aid Executive Function Development in Children 4 to 12 Years Old," *Science* 333 (2011): 959–64; T. Havnes and M. Mogstad, "No Child Left Behind: Subsidized Child Care and Children's Long-Run Outcomes," *American Economic Journal: Economic Policy* 3(2) (2011): 97–129. See also Kevin Gorkey, "Early Childhood Education: A Meta-Analytic Affirmation of the Short- and Long-Term Benefits of Educational Opportunity," *School Psychology Quarterly* 16(1) (2001): 9–30 (meta-analyses of all of the available short-term and long-term studies and data sets, prove that early childhood education "has a very positive influence on the lives of its participants transcendent of their scores on tests of intelligence or academic achievement").

98. See, e.g., Barnett and Masse, "Comparative Benefit-Cost Analysis"; C. Belfield, M. Nores, W.S. Barnett, and L.J. Schweinhart, "The High/Scope Perry Preschool Program," *Journal of Human Resources*, 41(1) (2006): 162–90; J.A. Temple and A.J. Reynolds, "Benefits and Costs of Investments in Preschool Education: Evidence from the Child-Parent Centers and Related Programs," *Economics of Education Review* 26(1) (2007): 126–44.

99. Hirokazo Yoshikawa et al., "Investing in Our Future: The Evidence Base on Preschool Education," The Society for Research in Child Development (October 2013), http://fcd-us.org/sites/default/files/Evidence%20Base%20on%20Preschool%20Education%20FINAL.pdf.

100. James Heckman and Lakshmi Raut, "Intergenerational Long-Term Effects of Preschool-Structural Estimates From a Discrete Programming Model" (working paper, National Bureau of Economic Research, 2013), 30, http://www.nber.org/papers/w19077.pdf.

101. Heckman and Raut, "Intergenerational Long-Term Effects," 35.

102. W.S. Barnett, "Preschool Education and Its Lasting Effects: Research and Policy Implications," Education and the Public Interest Center & Education Policy Research Unit Policy Brief (September 2008): 17, http://nepc.colorado.edu/publication/preschool-education.

103. W.S. Barnett, "Preschool Education and Its Lasting Effects," 21.

104. Hirokazo Yoshikawa et al., *Investing in Our Future*.

Chapter Five

The Relationship Between Investing in Early Childhood Education and Other Reforms

This chapter explores the relationship between investing in effective early childhood education programs and other current educational reform initiatives. In particular, the chapter takes seriously the following strategies:

1. "accountability," including the use of standardized testing to evaluate schools and teachers;
2. "privatization" or "school choice," including vouchers and charter schools; and
3. remedial education and vocational training programs.

These movements have generated tremendous debate, particularly about the efficacy of standardized tests, charter schools, and vouchers. As this chapter demonstrates, an investment in early childhood programs can bring together advocates with different perspectives on these issues.

A system of effective early childhood programs in which professionally trained educators make learning visible through documentation can serve as a model of genuine accountability. In addition, a system of effective early childhood programs in which government funds are made available to support both public and private providers can serve as a model of genuine school choice. Furthermore, a focus on early childhood education is based on a pre-distribution of resources and efficiently preempts the need for more costly remediation programs, thus providing a better return on investment than alternative reform strategies. Accordingly, advocates on all sides of the accountability and privatization debates have a shared interest in supporting an investment in early childhood education.

ACCOUNTABILITY

The first popular reform initiative is the call for greater accountability in education. There is little debate about the value of accountability. Yet calls for accountability are often limited to arguments for evaluating teachers and schools based on the test scores of their students.[1] When reformers advocate for "accountability," they tend to mean reliance on standardized tests.[2] While advocates for accountability through a regime of testing undoubtedly are well intentioned, the research has revealed some limitations on the value of standardized tests to assess student learning and teacher performance.

First, standardized tests do not usually assess social and emotional growth, including skills that reliably correspond to success such as motivation, perseverance, self-regulation, collaboration, and inter-subjectivity.[3] As James Heckman has concluded after conducting and analyzing numerous data sets, "using achievement tests alone to assess teacher effectiveness would miss important dimensions of teacher quality."[4] At best, standardized tests only assess student "academic" performance. And because of their nature, they assess student performance at only one moment in time, as long-term retention and ability to use this knowledge is not measured.

Second, students are tested on their "academic" performance in only a few of the many subjects covered in school.[5] Subjects such as math and literacy are emphasized while other subjects are not considered.

Third, even within each of the few subjects covered, the test questions do not cover the range of content within the subject itself.[6] A student's test scores thus do not measure the range and depth of student academic achievement in particular content areas.

Fourth, the test questions themselves are not objective. The authors of the test questions set the difficulty of the questions with reference to an anticipated range of student responses.[7] Successful questions are those that generate a significant percentage of incorrect answers.[8] The authors of the questions thus are incentivized to create questions that result in an easy stratification of student answers.[9]

Fifth, the choice of which questions to use in a particular test reflects a host of non-objective judgments. Particular subjects and narrow topics are privileged over numerous subjects and broad topics.[10] As Alfie Kohn has shown, high scores on typical standardized tests often signify superficial thinking.[11]

Sixth, a student's score on standardized tests is not predictive of that student's success in life, or even future academic success within different educational institutions.[12]

Seventh, student learning is not improved by high-stakes testing. Rather, in those states with high-stakes testing, student learning stays the same or "actually goes down."[13]

Eighth, the use of standardized tests as a sole measure of evaluating student and teacher performance can have unintended, negative consequences. As David Berliner and Audrey Amrein noted, "Because clear evidence of increased student learning is not found, and because there are numerous reports of unintended consequences associated with high-stakes testing policies (increased drop-out rates, teachers' and schools cheating on exams, teachers defection from the profession . . .), there is need for . . . transformation of current high-stakes testing policies."[14]

Ninth, as the significance assigned to test results increases, so too does the potential for abuse of those results. According to the "uncertainty principle," the likelihood of distortion and corruption of the political and social uses of test results increases when the consequences of those results increase.[15] When the "stakes" of standardized testing increased with No Child Left Behind, the distortion and corruption of the political uses of the test results predictably increased as well.

Tenth, the premise that a student's performance on a standardized test alone is a reliable indicator of the quality of a school or its teachers is flawed.[16] The test-based system of the No Child Left Behind Act has been extended by the Obama administration's Race to the Top program. Under the No Child Left Behind Act, the high-stakes tests are used to identify "nonperforming" schools with the stigma of failure and financial penalties. Under the Race to the Top program, states are incentivized to insure that their testing systems are used to evaluate not just schools, but individual teachers as well.

Under the two regimes together, the federal government rewards states that punish schools and teachers who fail to perform on standardized tests. While the benevolent assumption undergirding both the No Child Left Behind and Race to the Top is that every child can learn regardless of their socioeconomic conditions or their family circumstances,[17] the sole measure of whether or not a child is learning is his or her performance on these high-stakes tests. If the child's test scores do not improve, therefore, the child has not learned and the teachers must be the cause of this failure.[18]

Yet the opponents of the reliance on standardized tests to serve the need for accountability have argued that the problems with "value-added assessments of a teacher's performance are legion."[19] Even if the tests themselves were perfect, they contend, the data they produce cannot be legitimately used to measure teaching quality. While individual teachers undoubtedly have an enormous impact on a child's growth and development, that impact cannot be accurately measured by high-stakes tests across classrooms, schools, or grade levels. At best, "differences in the quality of schools can explain about one-third of the variation in student achievement."[20] Nonetheless, some advocates for testing insist that schools begin to discipline teachers whose students do not meet standards and reward teachers whose students do meet standards with merit-based pay.[21]

Eleventh, even within the school and the classroom, the variables cannot be sufficiently controlled to assess the "value" that any particular teacher in any particular year "adds." A student's performance on any given test can be shaped by factors in the school such as class size, class composition, instructional materials, availability of assistants, learning resources, wellness, peer culture, climate, prior teachers, prior in-school learning environments, and summer school programming. As one of the country's foremost education experts, Linda Darling-Hammond, has concluded: even when sincere efforts are made to control for student populations, test results "largely reflect whom a teacher teaches, not how well they teach."[22]

In fact, in a comprehensive study of teacher evaluation methods commissioned by proponents of using test scores to gauge teacher quality, the evidence indicates that test-based measures of student achievement cannot reliably be employed as the primary evaluation measure.[23] In fact, evaluation systems based primarily on student test scores were proven to be the least reliable teacher evaluation model relative to models that stressed a diversity of classroom observations and student surveys.[24] Teacher evaluation systems based on standardized test scores were particularly poor at measuring a teacher's ability to help students acquire higher-order thinking skills.[25] Such systems have proven to be ". . . inaccurate, unstable, and unreliable."[26]

Accordingly, while proponents of utilizing high-stakes tests argue that policy makers need a valid way to determine whether all students are meeting the same high standards,[27] the reliance on standardized tests alone provides an imperfect and incomplete measure of student learning. The legitimate goal of accountability can be better served if those tests are augmented by documentation of student learning.

As the researchers from Project Zero at the Harvard Graduate School of Education have demonstrated, the practice of documentation provides an authentic measure of student learning and therefore an extremely effective method of accountability.[28] Through documentation, highly skilled educators are able to record the process and products of student learning, and then share their assessments with multiple stakeholders, including community members, taxpayers, and policy makers.

As further detailed in chapters 9 and 10, educators in extremely effective early childhood education programs already use documentation to make learning visible. They carefully observe, record, interpret, and share the ways in which children construct their knowledge through meaningful relation-ships. The skilled use of documentation by those educators provides a model of authentic assessment and genuine accountability. Advocates on all sides of the accountability debate therefore share a strong interest in supporting the development of a system of early childhood programs that make student learning visible through documentation.

PRIVATIZATION

The second reform initiative that has generated substantial debate is the movement toward privatization or school choice, which includes vouchers and charter schools. Some advocates favoring the expansion of vouchers and charter schools argue that they offer a market-based solution to the problems associated with public education, and can offer families educational op-portunities not otherwise available in the public schools. On the other hand, some advocates opposing the development of voucher programs and charter schools argue that the evidence does support these claims. Advocates on all sides of the privatization and school choice debate, however, can find com-mon ground in their support for investing in government-funded early child-hood programs which provide a model of genuine choice.

Vouchers

Vouchers enable parents to take some or all of the money that would have been allocated to a public school to educate their children and use it for private school education.[29] Vouchers typically do not represent cash pay-ments directly to parents. Rather, the state or the district in which the child otherwise would have been enrolled transfers funding from public to private school. The amount of the voucher often represents either some portion of state or local funding or the amount of state aid that would have been paid for the child to attend public school in his or her school district. The actual cost to the school district can vary. In some programs, those costs exceed the amount of the voucher.

Although vouchers are frequently compared to tuition tax credit and tax deduction plans, they are different in several respects. Tax credit and deduc-tion plans do not transfer funds from the state to a private institution. In effect, parents receive a discount from their tax obligations for tuition paid in a prior year rather than a grant or subsidy from a public agency that is remitted to a private school. Private schools tend to prefer vouchers because the schools receive the funds directly. Further, since vouchers are not derived from parents' income, they allow private schools to raise tuition more easily than do tax deductions or tax credits.

Vouchers also are often confused with charter schools and choice programs. More than half the states have passed laws allowing parents and teachers to establish charter schools at some cost to the public. Charter schools operate relatively independently of the public school system, and commonly receive public funds on a per-pupil basis.

At first glance, vouchers appear to resemble charter schools and thereby may add to state pressures to adopt them. However, there are several key distinctions. Most charters are granted by a public agency, such as a local school board. Charter schools are subject to criteria, expectations, operating conditions, and monitoring that are not required of private schools. Further, most charters are staffed by public employees, cannot charge tuition, and are subject to many of the same admissions requirements as public schools.

However, there are some areas where the distinctions between charters and vouchers become blurred. Several states, including Arizona, Minnesota, and Wisconsin, allow private schools to become charter schools. Additionally, a distinction should be made between public charter schools that are created by local school boards and those created by other entities, such as the state or a public university. Although public in character, these charter schools, like private school vouchers, redirect local school district finances without traditional legal, fiscal, or performance accountability to the voters in the community.

Finally, vouchers should not be confused with public school choice programs. Choice programs can include public charter schools, magnet schools, and other public schools within the district and in other school districts. In these choice programs, students remain within the public school system, and public resources are not redirected outside of the public school system.

In 1996 Cleveland, Ohio, instituted a voucher program that limited eligibility to low-income students. In its *Zelman* decision, the U.S. Supreme Court voted 5-4 to uphold the constitutionality of the Cleveland voucher program.[30] Although most of the voucher recipients used their subsidies to pay religious school tuition, the Supreme Court concluded that Cleveland's voucher program involved strictly individual, private choices and therefore did not offend the Establishment Clause of the First Amendment.

Milwaukee has operated a voucher program since 1990, and over the years, the legislature has expanded the original program. The Supreme Court in *Zelman* refers to Milwaukee's voucher program, suggesting that it has been successful. The program was amended in 1995 to apply to any child residing in Milwaukee whose family's income is below 125 percent of the poverty level. In 2011 the program was expanded to any child whose family's income is below 300 percent of the poverty line. For high school students whose family's income is below 300 percent but above 220 percent of the poverty line, however, participating private schools may charge tuition.

The program initially was open to all eligible public school children in grades K-12, with the maximum number of vouchers set at 7 percent of public school enrollment or a maximum of 7,250 students. The scope of the program was then allowed to double to 15 percent (or about 15,000 students in 1996–1997). In 2011 the cap on enrollment in the program was removed and the geographic boundaries were expanded to include students whose families reside in Racine as well as those with families in Milwaukee. Students are selected by random lottery.

Enrollment of voucher students in any one school initially was limited to 50 percent, then to 65 percent. Currently, there is no limit on the portion of the student body that can include voucher students. The amount of the voucher, which is nearly $6,500 per pupil (full-time equivalent), is equal to the amount of per-pupil state aid that would have been paid to the Milwaukee school system, but not greater than the cost of educating a child at the private school.

Over the first four years, the program grew from 341 to 802 students, or about half the authorized level. During that time, the number of participating schools expanded from 6 to 12. By comparison, Milwaukee's 130 private schools enrolled more than 24,000 students in 1995, or about 30 percent of the city's middle- and upper-income children and 7 percent of the children from the city's poorest neighborhoods. In the 2011–2012 school year, following the income level and geographic expansion of program eligibility, 22,762 students used vouchers at 106 participating schools located in Milwaukee and the surrounding area. Seventy-one percent of these students attended religious parish schools.

The Milwaukee voucher program is one of the longest running and closest studied in the nation. By all legitimate measures, the program has not been as successful as was hoped. Voucher students have not outperformed public school students from the same area.[31] While utilizing resources from the public schools, the Milwaukee voucher program has produced little empirically sound advantages to its students relative to the corresponding public schools.[32]

The Milwaukee experience with vouchers is not atypical.[33] In 2004 there were more than two dozen privately funded voucher programs in the country. Two of the more established programs were in San Antonio and Indianapolis.

San Antonio set up a public school choice program emphasizing immersion into Latino language, culture, and history. In addition, the business community created a program to allow 2,000 poor children to attend private schools through a private scholarship program. Parents paid about one-half the tuition cost. In this program, 99 percent of the students were enrolled in sectarian schools, mainly Catholic, and 95 percent of the parents rated religious training as very important or important.

In Indianapolis, a privately financed trust was established in 1991 that supported the enrollment of about 1,000 children from low-income families in 67 private schools. As in San Antonio, parents paid about one-half the tuition cost. The private schools were overwhelmingly sectarian and enrolled 75 percent of the children involved in the program. Forty percent of non-Catholic parents participating in the voucher program sent their children to Catholic schools.

School voucher programs in Indiana have expanded and are receiving state support. There are now several "scholarship granting organizations," similar to this original privately financed trust, that operate across the state to provide vouchers to students. In the summer of 2009 the Indiana legislature approved a generous tax deduction for donations to these scholarship granting organizations. Additionally, in 2011 Indiana began operating a statewide publicly funded voucher program. In the 2012–2013 school year, this program served 9,324 families.

Proponents of these voucher programs contend that they will: (1) enhance parental choice; (2) spur competition between public and private education, thereby improving the academic achievement of all students as measured primarily by standardized test scores; (3) increase parental control over tax dollars; (4) open opportunities for minority and low-income families; (5) offer help for low-income parents whose children are currently in private school; (6) save money for public education; (7) save taxpayers' money; and (8) rescue public education.

Independent research demonstrates that these benefits have not materialized.[34] The voucher students in the Cleveland plan upheld by the Supreme Court in *Zelman*, for example, have performed worse on state achievement measures than those students left in the Cleveland public schools.[35] Even the voucher program in the District of Columbia created by Congress has produced "no conclusive evidence" of any impact on student achievement.[36]

According to the National School Boards Association (NSBA), vouchers weaken, not improve, public education because they re-direct much-needed public financial resources to private schools.[37] The NSBA has argued that, as such, vouchers do not improve public education but rather undermine the public schools' capacity to compete and improve.

Moreover, vouchers have not fulfilled their promise of providing genuine school choice. Geography and family finances limit most low-income students to a very narrow range of private schools. Even then, the private school, not the parent, determines which child is admitted and retained. Therefore, vouchers do not broaden the choices available to children from low-income families or those who do not meet the profile of private schools. Rather, vouchers provide more choices to private institutions to determine which children to accept or reject. In fact, according to the NSBA, vouchers reduce equity in educational opportunity. Even with vouchers, some low-income families still are unable to have access to realistic choices regarding their school enrollment.

In fact, vouchers force taxpayers to support two education systems. With about 5.5 million children currently enrolled in private schools, a universal voucher of $3,000 per child would immediately reallocate over $16 billion from public to private schools. Such a reduction in public school funds would not help to improve the education of children enrolled in public schools. In fact, such shortfalls already have forced state legislatures and school boards to raise taxes to make up for at least some of the lost revenue. Given a finite amount of public money, the pressure to fund this growing entitlement comes at the expense of general funds for public schools.

Recognizing that the Louisiana voucher program diverted public funds dedicated to the minimum foundation level for public education and redirected them to private and religious school tuition, the Supreme Court of Louisiana recently declared that program unconstitutional.[38] As the Louisiana Supreme Court understood, voucher programs necessarily allow the re-distribution of scarce public education funds to private purposes.

In addition, according to U.S. Department of Education statistics, four out of every five students in private schools come from families whose annual incomes exceed $50,000. In the public schools, only about one out of five students come from families at that income level. High-income families, therefore, are the primary beneficiaries of vouchers.

Furthermore, arguments favoring and opposing private choice in the form of vouchers have been divisive. By encouraging more students to enroll in a diffuse collection of private schools, voucher systems dilute the public interest in promoting an American culture and identity. As the breadth of the voucher debate suggests, the issue of vouchers raises questions about the fundamental value of public education and the political will to share in the education of the community's children.

In their path-breaking article, *The Political Economy of School Choice*, James Ryan and Michael Heise show that proponents and opponents of voucher programs have a shared interest in supporting the expansion of government-funded early childhood education programs. Publicly funded early childhood programs can provide a model of genuine and successful school choice. These programs demonstrate the value of providing families access to a range of publicly funded programs that are delivered by public providers, private providers, religiously affiliated providers, and public-private partnerships. After analyzing the interests of all of the stakeholders in the debate over school choice, Ryan and Heise therefore conclude: "Our message to those seeking to expand school choice is simple: Support and try to shape efforts to expand access to government-funded preschools."[39]

Charter Schools

As Ryan and Heise further suggest, advocates supporting and opposing charter schools also can find a shared interest in supporting investments in early childhood education programs. Charter schools are "publicly funded elementary or secondary schools that have been freed from some of the rules, regulations, and statutes that apply to other public schools, in exchange for some type of accountability for producing certain results, which are set forth in each school's charter."[40]

The National Educational Association has recognized that "charter schools and other nontraditional public school options have the potential to facilitate education reforms and develop new and creative teaching methods that can be replicated in traditional public schools for the benefit of all children. Whether charter schools will fulfill this potential depends on how charter schools are designed and implemented, including the oversight and assistance provided by charter authorizers."[41]

Proponents of expanding charter schools seek to rely on standardized test scores to claim that charter schools outperform their public school counterparts.[42] Charter schools attempting to justify their charters have a particular incentive to produce the kind of results that are measured by standardized tests. They also tend to attract the kind of students whose families self-select charter schools that promise those kinds of test results, and they accept and retain fewer students who are at risk of school failure as measured by standardized test scores.[43] The flaws in those standardized tests identified in this chapter therefore would tend to skew those scores in favor of charter school students.

Nonetheless, standardized test scores do not provide support for the expansion of charter schools. In 2004, the National Assessment Governing Board (NAGB) released an analysis of charter school performance based on the 2003 National Assessment of Educational Progress (NAEP), also known as "The Nation's Report Card." The report found that charter school students, on average, score lower than students in traditional public schools. While there was no measurable difference between charter school students and students in traditional public schools in the same racial or ethnic subgroup, charter school students who were eligible for free or reduced-price lunch scored lower than their peers in traditional public schools, and charter school students in central cities scored lower than their peers in math in the fourth grade.

NAGB looked at the impact of school characteristics and found that:

- Charter schools that were part of the local school district had significantly higher scores than charter schools that served as their own district.
- Students taught by certified teachers had roughly comparable scores whether they attended charter schools or traditional public schools, but the scores of students taught by uncertified teachers in charter schools were significantly lower than those of charter school students with certified teachers.
- Students taught by teachers with at least five years' experience outperformed students with less experienced teachers, regardless of the type of school attended, but charter school students with inexperienced teachers did significantly worse than students in traditional public schools with less experienced teachers. (The impact of this finding is compounded by the fact that charter schools are twice as likely as traditional public schools to employ inexperienced teachers.)

Recent evidence confirms that most charter schools do not perform as well as their public school counterparts. After conducting a meta-analysis of all of the available data, the National Alliance for Public Charter Schools and the Center for Research on Education Outcomes both concluded that the majority of charter schools do the same or worse than their public school feeders. In fact, 37 percent of charter schools performed "significantly worse" than public schools in math and literacy.[44]

Opponents of the expansion of charter schools also have raised concerns regarding student attrition, high rates of teacher turnover, student access, and inclusiveness. In particular, they argue that some charter schools are able to skim the highest-performing students from public schools by discouraging other students from applying or by "counseling out" students with educational disabilities. In *Schools Without Diversity: Education Management Organizations, Charter Schools, and the Demographic Stratification of the American School System* (2010), the authors conducted a comprehensive study of charter schools and concluded that they have produced stark segregation by race, income, English language acquisition, and disability.[45]

Despite the data challenging charter school performance, charter schools continue to garner public support. The number of students served by charter schools has continued to grow rapidly. In the 2011–2012 school year, more than 2 million students—nearly 5 percent of total enrollment in public schools—attended charter schools in 41 states and the District of Columbia. More than 100 school districts have at least 10 percent of their students in charter schools.[46]

The debate over the effectiveness of charter schools is intense and sometimes divisive. But advocates on all sides of that debate have a mutual interest in supporting a substantial investment of resources in effective early childhood education programs. Those programs can provide a laboratory for the kind of innovative, research-based teaching practices that were the original promise of charter schools.[47] As Ryan and Heise have shown, a vibrant system of government-supported early childhood programs also will serve as a model, demonstrating that the investment of public funds to support a range of genuine educational choices for families can produce significant benefits for children and for the country.

REMEDIAL EDUCATION AND VOCATIONAL TRAINING PROGRAMS

Even if the accountability and privatization initiatives were successful in improving educational opportunities for all children, these strategies would not be as cost-effective as an investment in early childhood education. The evidence adduced by James Heckman and others demonstrates that interventions early in the lives of children are much more efficient than later educational interventions. Heckman specifically analyzed the relative costs and benefits of efforts to remediate a deficient early learning environment, including GED programs, job training, educational rehabilitation, adult literacy, and tuition subsidies.[48]

These efforts to correct deficiencies in early learning environments may be effective, but they are not as cost-effective as early childhood education programs.[49] As James Heckman concludes: "for studies in which later intervention showed some benefits, the performance of disadvantaged children was still behind the performance of children who experienced earlier interventions in the preschool years."[50] Moreover, "[e]arly interventions promote economic efficiency and reduce lifetime inequality." Remedial interventions, by contrast, can reduce inequality somewhat, but "are difficult to justify on the grounds of economic efficiency."[51]

The most recent evidence demonstrates that "Only early interventions . . . improve IQ in a lasting way, consistent with the evidence that early childhood is a critical period of cognitive development. . . . The most successful interventions target preschoolers and primary school children. They improve later-life outcomes by developing character skills."[52] The most effective adolescent remediation programs are those that develop character by integrating work and education.[53]

But the development of essential character skills in pre-K is much more cost effective than their remediation later in life. The positive effects from effective early childhood programs "arise primarily from lasting changes in character skills, not from changes in IQ."[54] The acquisition of general knowledge depends on "persistence, curiosity and focus."[55] There is "substantial evidence that high-quality early childhood programs have lasting and beneficial effects on character skills."[56] Early childhood education programs that develop essential relationship-building skills thus show significant positive long-term educational, social, and economic benefits. The bottom line is that:

> Most successful remediation programs are not as effective as the most successful early childhood programs. Building on an early base of skills that promote later-life learning and engagement in school and society is a better strategy. Prevention is more effective than remediation.[57]

Based on his careful analysis of the most significant education reform initiatives, David Kirp, one of the world's foremost education experts, has arrived at the same conclusion: "Every successful educational initiative of which I'm aware aims at strengthening personal bonds by building strong systems of support in the schools. The best preschools create intimate worlds where students become explorers and attentive adults are close at hand."[58]

As Kirp insightfully demonstrates, "It's impossible to improve education by doing an end run around inherently complicated and messy human relationships. All youngsters need to believe that they have a stake in the future, a goal worth striving for, if they're going to make it in school. They need a champion, someone who believes in them, and that's where teachers enter the picture. The most effective approaches foster bonds of caring between teachers and their students."[59] Accordingly, an investment in the "best" early childhood programs—ones designed to build those indispensable bonds—will provide a model of success that will advance the shared goals of all advocates of genuine education reform.

NOTES

1. Phillip Harris, Bruce M. Smith, and Joan Harris, *The Myths of Standardized Testing: Why They Don't Tell You What You Think They Do* (New York: Rowman & Littlefield, 2011).

2. Diane Ravitch, *Reign of Error: The Hoax of the Privatization Movement and the Danger to America's Public Schools* (New York: Knopf, 2013), 34.

3. Ibid.

4. James J. Heckman and Tim Kautz, "Fostering and Measuring Skills: Interventions That Improve Character and Cognition" (working paper, National Bureau of Economic Research, 2013), 86, http://www.nber.org/papers/w19656.pdf.

5. Harris, Smith, and Harris, *The Myths of Standardized Testing*, 31.

6. Ibid.

7. Ibid.

8. Ibid.

9. Ibid.

10. Ibid.

11. Alfie Kohn, *The Case Against Standardized Testing: Raising the Scores, Ruining the Schools* (Portsmouth, NH: Heinemann, 2000).

12. Ibid.

13. Audrey Amrein and David Berliner, "High-Stakes Testing, Uncertainty, and Student Learning," *Education Policy and Analysis* 10(2) (2002).

14. Ibid., 2.

15. Ibid., see also Pelletier et al., "Pressure From Above and Pressure From Below as Determinants of Teachers' Motivation and Teaching Behaviors," *Journal of Educational Psychology* 94 (2002):186–96.

16. See e.g. John Ewing, "Mathematical Intimidation: Driven by the Data," *Notices of the AMS* 58(5) (May 2011): 667, http://www.ams.org/notices/201105/rtx110500667p.pdf.

17. Ravitch, *Reign of Error*, 100.

18. Ibid.

19. Ibid., 108.

20. Richard Rothstein, "How to Fix Our Schools," *Economic Policy Institute*, October 14, 2010, http://www.epi.org/publication/ib286/.

21. Ravitch, *Reign of Error*, 103–6.

22. Linda Darling-Hammond, "Value-Added Evaluation Hurts Teaching," *Education Week*, March 20, 2012, http://www.edweek.org/ew/articles/2012/03/05/24darlinghamm ond_ep.h31.html.

23. See "Ensuring Fair and Reliable Measures of Effective Teaching," *Bill and Melinda Gates Foundation Measures of Effective Teaching Project*, 2013, 10, http://www.metproject.org/downloads/MET_Ensuring_Fair_and_Reliable_Measures_Practitioner_Brief.pdf ("Teaching is too complex for any single measure of performance to capture it.").

24. Ibid., 11–12.

25. Ibid.

26. Ravitch, *Reign of Error*, 113.

27. See, e.g., "Accountability Systems," Democrats for Education Reform Education Equality Project, March 2010, http://www.dfer.org/docs/DFER.EEP.Accountability. ESEA.March.2010.pdf.

28. See M. Krechevsky, B. Mardell, M. Rivard, and D. Wilson, *Visible Learners* (San Francisco: Jossey-Bass, 2013); Project Zero and Reggio Children, *Making Learning Visible: Children as Individual and Group Learners* (Reggio Emilia, Italy: Reggio Children, 2001).

29. The National School Boards Association has prepared excellent materials regarding the political economy of vouchers. See, e.g., National School Boards Association Advocacy Tools on Vouchers, www.nsba.org.

30. *Zelman V. Simmons-Harris*, 536 U.S. 639 (2002).

31. Ravitch, *Reign of Error*, 208–9, citing Matthew DeFour, "DPI: Students in Milwaukee Voucher Program Didn't Perform Better in State Tests," *Wisconsin State Journal*,

March 29, 2011, http://host.madison.com/news/local/education/local_schools/dpi-students-in-milwaukee-voucher-program-didn-t-perform-better/article_4f083f0e-59a7-11e0-8d74-001cc4c03286.html.

32. Ibid., 209.

33. See Alexandra Usher and Nancy Kober, *Keeping Informed About School Vouchers: A Review of Major Developments and Research* (Center on Education Policy, July 27, 2011), www.cep-dc.org/displayDocument.cfm?documentID=369.

34. Ibid.

35. Ravitch, *Reign of Error*, 210.

36. Ibid.

37. Michael A. Resnick, *Why Vouchers Won't Work* (National School Boards Association, 1998).

38. *Louisiana Federation of Teachers v. State of Louisiana*, No. 2013-CA-0120 (May 7, 2013).

39. See James E. Ryan and Michael Heise, "The Political Economy of School Choice," *Yale Law Journal* 111 (2043) (2002).

40. See "Charter Schools," National Educational Association, www.nea.org/charter.

41. Ibid.

42. See e.g., G. Tirozzi, "It's Déjà Vu All Over Again for Charter Schools," *Education Week*, August 27, 2014, 22.

43. Ibid., 23.

44. See, e.g., Tirozzi, "It's Déjà Vu All Over Again for Charter Schools"; Scott A. Imberman, "Achievement and Behavior in Charter Schools: Drawing a More Complex Picture," *Review of Economics and Statistics* 93(2) (2011), http://www.mitpressjournals.org/doi/abs/10.1162/REST_a_00077?journalCode=rest#.VAaDuRZJnG4.

45. See "Strengthening Charter School Policies," National Education Association Policy Brief, (2011), http://www.nea.org/assets/docs/PB33charterschoolpolicies2011.pdf; Ravitch, *Reign of Error*, 175.

46. "A Growing Movement: America's Largest Charter School Communities," National Alliance for Public Charter Schools (November 2012), http://www.edweek.org/media/napcsmarketshare-13charters.pdf.

47. See Richard D. Kahlenberg and Halley Potter, *A Smarter Charter: Finding What Works for Charter Schools and Public Education* (New York: Teachers College Press, 2014).

48. Heckman, "School, Skills and Synapses," 4, 21.

49. Ibid., 20–21.

50. Ibid., 21.

51. Heckman, "School, Skills and Synapses," 22. See also C. Raver, P. Garner, and R. Smith-Donald, "The Roles of Emotion Regulation and Emotion Knowledge for Children's Academic Readiness: Are the Links Causal?" in *School Readiness and the Transition to Kindergarten in the Era of Accountability*, ed. Robert Pianta, Martha Cox, and Kyle Snow (Baltimore: Paul H. Brookes, 2007).

52. Heckman and Kautz, "Fostering and Measuring Skills."

53. Ibid., 35, 66.

54. Ibid., 44.

55. Ibid., 45.

56. Ibid., 89.

57. Ibid.

58. David Kirp, "Teaching Is Not a Business," *New York Times*, August 16, 2014, http://www.nytimes.com/2014/08/17/opinion/sunday/teaching-is-not-a-business.html. See also David L. Kirp, *Improbable Scholars: The Rebirth of a Great American School System and a Strategy for America's Schools* (New York: Oxford University Press, 2013).

59. Kirp, "Teaching Is Not a Business."

Section 2

THE PROVEN BENEFITS OF EARLY CHILDHOOD EDUCATION PROGRAMS THAT ENCOURAGE CHILDREN TO CONSTRUCT KNOWLEDGE BY BUILDING MEANINGFUL RELATIONSHIPS

This section begins by presenting a range of pedagogical approaches to early childhood education on a continuum from direct instruction of traditional academic skills to social constructivist practices. Chapter 6 describes the foundations for each approach and provides exemplars of the approach in practice. Chapter 7 then shows how and why the social constructivist approach produces particularly robust educational, social, and economic benefits for children and for the country.

Chapter Six

Pedagogical Approaches to Early Childhood Education

Early childhood education programs offer a wide range of educational approaches.[1] Some of these approaches emphasize long-term social and emotional development, while others prioritize shorter-term academic performance. This chapter presents a continuum of pedagogical approaches, from those that tend to utilize direct instruction of traditional academic skills to those that emphasize social constructivist practices.

These demarcations are admittedly somewhat artificial. Many outstanding early childhood programs employ a variety of these approaches. While some programs along this continuum utilize a canned pre-set curriculum, others provide to highly skilled educators the professional training and the discretion to interweave a variety of these approaches to meet the particular, emergent interests and needs of their students.

All of the methods described in this chapter have strengths, and an investment in any of them would produce substantial benefits for children. With proper training and professional development, for example, educators can be given the respect and professional autonomy to use direct instruction, constructivist, and social constructivist practices together in an environment in which children are encouraged to construct knowledge by building meaningful relationships.

DIRECT INSTRUCTION OF TRADITIONAL ACADEMIC SKILLS

The direct instruction approach prioritizes the development of traditional academic skills, particularly those characterized as literacy and math. In these classrooms, the teacher often functions as the authoritarian figure while the

106

students are expected to be consumers of information. Under this traditional academic method, there is often an emphasis on testing, predetermined curricula, and standardized assessments to measure student outcomes. Some aspects of various Head Start programs and the Harlem Children's Zone exemplify this approach.

The Foundations of the Direct Instruction Approach

The direct instruction approach is founded on behaviorism, or the belief that learning is defined as a change in observable behavior. In this approach, the role of the teacher is to provide direct instruction of information and to use positive and negative reinforcements to reward or punish student conduct. The teacher is often the dominant source of information to the students, primarily through lecture. To reinforce certain behaviors, teachers provide particular pieces of information in a sequential order and present their instruction in a linear way so that they can ensure that one particular desired behavior is observed before proceeding to the next.

Exemplars of the Direct Instruction Approach

Head Start

Head Start, a United States Department of Health and Human Services program, is the largest federal early childhood program in the United States.[2] Established in 1965 as a key part of the nation's War on Poverty, Head Start promotes school readiness for children in low-income families by offering educational, nutritional, health, social, and other services.[3] Early Head Start, a program that serves low-income pregnant women and families with children three years of age or younger, was established in 1995.[4]

Since its inception, Head Start has served more than 30 million children and their families.[5] In 2012 alone, Head Start enrolled over 950,000 children,[6] 51 percent of which were four years old and 36 percent of which were three years old.[7]

Head Start is primarily federally funded but locally operated. Head Start can be financed up to 80 percent of total program costs by federal funds—at least 20 percent of the funds must come from nonfederal sources.[8] The Office of Head Start, a part of the U.S. Department of Health and Human Services, administers Head Start federally.[9] Local programs are operated through grants to public agencies, private nonprofit organizations, faith-based organizations, and school systems.[10] Because they are locally operated, Head Start programs vary significantly from one to the next. Most Head Start programs operate a part-day program.[11]

Head Start programs take a comprehensive approach to early childhood education, including health services, nutrition, wellness, parent education, and
social services. In recent years, however, the federal Department of Health
and Human Services has promulgated Head Start "performance standards"
that emphasize academic achievement, particularly in the area of traditional
literacy skills.[12]

Specifically, in its 1998 Reauthorization, Congress mandated that the
Program Performance Standards be expanded to require that children: (1) develop print and numeracy awareness; (2) understand and use an increasingly
complex and varied vocabulary; (3) develop and demonstrate an appreciation
of books; and (4) for non-English-speaking children progress toward acquisition of the English language.[13] Congress also augmented the learning outcomes to include "that children know that letters of the alphabet are a special
category of visual graphics that can be individually named, recognize a word
as a unit of print, identify at least 10 letters of the alphabet, and associate
sounds with written words."[14]

In order to provide further uniformity and to achieve these goals, Head
Start has long embraced a set of objectives focused on the development and
learning outcomes of low-income children.[15] In 2000, the federal Office of
Head Start issued a Child Outcomes Framework of building blocks deemed
important for success.[16] The revised framework, issued in December 2010, is
organized into 11 general domains, 37 domain elements, and more than 100
examples of specific indicators of children's skills, abilities, knowledge, and
behaviors.[17] The 11 domains are:

- Language development;
- English language development (for dual language learners);
- Literacy knowledge and skills;
- Mathematics knowledge and skills;
- Science knowledge and skills;
- Creative arts expression;
- Social studies knowledge and skills;
- Physical development and health;
- Social and emotional development;
- Approaches to learning; and
- Logic and reasoning.[18]

A core tenet of Head Start is that local programs need flexibility to meet
the particular needs of the communities they serve.[19] Flexibility, however, occurs within firm parameters set forth in the Head Start Program Performance

Standards: Early Childhood Development and Health Services, Family and Community Partnerships, and Program Design and Management.[20]

Early Childhood Development and Health Services

Local Head Start programs are given a good deal of flexibility to select or design and implement a developmentally appropriate curriculum consistent with children's interests, temperaments, and backgrounds.[21] Head Start strives to balance child-initiated and adult-directed activities, including individual and small-group activities, in the daily program.[22] The program proceeds as follows:

> Social and emotional development is to be supported by building trust; fostering independence; encouraging self-control by setting clear, consistent limits and having realistic expectations; encouraging respect for the feelings and rights of others; and providing timely, predictable, and unrushed routines and transitions.
>
> Each child's learning is to be supported through experimentation, inquiry, observation, play, exploration, and related strategies. Art, music, movement, and dialogue are viewed as key opportunities for creative self-expression, and language use among children and between children and adults is promoted. Developmentally appropriate activities and materials are to be provided for support of children's emerging literacy and numeracy development.
>
> Center-based programs are to provide sufficient time, space, equipment, materials, and adult guidance for active play and movement that supports fine and gross motor development. Provisions and encouragement for social and symbolic forms of play help young children's self-regulation and social competence. Home-based programs are to encourage parents to appreciate the value of physical development and to provide opportunities for safe and active play.[23]

Family and Community Partnerships

Head Start views the family, parents, and primary caregivers as essential partners in achieving improved outcomes for children.[24] Accordingly, the program provides numerous opportunities for parents to be involved in program decisions and activities and to develop their own strengths and interests.[25] All center-based programs are expected to provide a minimum of two home visits annually, and a relatively small number of programs provide significant home-based services.[26]

Parent involvement is a cornerstone of Head Start's success.[27] Head Start therefore emphasizes two parental roles: the parent as an active contributor to program practices and the parent as a competent supporter of his or her child's growth and development.[28]

Head Start seeks to establish a partnership with parents based on trust and understanding of family goals and necessary supports. Accordingly, programs offer parents an opportunity to develop and implement an individual-ized Family Partnership Agreement that sets forth family goals and responsi-bilities as well as timetables and strategies for achieving these goals.[29]

Program Design and Management

Each program is to develop and implement a process of program planning that includes consultation with the program's governing body, policy groups, program staff, and other community organizations.[30] Program planning should include:

- An assessment of community strengths, needs, and resources;
- The development of both short- and long-range program goals and objec-tives;
- Written plans for implementing services; and
- A review of progress in meeting goals at least annually.[31]

A self-assessment of program effectiveness and progress in meeting goals and objectives is to be conducted at least annually.[32] The 2007 reauthorization of Head Start also stipulates that at least 50 percent of Head Start teachers na-tionwide in center-based programs should have a bachelor's or an advanced degree in early childhood education or related filed by 2013.[33]

Findings

The impact of Head Start is difficult to measure because of the variety of programs and the inadequacy and unevenness of funding. Nonetheless, the best evidence available shows significant positive differences in outcomes between children who had access to Head Start and those in the control group who did not have such access.[34] Moreover, results of the large-scale Head Start Impact Study indicate that Head Start had positive impacts on several aspects of children's school readiness during their time in the program.[35] Even detrac-tors who question whether some aspects of a child's gains in Head Start can be sustained must acknowledge that those gains have been achieved.

Harlem Children's Zone

The Harlem Children's Zone is an educational and social service organiza-tion that seeks to transform central Harlem in New York City by providing support services for the children and families that live there.[36] The Children's Zone began in the 1970 as the Rheedlen Centers for Children and Families. Geoffrey Canada, a social activist and educator, started as president in 1990 and sought to expand the scope of the program. Under his direction, in the early 1990s, the Harlem Children's Zone ran a pilot project that brought a wide range of support services to a single block in New York City in order to address problems that poor people were having.[37]

The Harlem Children's Zone created a 10-year business plan and partnered with nonprofits that tracked and evaluated their work.[38] In 1997, the Harlem Children's Zone began a network of programs for a 24-block area—the Harlem Children's Zone Project.[39] In 2007, the Harlem Children's Zone project grew to almost 100 blocks.[40] Today, the Harlem Children's Zone serves more than 8,000 children and 6,000 adults.

Mr. Canada wanted the Harlem Children's Zone children to be able to compete with middle-class children who are surrounded by a "cocoon" of educational support, emotional support, and medical support that starts at birth and never stops.[41] In order to do this, "[t]he only way for his kids to catch up and keep up, he believes, is for his organization to emulate that cocoon as closely as possible, to create an alternative ongoing safety net to the one that invisibly supports middle-class kids all the way through childhood."[42] Accordingly,

> Geoff's project is based on the idea that schools alone can't solve all the problems facing poor children. Which is why he runs not just a charter school but also a parenting program and an all-day prekindergarten and an after-school tutoring program and family-support centers. He thinks that in order to succeed with big numbers of kids, you need to do it all.[43]

Harlem Children's Zone is thus a continuous series of integrated interventions—a safety net—beginning with prenatal parenting classes and intensive early childhood programs up to college.[44] Its programs have a relatively academic focus.

Program

The early childhood outreach of Harlem Children's Zone consists primarily of its Baby College and Harlem Gems. The Baby College provides a nine-week parenting workshop to expectant parents and those raising a child up to three years old.[45] The workshops, among other things, promote reading to children and verbal discipline over corporal punishment.[46]

Mr. Canada sees attentive, careful parenting as the first step toward overcoming poverty and thus wants his parents to have the same information middle-class and other parents do.[47] The Baby College thus seeks to equip parents with the skills and knowledge to give children the tools they need to be school ready.[48] Harlem Children's Zone notes that the Baby College "works to ensure that, from the time they are born, our kids are immersed in healthy, supportive environments that will enable them to thrive and set them on the path to school and college readiness."[49]

At age three, children can enter the lottery for one of the "Promise Academies," the charter schools established by the Harlem Children's Zone.[50] If admitted, the child enters an 18-week Three-Year-Old Journey class for parents that covers many of the same topics as Baby College and then the "Get Ready for Pre-K" program, a six-week summer session that prepares students for Harlem Gems.[51]

Harlem Gems is the Harlem Children's Zone's all-day pre-K program.[52] Classes have a 4:1 ratio and operate from 8 a.m. to 6 p.m.[53] It is an "academically intensive" program that emphasizes language immersion.[54] The "ultimate goal" of the pre-K program is "[s]chool readiness."[55] The primary focus of the curriculum is traditional "[e]arly literacy skills" and traditional number skills.[56]

Author Paul Tough notes that:

> Geoffrey Canada and his staff collect a lot of data, but the only markers of success that really matter to them are the ones measuring educational attainment: higher college-graduation rates, lower high-school drop-out rates, better scores on tests of school-readiness in the prekindergarten or of math and English ability in the middle school. Hypothetically, Canada could be accomplishing all sorts of good and worthy things in Harlem—reducing asthma, improving nutrition and dental care, providing job training to young adults, cleaning up parks and streets—but if he wasn't raising test scores and graduation rates, he would consider his whole operation to be a failure. Every one of the organization's disparate initiatives, from the health clinic to the parenting classes to the prekindergarten, exists for the same reason: to give children in Harlem the skills and support they need to succeed in school and to graduate from college.
>
> Canada's single-minded focus is based not on a particular love of standardized tests or on a sentimental belief in the importance of education. It is rooted instead in a fundamental economic understanding: in the twenty-first century, in low-income urban neighborhoods like Harlem, the best way for children to escape poverty is through educational achievement.[57]

Findings

The Harlem Children's Zone data indicate that 100 percent of Harlem Gems pre-kindergartners were assessed as "school ready."[58] Ninety-five percent of the HCZ high school seniors were accepted into college, and $20 million in scholarships and grants were awarded to HCZ's most recent college freshmen.[59]

THE CONSTRUCTIVIST APPROACH

In constructivist programs, children construct knowledge individually with the teacher as a supervisor rather than an authoritarian figure.

The Foundations of the Constructivist Approach

Jean Piaget was among the first to demonstrate that children learn through developmental stages by constructing knowledge, rather than receiving it through direct instruction. Based on his observations of young children, Piaget delineated four stages of growth, from sensorimotor to preoperational, to concrete operations, and to formal operations. Children from ages three through five typically are in the preoperational stage of development in which they learn by social interactions and role-playing.[60] Piaget also believed that children must first develop the ability to speak privately before they can use their speech to communicate with others.[61] He claimed that the child had to graduate from an "egocentric" developmental phase before employing language as a mental processing and communicating tool.[62]

For Piaget, thought is constructed within each individual child's mind, and then the child develops language to repeat that thought to others.[63] Piaget believed that children construct their knowledge primarily through their interactions with inanimate materials.[64]

Piaget's research provided substantial support for the growth of the constructivist approach founded by Maria Montessori. In 1907, Montessori, a physician and anthropologist, created a program for low-income children who resided in a housing project in Rome.[65] She developed a Children's House in which educators enabled children to construct their own knowledge and life skills through involvement in the practical experiences necessary for everyday life.[66]

This element of individual freedom, therefore, is the first of six essential components of a constructivist Montessori learning environment:

- **Freedom:** Montessori believed that the natural thrust of children is toward independence and that educators should follow the child. Children possess the blueprint for their own development, which will unfold naturally in an appropriate environment.[67] Freedom is necessary in a Montessori environment so that children may choose among the materials and experiences offered.[68] Where a child takes on a task, attention is fixed on that task to strengthen the child's focus and self-discipline.[69] In this sense, a child's learning is individualistic and self-directed.

- **A Structured Environment:** Montessori believed that the external organization of the environment should mimic and promote the internal organization within the child.[70] Rhythms and routines should be predictable,
  learning materials should be organized, and delivery of lessons should be
  exact and concise.[71]
- **Reality:** Montessori felt strongly that young children should be immersed
  in a world of reality rather than fantasy because the child's imagination develops from a foundation in real-world experiences.[72] Children should work
  with authentic materials like brooms and glassware that tangibly represent
  the real world.[73]
- **The Natural World:** Similarly, Montessori felt that nature should be part
  of the learning environment because the child is inherently drawn to the
  natural world.[74] Many Montessori classrooms have plants, animals, and
  small gardens that are cared for by the children.[75] Montessori believed
  the environment should be clean, attractive, well cared for, colorful, and
  uncluttered.[76]
- **Materials:** Didactic materials generally progress from simple to complex.
  When a child masters a skill, material, or concept, that child may then move
  on to an activity that requires more steps or requires more judgment.[77]
- **Productive Sociability:** In a Montessori classroom, socialization is not
  designed to support "mere togetherness"; rather children may interact with
  each other to assist their productivity by coordinating work and helping
  each other use materials.[78]

The Montessori Exemplar

The contemporary Montessori movement in the United States began in the
late 1950s and, in 1959, the American Montessori Society was established.
Today, the combined total of public and private Montessori schools in the
United States is just under 5,000.[79]

In a Montessori program, the child is a constant inquirer who does not
passively receive experience but rather interacts purposefully and freely
within a specifically designed environment.[80] The Montessori environment is
designed to be ordered, proportioned to the child's size, aesthetically pleas-
ing, and visually harmonious.[81] The environment should invite, support, and
make possible learning.

The teacher's job is to be a careful observer and manager of each child's
development.[82] The teacher carefully prepares and maintains a classroom that
is interesting and safe, responds to disorderly children, and presents lessons
with didactic materials to children who are interested.[83] Individual responsibility is strongly emphasized.[84] Children return materials to their place after

using them, they help clean and maintain the classroom, and they help develop the classroom rules.[85]

The Montessori program is generally divided into practical life, sensorial, language, and mathematics.[86]

Practical Life

Practical life is an essential component of a Montessori education.[87] Through involvement with familiar home-based activities, the child begins to focus attention on a single activity, learns to follow a sequence, to coordinate movements, and to organize each step of a given task.[88] Specific activities involve self-care, care of the environment, life skills, fine-motor development, and community living.[89] Children for instance may be taught to spoon, to pour, and then to cook. They acquire the skill of tracing letters, numbers, and shapes. They practice using zippers or buttons to prepare them to learn how to clothe themselves.[90]

Sensorial

Montessori believed that, from birth, children are immersed in a stimulus-rich environment and unconsciously use all of their senses to absorb these stimuli.[91] Children in a Montessori program therefore are given a series of sequenced exercises and materials so that they can catalog, classify, and sharpen their sensory impressions.[92] Materials appealing to the visual, muscular-tactile, auditory, gustatory, and olfactory senses are presented consecutively, each isolating one specific concept or sensory perception.[93] For example, children may be asked to identify different sounds made by different materials placed within cones or cylinders.[94] As the child progresses through the series, increased judgment and refined perception gained from previous exercises guide the child.[95]

Language

In a Montessori classroom, language development is also fostered through the structured environment. Specific didactic materials are introduced to promote language and literacy development.[96] In order to learn to write, for example, the child must first acquire the mechanics of writing by using metal geometric templates that allow for a large number of tracing and drawing skills, handling individual wooden letters, and tracing sandpaper letter forms.[97] Later, the child begins to investigate printing language by "writing" words by using a large box of wooden letters and, still later, forming words with a writing utensil.[98] The Montessori language sequence assumes that writing generally precedes reading, but that the two are highly interrelated.[99]

Mathematics

Montessori felt that the order, precision, attention to detail, and sequencing skills fostered through practical life and the sensorial materials created the foundation for the "mathematical mind."[100] "The child explores and compares similarities and differences through all gathering and sorting activities, explores spatial relations through making patterns, and explores temporal relations through experiencing the pattern of daily routines."[101]

Artistic Expression

Contemporary Montessori programs emphasize child self-expression through the visual arts, music, dance, and drama.[102] Montessori classrooms focus on aesthetics and reflect an awareness of the importance of the visual arts to a child's self-expression.[103] A wide range of expressive art media is generally available to children in contemporary Montessori environments.[104]

The core Montessori curriculum continues to be developed and expanded to new situations.[105] Over the past twenty years, Montessori programs have been incorporated into many public school systems as an experimental model, expanding the availability of what is primarily a private school movement.[106]

THE SOCIAL CONSTRUCTIVIST APPROACH

In social constructivist programs, the role of the teacher is to be a partner in learning with the student, who is a designer, builder, and inventor. The core tenet of social constructivist programs is to build knowledge through meaningful relationships.

The Foundations of the Social Constructivist Approach

Lev Vygotsky created the foundations for the social constructivist approach by building upon Piaget's research demonstrating that children construct their own knowledge. Vygotsky proved that this construction takes place primarily through social interactions.

Vygotsky was born in Orsha, Belorussia, in 1896, and was graduated from Moscow University with a degree in law. Upon graduation, he turned his research and teaching toward psychology. Although he died at the early age of 37 from tuberculosis, he authored more than 180 path-breaking articles and books on child psychology and human development.[107] After he reviewed

Vygotsky's work, Piaget refined his constructs to recognize the primal role of social relationships in the development of mental processes and language.[108]

Vygotsky demonstrated and ultimately convinced Piaget that learning is a social construct. He finds that all of "[h]uman learning presupposes a specific social nature and a process by which children grow into the intellectual life of those around them."[109] The social, interpersonal process of the construction of knowledge is transformed by the child into an internal one.[110] Every function of a child's development happens twice: "first *between* people . . . and then inside the child."[111] In fact, all of the higher mental functions, including attention, memory, and the formation of concepts "originate as actual relations between human individuals."[112]

Vygotsky's research revealed that "human beings become ourselves through others."[113] This fundamental rule that knowledge is constructed through meaningful social relationships "applies not only to the personality as a whole, but also to the history of every individual function."[114]

The finding that knowledge is co-constructed between human beings was confirmed by Vygotsky's research regarding the interplay between thought and speech. As Vygotsky concludes: "thought does not express itself in words, but rather realizes itself in them."[115] In other words, a child constructs thought by communicating with others. The social construction of knowledge through language is a process of continual movement back and forth from speech to thought.[116] Hence, "[t]he relation between thought and word is a living process; thought is born through words."[117]

The child's social context is an integral part of the construction of knowledge and the very process of cognition. That context includes the child's direct interactions with individuals and materials that are proximate to the child. Yet the social context also includes the child's family, school, culture, and society. All of these social networks are not merely received by a child, they shape the way in which the child thinks.[118] Because the culture surrounding a child evolves over time, Vygotsky also demonstrated that a child's mental processes are shaped in part by the body of accumulated knowledge passed historically from one generation to the next.[119]

Significantly, Vygotsky revealed how a child's mental processes are actually shaped by social interactions. Mental processes grow in an exchange among human beings. Children "acquire a mental process by *sharing*, or using it when interacting with others."[120] The child must first share an experience with another human being before internalizing the mental process and being able to perform that process independently.[121] Without a shared, social experience, knowledge cannot be genuinely constructed.[122]

As a consequence, a child's mental processes also are bound up with the multiple languages in which the child shares his or her experiences with others. Because knowledge is constructed in social relationships, knowledge is dependent upon communication. In order to share an experience, individuals must develop a meaningful language. The child therefore first discovers how to communicate an experience to another, and then internalizes the means of communication. Language cannot be developed without social relationships. The very process of developing a method of social communication is a prerequisite to the construction of knowledge itself.

Based on Vygotsky's work, the step-by-step process by which knowledge is constructed can be mapped as follows:

1. The child is naturally driven toward meaningful social relationships;
2. The child encounters meaningful social relationships;
3. The child naturally desires to share his or her experiences with others in that meaningful social relationship;
4. The child naturally seeks to represent to others the child's perceptions;
5. The child develops multiple languages to communicate his or her perceptions to others;
6. The child develops the mental process used to communicate successfully his or her experience to others including the mental process required to receive input from others;
7. The child develops the mental process necessary to replicate the communications;
8. The child internalizes the shared experience and the mental process by communicating the experience to himself or herself within the child's own mind;
9. The child's mind has been reshaped by the experience;
10. The child has constructed language;
11. The child has constructed knowledge.[123]

Exemplars of the Social Constructivist Approach

Tools of the Mind

The foundation for Tools of the Mind comes primarily from Lev Vygotsky's theory of development.[124] Schools that employ the Tools of the Mind curriculum exemplify three primary concepts underlying the Vygotskian approach: a cultural-historical view of development; a focus on "tools"; and an attention to lower and higher mental functions.

First, Vygotskians have a cultural-historical view of development. "History" refers to Vygotsky's idea that to truly understand human psychological processes, we must study the history of the development of these processes.[125] "Culture" focuses on various signs and symbols that serve as cultural tools and their role in the development of uniquely human mental processes that he called higher mental functions.[126] Vygotskians also look at the specific sociocultural context of learning and development to see how specific cultural tools and practices affect the development of higher mental functions.[127]

Second, Vygotsky believed that the difference between humans and lower animals is that humans use tools, make new tools, and teach others how to use them.[128] Tools extend human abilities by enabling people to perform tasks they could not do without them.[129] Physical tools can act as an extension of human bodies; similarly, mental tools extend our mental abilities by acting as an extension of our mind.[130] For Vygotsky, one of the major goals of education is to help children acquire the tools of their culture.[131] As children are taught and practice mental tools, their minds are transformed, leading to the emergence of higher mental functions.[132]

Third, Vygotsky divided mental processes into lower and higher mental functions.[133] Lower mental functions were thought to be those that manifested in reflex, perceptual, and motor behaviors that are easy to observe and measure.[134] Higher mental functions were thought to be more complex processes which could only be accessed through a person's self-report.[135]

Vygotsky describes lower mental functions as common to human beings and higher animals.[136] He describes higher mental functions as deliberate, meditated, and internalized behaviors.[137] "For Vygotsky, higher mental functions do not appear in children in their fully developed form. Instead, they undergo a long process of development in the course of which a fundamental reorganization of lower mental functions occurs."[138] As children start using higher mental functions more, their lower mental functions are used less and less.[139]

In contrast to other psychological theories, Vygotsky believes that not only what a child knows but also how the child thinks and remembers is shaped by the child's prior interactions with other people, such as parents, teachers, and peers.[140] Accordingly, Vygotskians think of early childhood education as the first step in which children engage in the acquisition of "tools" and the development of higher mental functions that are learned from others.[141]

Furthermore, Vygotsky believed that the role of the teacher is more than teaching facts or skills. Teachers can actually shape children's development by helping them acquire mental tools. This view is reflected in the three main principles of Vygotskian-based Tools of the Mind education:

- **Teachers and Children Co-Construct Knowledge:** Vygotsky believed that children construct their own understandings rather than passively reproducing whatever is presented to them.[142] For Vygotsky, though, this process takes place in a cultural context and is mediated by other people.[143]

Chapter Six

In the classroom, for example, a teacher can affect a child's construction of knowledge by using specific words or orchestrating the context for the child's interactions with other children.[144]

- **Scaffolding Helps Children Make a Transition From Assisted to Independent Performance:** For most children, the transition from assisted to independent learning is gradual and involves moving from using a great deal of assistance before no assistance is needed.[145] For a teacher, this means the teacher needs to scaffold student learning by first designing and then following a plan for providing and withdrawing assistance over time.[146]
- **Instruction Should Amplify Child Development and Not Accelerate It:** Vygotsky's students extended his idea of effective teaching by condemning the idea of accelerating development—something that intends to prematurely turn a toddler into a pre-K student.[147] Instead, a child's development should be amplified by using the child's "zone of proximal development" or "ZPD" to its fullest.[148]

Based on Vygotsky's evidence, the Tools of the Mind approach is designed to: (1) foster child development by engaging children in leading activities; (2) promote children's acquisition of higher mental functions and mental tools; and (3) focus on re-mediation as the core principle of special education.[149]

Teachers Promote and Foster Development by Engaging Children in Activities That Are Leading Activities for Their Age

Make-believe play is the leading activity for pre-K and kindergarten-aged children.[150] As such, supporting play is a priority in a Vygotsky-based early childhood classroom.[151]

- **Vygotskian Definition of Play:** Vygotsky's definition of play is limited to dramatic or make-believe play.[152] "Real" play has three components: (1) children create an imaginary situation; (2) children take on and act out roles; and (3) children follow a set of rules determined by specific roles.[153]
- **Make-Believe Play as a Source of Development:** Play is one of the social contexts responsible for creating young children's ZPD.[154] Young children's performance in play is higher than their performance in nonplay contexts.[155] For Vygotsky, mastery of academic skills is not as good a predictor of children's scholastic abilities as the quality of their play.[156]
- **Implications of Vygotsky's Theory of Play for Early Childhood Educators:** Play is valuable for child development in part because it develops the competencies that make children ready for formal schooling.[157]

- **Self-Regulation:** Play helps children develop the ability to self-regulate their behaviors rather than acting on impulse.[158] Current studies confirm Vygotsky's belief that make-believe play can improve self-regulation, especially in highly impulsive children.[159]
- **Abstract Thinking:** Make-believe play also encourages abstract thinking.[160] For example, when a child pretends to "drive" a block as if it were a truck, the child separates the idea of "truckness" from the truck and attaches it to the block—a precursor for the development of abstract thought.[161]

Teachers Focus on Promoting the Development of Higher Mental Functions and Children's Acquisition of Cultural Tools

For Vygotskians, the goal of education is to help children acquire mental tools and higher mental functions.[162]

- **Private Speech as a Mental Tool:** For Vygotsky, many mental tools are language-based.[163] Major transformation in a child's mind depends on how well the child masters the use of speech.[164] According to Vygotsky, during the pre-K years, children start using their speech both for communicating to others and for communicating to themselves ("private speech").[165] During the pre-K years, the function of private speech changes—initially used just to accompany children's practical actions, it later becomes exclusively self-directed and organizes children's own behaviors.[166] Private speech also changes from complete sentences to abbreviated phrases and words, and later to verbal thought.[167] Because, for Vygotsky, young children "think as they talk," teachers should not try to keep children quiet when they are thinking and problem solving.[168]
- **Written Speech as a Mental Tool:** Vygotsky asserts that children learn to employ the function of written speech to expand their mental capacities.[169] Vygotsky thus emphasizes that the goal of the instruction should be to teach a child written language and not simply how to write the alphabet.[170]

The HighScope Perry Model

The HighScope model, which was created by David P. Weikart and his colleagues, is based upon the child development theories of Piaget and Vygotsky as well as the progressive educational philosophy of John Dewey.[171] The catalyst for its development was the concern of the Ypsilanti, Michigan Public Schools Special Education Director that easily identifiable children were failing in school and turned to the pre-K years as a way of reaching children early.[172]

Thus the HighScope model began to be developed in 1962 with the High-Scope Perry Preschool program, a program for three- and four-year-olds in Ypsilanti. This program was one of the first designed to help children overcome the negative effects of poverty on schooling.[173] The HighScope Perry model provides teachers with a framework of educational ideas and practices based on the development of young children.[174]

Study participants and families were recruited for this early childhood education program, which was staffed by research psychologists and teachers.[175] The study showed that the HighScope Perry Preschool program provided participants with better preparation for school, greater success throughout schooling and in adulthood, a lower arrest rate, a higher employment rate, and a lower welfare rate.[176]

As the HighScope Perry Preschool program entered its second year, the staff embraced Piaget's idea of the child as an active learner.[177] Later, Vygotsky's work became the foundation for the HighScope Perry teaching model, particularly his idea that development occurs within sociocultural settings in which adults scaffold each child's learning.[178]

Program

The HighScope model recognizes children as active learners who learn best from activities that they themselves plan, carry out, and reflect on.[179] The HighScope model's daily routine is thus made up of a plan-do-review sequence, group times, and several additional elements.[180]

- **Planning Time: Stating an Intention**: The HighScope Perry program provides for planning time—a way for children to think about their decisions in a systematic way and helps them realize the possibilities and consequences of these choices.[181] Planning time gives children a consistent, predictable opportunity to express their ideas and also provides the power of independence.[182] The teacher talks over the plans with the children before they carry them out, helping the children form a picture of their ideas and determine how to proceed.[183] The teacher accepts the plans and their limits as determined by the children.[184] As such, the children feel reinforced and ready to start their plans, and the teachers know what to look for and where help might be needed.[185] Planning time thus provides for shared control.[186]
- **Work Time: Executing the Intention**: Work time is the "do" part of the plan-do-review sequence.[187] Work time is the longest time period in the daily routine and is an active period of work and play for children and adults.[188] Children execute their own plans of work while the teacher observes the children and then enters into the children's activities to scaffold

learning by encouraging, extending, setting up problem-solving situations, and engaging in conversation.[189]

- **Cleanup Time:** During cleanup time, which is integrated into the plan-do-review sequence, children return materials and equipment to their labeled laces and store their incomplete projects.[190] This process has the benefit of both restoring order to the classroom and providing an opportunity for children to learn and use many basic cognitive skills like ordering objects.[191]
- **Recall Time: Reflecting on Accomplishments:** Recall time, the final phase of the plan-do-review sequence, is the time when children reflect on what they have accomplished.[192] The children represent their experience in a variety of developmentally appropriate ways: naming the children they involved in carrying out their plan; dictating the story of their activity; recounting the problems they faced; drawing pictures or making models of what they did; or reviewing or recalling past events. Recall time is essential because it brings closure to the children's work activities and provides them opportunities to use language and express insights on their experience.[193]
- **Small-Group Time:** During small-group time, the teacher creates an activity drawn from the children's interests, backgrounds, materials, or experiences that they participate in for a set period of time.[194] Children are encouraged to contribute ideas and solve problems presented by the small-group activities the teacher coordinates.[195] Once a child has had an opportunity to solve a problem, the teacher extends the child's ideas by asking questions, conversing, and supporting additional problem-solving situations.[196]
- **Large-Group Time:** During large-group time, the whole group meets to play games, sing songs, do finger plays, play instruments, act out stories, or reenact special events.[197] Each child shares and demonstrates ideas and imitates the ideas of others.[198]

To support this model, teachers use complex language as they observe, support, and extend the child's work.[199] Teachers:

- Arrange interest areas in the learning environment;
- Maintain a daily routine that allows children to plan, carry out, and reflect on their own activities;
- Join in children's activities, engaging with children to help them think them through; and
- Encourage children to make choices, solve problems, and engage in curriculum activities.[200]

The HighScope model is organized around a set of key developmental indicators acquired through research and aligned with standards for early learning.[201] These key developmental indicators—which are organized in domains such as social and emotional development, language, literacy and communication, and approaches to learning, to name a few—are both the central feature for the teacher to implement the curriculum and a way of helping the teacher support and extend the child's activity so that growth is always available to the child.[202]

Parent participation is vital to the HighScope model.[203] HighScope staff teachers are provided strategies to involve parents in supporting their child's early learning in ways that are meaningful and appropriate.[204] Essential to effective parent involvement is the focus on the child and the dual nature of information flow—the staff is trained to provide to the family, but the staff must also learn from the family about the child.[205]

The HighScope model is centered upon providing a setting in which children learn actively and construct their own knowledge.[206] Much of the child's knowledge comes from personal interaction with ideas, direct experiences with objects and events, and application of logical thinking to these experiences.[207] The teacher's role is to supply context for these experiences and allow the child to think about them logically while scaffolding further learning for the child.[208]

The teachers of the HighScope model are also active learners.[209] By daily evaluation and planning using the HighScope key developmental indicators, teachers assess the children's experience and activities to try to bring about new insights in the students.[210]

HighScope teachers do not have a precise script for teaching children.[211] Instead, teachers listen closely to what children plan and actively work with them to extend their activities to more challenging levels.[212] In doing so, the adult emphasizes questions that seek information from the child that will help the adult participate in the interaction.[213]

Conversation is essential, as the teacher is a participant in the interaction rather than an imparter of knowledge.[214] This questioning and conversation style both permits free interaction between the teachers and children and models language for the children.[215] Teachers and students are thinkers and doers rather than assuming roles as "active teacher" and "passive pupil."[216]

To create an environment where active learning is paramount, a consistent daily routine is maintained.[217] This routine varies only when children have fair warning that the classroom routine will be different the next day.[218] This commitment to routine gives children the security and control necessary to be responsible and independent.[219]

Findings

There is ample research on this model that demonstrates its positive results. Specifically, the HighScope Perry Preschool Study found that the HighScope program group significantly outperformed the no-program group on the highest level of schooling completed.[220] Additionally, significantly more of the program group than the no-program group was employed at age 40.[221]

The study also presented strong evidence that the Perry Preschool program played a significant role in reducing overall arrests and arrests for violent, property, and drug-related crimes.[222] The major conclusion of this study was that "high-quality preschool programs for young children living in poverty contribute to their intellectual and social development in childhood and their school success, economic performance, and reduced commission of crime in adulthood."[223]

The Reggio Emilia Experience

The Reggio Emilia experience with early childhood education has become the gold standard, and these programs have been deemed to be the best in the world.[224] The "Reggio Emilia experience" is named after the city in which it originated and for the community of people who were dedicated to changing the culture of early childhood.[225]

After World War II had seriously damaged their city, the community of Reggio Emilia came together and decided that the rebuilding process must be focused on children and their early education. In a city torn by violence, the leaders were determined to place children at the center of policymaking. They dedicated themselves to establishing a new kind of education in which children are vital, contributing members of the democratic community and in which the community is an active participant in the development and well-being of children and their families.[226]

Loris Malaguzzi played a leading role in articulating and realizing these goals. He first supported one of the communities in the countryside near the city that started with "an army tank, six horses and three trucks," and then led his own community in the city to develop an extraordinary network of learning centers for young children.[227]

With Malaguzzi's assistance, the city of Reggio Emilia created and officially opened the city's first municipal preschool in 1963 and played a leadership role in the establishment of Italy's national system of early childhood services.[228] Today in Reggio Emilia there are currently more than three dozen *scuole*, which are pre-primary schools, and *nidi*, which are infant-toddler centers.[229]

The educators in Reggio Emilia were guided by the fundamental image of the child as a capable, caring, creative, curious, and connected member of the community who has "legitimate rights."[230] Their schools were designed to realize the "universal aspiration" of parents that their children be taken seriously, believed in, and encouraged to reach their rich and overlooked potential.[231]

The Reggio Emilia early childhood centers originally envisioned by Malaguzzi now have greatly expanded with municipal support and public funding. The Reggio Emilia experience has become a model for national and international campaigns for public early childhood programs for all children.[232]

As Lilian Katz as has declared:

> I cannot recall having seen anywhere before preschool children's work of such high quality as in Reggio Emilia. . . . But most important, teachers do not underestimate children's capacities for sustained effort in achieving understanding of what they are exploring nor do they underestimate children's abilities to capture and depict these understandings through a variety of art.[233]

Education experts throughout the world have visited Reggio Emilia's learning centers, and Reggio-inspired practices are now being used in outstanding early childhood education programs in the United States.[234]

As Carolyn Edwards, Lella Gandini, and George Forman have insightfully demonstrated, however, the "educators in Reggio Emilia prefer language in which we speak of their *experience* (as opposed to their *method* or *model*) and of their experience *entering into dialogue* with (as opposed to *instructing, improving, informing*) educators in other contexts."[235] Nonetheless, these leading experts in the Reggio experience also have recognized that it is "valuable" and "fruitful" for educators to set up schools or classrooms "that embody as closely as possible all of the important central premises of the Reggio Emilia experience" or to "incorporate one or a few insights gleaned from contact with the Reggio experience into their ongoing endeavors" within their particular context.[236] While it is virtually impossible to fully articulate the richness and depth of the teacher-child interactions that comprise the Reggio Emilia experience, it is possible to gather some "important central premises" and "pillars" from that experience.

The following premises for example seem central to Reggio Emilia experience:

- A critical importance of the "image of the child" that recognizes the child's creative, intellectual, and communicative abilities and potential;

- An interpretation of schools as systems of relations—the well-being of children is interdependent with the well-being of teachers and families; and
- The value of doubt and uncertainty as ethical premises and incentives for teachers to dedicate themselves to learning.[237]

Based on these premises, educators in Reggio Emilia have created early learning centers in which: (1) the environment is a "teacher" that encourages the co-construction of knowledge through relationships; (2) the curriculum emerges from and inspires children's curiosities, relies on teachers' collaborative research, and values multiple forms of representation; and (3) the learning of each child and the community is made visible through documentation.[238]

An Environment That Teaches

The Reggio Emilia experience supports the creation by professional and deeply valued educators of a learning environment that facilitates a child's co-construction of his or her own cognitive, social, and emotional powers through meaningful relationships with peers, teachers, and surroundings. Reggio Emilia's schools are purposefully designed to reflect and promote the values of the community.[239] Accordingly, the environment includes a large central space, natural lighting, and non-industrial furnishing and plants.[240] The phrase "space is our third teacher" is represented in the active use of school spaces to convey both "messages and possibilities."[241]

Materials for children's work and play (blocks, crayons, paint, paper, dishes, dolls, tools, raw materials, etc.) are within easy reach and purposefully and sometimes creatively arranged, stored, or displayed to convey the message that they are important.[242] The spaces for large- and small-group activities, play, and the display of child work are carefully and flexibly designed to promote child engagement.[243] There is a pervasive use of mirrors and other reflective surfaces in open spaces, classrooms, and bathrooms.[244] There are light boxes and light tables used to display artifacts and manipulations of objects with various degrees of translucency, demonstrating Reggio Emilia's appreciation for physics and light.[245]

Similarly, large windows allow shadows and light to enter classrooms and encourage observations of the outside world.[246] Dress-up clothes and other interesting materials for play are centrally located to invite children from different classes to play together.[247] Kitchens are highly visible places that are frequented by children "as helpers" and by parents on arrival.[248] Teachers have spaces to gather, work, and talk together. Adult-size furniture is placed in the central space and in classrooms to support adult relations.[249]

One of the most important messages conveyed by the environment is the value of the experiences children share in the classroom.[250] Teachers are trusted to thoughtfully construct the classroom space to encourage and guide children's exploration, to promote collaboration, and prominently display children's identities. The classroom environment promotes learning processes in which children are engaging with each other and with objects of interest, exploring, constructing, and representing their understandings. Photographs and examples of collaborative children's work are intentionally displayed.[251]

Reggio Emilia spaces are designed with consistent pedagogical aims and reflect the identity of their particular place.[252] As such, Italian educators often refer to their early childhood environments as *places* rather than *programs*.[253] In addition to the classroom, the children's environment also includes the school building, school grounds, neighborhood, and the city. All of these areas provide children opportunities to explore and learn.

A Reggio-inspired environment also includes attractive materials. These materials include natural, beautiful, and repurposed objects for children's expression. Natural items might include leaves, seeds, sticks, shells, and stones. Beautiful man-made objects ripe for expression might include ribbon and lace, buttons and foils, wire, and other metal objects. Repurposed materials might include safe industrial by-products and small pieces of plastic. In the hands of a child with an idea, an otherwise familiar plastic piece can represent something extraordinary.

As Cathy Topal and Lella Gandini illustrate in their influential book *Beautiful Stuff*, engaging children in the collection and sorting process inspires the children to use these materials to express their evermore complex ideas, often in three dimensions.[254] The teacher and the children engage together with those materials around questions or provocations that arise through dialogue. The classroom environment is designed to encourage children to engage in activities that allow them to pursue play individually or in small groups.

To promote play, the classroom is structured with small-group learning areas filled with interesting objects and materials (blocks, reading materials, water, or sand tables). The classroom has collaborative work surfaces, easily accessible and sorted materials for creating representations, an inviting atmosphere, and displayed and stored children's work. When possible, the classroom has a thoughtful use of light. The learning areas are positioned close to other learning areas to encourage children to join resources (combining a dress-up area and a book area or writing table).[255]

Classrooms also display children's work, their interests, thoughts, photographs, and panels of themselves and their families to create an identity and history of the classroom. The walls are usually neutral in color to allow children's work to stand out. Children decorate their cubbies or personal spaces with meaningful objects or photos of family and friends, or other personal symbols. Their photos adorn their personal mailboxes and nap spaces, and full-length mirrors are placed around the room to allow children to see their whole bodies from multiple perspectives while working.

The classroom also includes furniture that invites children to collaborate, engage, and discover their own capabilities. Ladders show children they are able to climb, adult-sized furniture and real utensils give children the opportunity to stretch their behaviors, and breakable glassware illustrates to all that young children can use and respect beautiful and delicate objects. All of these materials are accessible to the children in reachable spaces and transparent storage units. The children also have access to a variety of work surfaces, including tables of different heights. The environment includes mobile furniture and materials to facilitate learning relationships of various sizes and to enable children to observe themselves and their world from multiple perspectives.

The learning environment does not stop at the classroom walls. Where possible, common indoor and outdoor space is a vital part of the learning community. Entryways to the classrooms are designed to connect the school to the community and the classrooms to one another. Classroom doorways are often open, welcoming, engaging, and informative. These areas display children's work and portfolios of children's explorations over time. Parents and caregivers are invited in and made to feel welcome to speak with the teacher, view their children's work, and become active partners in the learning community. The learning environment also encompasses areas outside the school building, where children are encouraged to explore with all of their senses. Rain, puddles, dew, mud, flora, and fauna often capture the interest of children.

A Negotiated Curriculum: 100 Languages and Possibilities

Within a fully engaged environment, a Reggio-inspired early learning center also reflects: (1) a negotiated curriculum that emerges from dialogue among professional educators, children, and their families; (2) projects that arise naturally from the interests of groups of children and that are as short or long as seem constructive; (3) the representation and presentation of concepts in multiple forms of expression, materials and media, including spoken and written language, print, art, construction, music, puppetry, play, and drama; and (4) collaboration among children, among teachers, and among children and teachers, including dialogue, negotiation, problem solving, listening, and respect for different perspectives.

Loris Malaguzzi believed that a child has "one hundred languages . . . one hundred ways of thinking of playing, of speaking . . . and a hundred hundred hundred more."[256] A Reggio-inspired classroom does not deprive the child of these languages; rather, it encourages children to represent their understanding in multiple ways.[257]

Malaguzzi recognized the intimate relationship between creativity and intelligence and hired an atelierista, or art educator, to work closely with teachers and with children. Creative expression "should not be considered a separate mental faculty but a characteristic of our way of thinking, knowing, and making choices."[258] Educators ask children to communicate their knowledge through observational drawings and sculptures.[259]

Art is not construed as an activity separate and apart from disciplines such as mathematics and literacy. In fact, Reggio-inspired educators understand that learning for children includes aspects of all disciplines. Forms of expression that are traditionally categorized as "art" are a vital and integrated aspect of thinking, exploration, and communication in Reggio Emilia classrooms.[260]

Children have daily opportunities to experiment with a variety of materials and tools, including clay, paint, sculpture, and pen and pencil to represent and share their understandings.[261] Children are often challenged to revisit, revise, and reshape their own representations of their thinking.[262] Children's work serves as a valuable tool for the co-construction of new understandings with peers and adults.[263]

Curriculum goals in Reggio Emilia are defined in terms of broadly construed cultural values such as developing relationships or learning how to collaborate.[264] Long-term projects emerge from questions posed by children. The children share the project with their peers, teachers, families, and the surrounding community.[265] Teachers, working together, also use what they learn about children's interests and understandings in the course of explorations to design challenging additional project work that promotes the development of new skills and understandings.[266] In a Reggio-inspired early childhood learning environment, children are not only respected, they are given some control over their own learning. In one school in Reggio, for example:

> a child constructed a water wheel. The young boy had attached the water paddles at the wrong angle, and became frustrated with his work. The teacher, rather than telling him he had put them on incorrectly and giving him direct instruction, took him to the sink and allowed the water to run down the palm of his hand. She asked him to cup his hand to catch the water. Aha! He now understood why his paddles were not working. She facilitated the leap to his next level of understanding.[267]

Similarly, in Reggio schools, educators celebrate the diversity in backgrounds and perspectives that children and families bring to the learning environment. The city of Reggio Emilia has become increasingly diverse in the past decade. The educators in Reggio Emilia understand the integration of immigrant families into the centers and schools as an opportunity for tremendous growth and learning.[268] Moreover, "[c]hildren with special needs (or 'special rights' as they are called in Reggio Emilia) are not limited by adult perceptions of their cognitive functioning and are included in all activities."[269]

Children with special rights are not defined by perceived limitations. Rather they are fully included in a classroom in Reggio Emilia, and are respected for their capability to use all their senses to learn, through play, touching, dancing, moving, listening, seeing, and creating.[270]

Educators in Reggio welcome parents and guardians as partners in designing and implementing the negotiated curriculum. Regular meetings are scheduled to encourage all to come together. The school becomes the hub of the community, fostering developmentally appropriate learning for children and adults.

Making Learning Visible through Documentation

The Reggio Emilia experience also reflects the work of highly skilled educators who research and learn along with students while listening, observing, and documenting the growth of community in the classroom. These teachers provide authentic assessment through documentation of a variety of learning experiences, which is then used as a tool for additional learning and advocacy for children.

Documentation is the practice of observing, recording, interpreting, and sharing through a variety of media the process and products of individual and community learning. It makes visible to multiple stakeholders the learning that takes place in an early childhood education program. Documentation is central to teachers' roles as researchers in the classrooms.[271] Teachers take photographs, collect artifacts, and record the children's conversations.[272] They then reflect on this data—sometimes with other teachers and frequently with the children's parents and family members—to make sense of what has been learned and to plan next steps.[273]

The art educator, or atelierista, is also a part of the process and records the children's activities.[274] As Rebecca New has observed, documentation enables all members of the learning community to construct and to share their knowledge:

> As teachers collected and contemplated transcripts of children's conversations and detailed renderings of their developing understandings, they, too, began to refine their own form of symbolic representation. Their elegant and compelling forms of documentation represent their understandings about children's learning, their questions about their own teaching, and their advocacy for more sincere and reciprocal adult-adult and adult-child conversations.[275]

Documentation efforts are used as a professional development tool and are also used to make learning visible in shared spaces. Documentation also functions as: advocacy for Reggio Emilia's high-quality services; information to guide curriculum planning; and an invitation for parents to participate in the process.[276]

In Reggio Emilia, documentation is a means of keeping parents involved in and informed about their children's experiences.[277] Images of families and artifacts from the families' homes are shared in the classroom.[278] Parents are informed about and contribute to curricular decisions because of documentation and meetings focused on ongoing events in the classroom.[279] Where appropriate, meetings with the wider school community also are documented and shared.[280]

Vital to the development of a Reggio-inspired social constructivist learning environment are relationships between teachers, children, families, and the community. Documentation is a critical part of creating these connections. Although, as Carolyn Edwards, Lella Gandini, and George Forman have cautioned, it is extremely difficult to capture the essence of the Reggio Emilia experience in a series of premises; it is possible to recognize that underlying that experience is the fundamental shared belief that children construct their knowledge by building meaningful relationships.

As Loris Malaguzzi fully realized, that pedagogical understanding also has a profound political consequence. He believed that children, like adults, should have "the right to participate; the right to participate actively; the right to constantly discover; the possibility to make a decision and to choose."[281] If a community's schools recognize and develop in children their capacity to be active participants in the construction of their own knowledge, those schools also will prepare children to become active and empowered participants in a truly democratic regime. Accordingly, the Reggio Emilia experience is built on a strong social constructivist foundation and the following "democratic" pillars:

Documentation: Teachers actively listen and observe children's learning in order to make learning visible to multiple stakeholders and to decipher children's interests, feelings, and ideas. To create such records, teachers take notes, photos, or videotape children's learning. This documentation can be shared with other teachers, children, and parents, and can also be displayed as formal public communications in the form of books, blogs, or slideshows.

Emergent Negotiated Curriculum: What has been described in the United States as emergent negotiated curriculum is an extended learning process, given shape by educators, that is driven by children's interests and discoveries as they tackle a particular question, posed by a child or an adult. It requires teachers and children to listen, observe, reflect, negotiate, and respond to one another in real time. As teachers scaffold the learning process, they observe and document what the children are pursuing and representing, and guide children according to certain learning objectives. Teachers do not set a predetermined outcome. Rather, the learning process changes based on children's discoveries and questions that follow. Teachers take the child's perspective, while relying for direction on their own reflection and documentation of student learning.

This way of teaching and learning by teachers with children cycles through several steps, not necessarily in a linear fashion: listening, observing, documenting, interpreting, projecting, deciding, planning, hypothesizing, scaffolding, and back to listening and observing. The first part of the emergent curriculum requires teachers to observe and document children's actions, interactions, and representations though various media. Teachers then reflect upon and interpret the interests being expressed by the child or children. Teachers next interpret and confirm that interest with the children, and provide opportunities for children to participate, often in small groups, in collaborative related activities.

Throughout the activities, teachers and children interact and co-construct understandings. During this time, teachers continue to observe and document the children's behavior and engagement, and take note of any newly expressed interest or ideas. Teachers then use any newly formed or expressed interests to create different, additional activities.

While in this process, teachers also develop in children the ability to experience themselves as active, self-directed agents who can, individually and in collaboration with others, formulate personally meaningful learning goals, figure out strategies to achieve them, engage the world to pursue them, construct understandings, and communicate the newly developed understandings to others.[282] Children strengthen their capacity to make connections, to communicate, to observe, to reason, and to represent their ideas in various media, and to share these ideas with peers and adults.

Multiple Perspectives: Reggio-inspired teachers encourage children to consider multiple points of view when pondering a question or object of inquiry in order to expand the children's range or depth of their understanding. Children can then compare their viewpoints and learn that their own views may differ from those of their peers.[283] This dialogue is important for children to engage in, as it is crucial for children, like adults, to connect with other children, and become more aware of others' perspectives.[284]

One Hundred Languages: Reggio-inspired educators are inspired in their practice with children by the insight in Loris Malaguzzi's poem entitled *No Way. The Hundred Is There*.[285] They believe it is their responsibility to provide opportunities for children to express their ideas in countless ways. The poem's metaphor of "one hundred languages" also leads educators to reject arbitrary separation of head and hands, listening and speaking, science and imagination, and work and play. In its place, these educators embrace the whole child and recognize that children are always constructing knowledge across traditional disciplines.

Collaboration: The educational environment is infused with collaborations between children, between children and teachers, between teachers and families, and between the school and the community.[286] Small groups provide opportunity for meaningful interactions and shared discovery. Moreover, teachers model collaboration by sharing with each other their research about learning. After documenting their observations, for example, teachers reflect with one another on their findings, plan extensions of children's learning, hypothesize possible outcomes, and collaborate to implement activities and different ways to structure their classrooms.

Researchers: Children are natural "researchers" as they question what they see, predict outcomes, experiment, and dissect their discoveries. When children participate in long-term learning projects, they have an opportunity to continue to become a "researcher" as they learn, explore, and look closely at their understanding of the world around them.[287] As highly respected researchers, teachers also approach their work with children with inquisitive minds, rather than with preset assumptions and goals.

Atelier: Reggio-inspired schools have or aspire to have an atelier, or at least some common space for students to work on projects involving several different mediums, such as clay, wire, mirrors, paper, paints, and other objects.[288] When not possible, mini-ateliers in classrooms or mobile studios are developed. Ideally, each school would also have an Atelierista, or studio educator with a strong background in visual arts. The studio educator supports the children and teachers by finding commonalities in children's interests across classrooms, by providing an artist's knowledge of a wide range of materials, and by offering a shared space for expression.

Time to Explore: Teachers have sufficient time to follow the curiosities of children inspired to pursue long-term projects, or in-depth studies of a question or provocation. Children engaged in projects have an opportunity to become disciplined researchers; they observe, hypothesize solutions, reflect on their findings, and reanalyze their original hypotheses.[289]

Image of the Child: Reggio Emilia educators understand that children are capable, creative, curious, caring, and connected members of their community who have tremendous strengths and capabilities.[290] As further demonstrated in the next chapter, that image of the child has been confirmed by the most recent evidence from cognitive neuroscience and developmental psychology. With that proper image, teachers aim to challenge children's thinking, empower children to be curious, and facilitate children's ability to connect with the world and create understandings. As a teacher continues to view children as strong, deep, and powerful, the children will become this image, and become active questioners who construct knowledge and meaning.

Community: This genuinely democratic early childhood education requires a professional educator who partners with families and the community. Teachers view parents or guardians as fully engaged participants in their children's education. Teachers engage in a regular meetings with parents, teachers, and other staff members for everyone to share perspectives, learn, and deepen their understanding of this learning approach. The meetings often include whole-group dialogues that relate to some portion of child development. During this time, shared documentation of children's learning, such as a drawn representation of an object in nature, enables many to reflect on children's deep thinking. This type of community discussion exposes parents to others' perspectives and provides a forum to discuss the goals of education.

Teachers create a classroom environment that is welcoming to parents and encourages them to engage with teachers. Family members are invited into the classroom to share experiences and cultural practices. Once a relationship is developed between a teacher and parent, teachers can more easily make visible to the parent the child's interests and growth. Parents, in turn, after learning of new interests, are then able to engage their children at home around these interests.

Teachers share children's learning and exploration with parents through portfolios that document children's pleasure of learning and growth. They are kept in the classroom of the children with each child's name, visible to children and to families. They will be kept in the school until the end of the time the children are in the learning center, and then the children themselves will hand them to their families the last day at the center to celebrate their work and take them home.

Portfolios are designed to share the strengths and interests of a child operating as a member of a learning community. Teachers also engage family members by asking them to enter in the classroom every day—for a few minutes if possible—when they accompany them. In Italy, grandparents may play that role as Italian extended families tend to live close and help young working parents. Parents also form an organization and elect representatives among them that are in dialogue with the city school administration.

All of these interactions allow teachers to understand parents' feelings and ideas, while also allowing parents to value the abilities of their child. Parents and teachers "co-construct" understandings about children. Lastly, these parent-teacher interactions provide teachers with opportunities to share their perspectives of teaching and learning with parents. Parents then are better

Table 6.1.

Approach	Foundations	Teacher's Role	Student's Role	Assessment	Exemplars
Direct Instruction— Children receive information passively from an authority figure	Behaviorism (Pavlov, Skinner)	Authoritarian	Consumer	Standardized Tests	Some aspects of HCZ and some Head Start programs
Constructivist— children construct knowledge individually	Jean Piaget	Supervisor	Producer	Outputs	Montessori
Social Constructivist— Children construct knowledge through meaningful relationships	Vygotsky, neuroscience, behavioral science	Partner	Leader, Designer, Builder, Inventor	Documentation	Reggio Emilia, Tools of the Mind, Perry School

able to incorporate what they learn from teachers and the educational process into their relationship with their children.

In a Reggio-inspired early childhood education program, the community beyond the doors of the school is a vital partner in the learning. The community provides a forum for children's expression in common spaces. The city or town surrounding the school may become involved in a community-wide activity. For example, if children begin to explore their questions about bicycles and how they work, the community may decide to explore those same questions. The children's representations drawn during their studies may be displayed for adult reflection in shared space (e.g., on walls of a railroad underpass). Or, where children and teachers explore questions about lines in leaves, the surrounding city may explore questions about lines of transportation or lines of authority.

Not only do children learn outside of their school walls, but community members learn to appreciate the abilities of young children to construct knowledge. Through documentation, Reggio-inspired educators make visible to the community surrounding the school the learning that takes place within. This form of authentic assessment provides to community stakeholders, including policy makers, taxpayers, and funding sources, evidence of the profound effectiveness of the children's experience.

Children emerge from a Reggio-inspired early childhood experience with the executive functioning skills that they need to lead, to create, to problem solve, to collaborate, to express themselves, to negotiate, to build alliances, to focus, to listen, to absorb, to relate to adults, and to find joy in learning. They also develop a deeply rooted sense of self-confidence and an authentic sense of self-respect and self-esteem. By creating a community of early learning environments in which children are encouraged to construct their own knowledge through meaningful relationships, the educators in Reggio Emilia have developed an exemplary experience founded upon social constructivist premises and democratic pillars. As Gunilla Dahlberg and Peter Moss have eloquently concluded:

> In their work, the teachers of Reggio have struggled to raise the emancipatory potential of democracy, by giving each child possibilities to function as an active citizen and to have the possibility of a good life in a democratic community.[291]

NOTES

1. See, e.g., Roopnarine and Johnson, Approaches to Early Childhood Education.

2. Douglas R. Powell, "The Head Start Program," in Roopnarine and Johnson, Approaches to Early Childhood Education, 61.

3. "Head Start Program Facts, Fiscal Year 2012," Head Start, An Office of the Administration for Children and Families Early Childhood Learning & Knowledge Center (ECLKC), http://eclkc.ohs.acf.hhs.gov/hslc/mr/factsheets/docs/hs-program-fact-sheet-2012.pdf

4. Powell, "The Head Start Program," 67.

5. Ibid.

6. Ibid

7. Ibid., 66.

8. Ibid.

9. Ibid.

10. Ibid., 67.

11. Ibid., 66.

12. See, e.g., 45 C.F.R. Section 1304.21 (2007).

13. Helen H. Taylor, "Head Start Bulletin, #67," Curriculum in Head Start, Head Start, An Office of the Administration for Children and Families Early Childhood Learning & Knowledge Center (ECLKC), http://eclkc.ohs.acf.hhs.gov/hslc/tta-system/teaching/eecd/Curriculum/Definition%20and%20Requirements/CurriculuminHea.htm.

14. Ibid.

15. Powell, "The Head Start Program," 64.

16. Ibid.

17. Ibid.

18. The Head Start Child Development and Early Learning Framework, Promoting Positive Outcomes in Early Childhood Programs Serving Children 3–5 Years Old, U.S. Department of Health and Human Services, Administration for Children and Families, and Office of Head Start, December 2010, http://eclkc.ohs.acf.hhs.gov/hslc/tta-system/teaching/eecd/Assessment/Child%20Outcomes/HS_Revised_Child_Outcomes_Framework(rev-Sept2011).pdf.

19. Powell, "The Head Start Program," 67.

20. Ibid. See also Head Start Performance Standards, 45 CFR Chapter XIII, U.S. Department of Health and Human Services, Administration for Children and Families, and Office of Head Start, October 1, 2009, https://eclkc.ohs.acf.hhs.gov/hslc/standards/hspps/45-cfr-chapter-xiii/45-cfr-chap-xiii-eng.pdf.

21. Powell, "The Head Start Program," 68.

22. Ibid.

23. Ibid.

24. Ibid., 65.

25. Ibid.

26. Ibid., 65–66.

27. Ibid., 70.

28. Ibid., 71.

29. Ibid., 70–71.

30. Ibid., 72.

31. Ibid., 72–73.

32. Ibid., 73.

33. Ibid.

34. Ibid., 74.

35. Ibid., 73.

36. Danielle Hanson, "Assessing the Harlem Children's Zone," The Heritage Foundation, March 6, 2013, http://www.heritage.org/research/reports/2013/03/assessing-the-harlem-childrens-zone.

37. "History: The Beginning of the Children's Zone," Harlem Children's Zone, http://www.hcz.org/index.php/about-us/history.

38. Ibid.

39. Ibid.

40. Ibid.

41. Paul Tough, *Whatever It Takes: A New Afterward* (New York: Harlem Children's Zone, 2014), 5–6, http://hcz.org/wp-content/uploads/2014/04/Whatever-It-Takes-Afterword.pdf.

42. Ibid.

43. "Whatever It Takes: A Conversation with Paul Tough," http://www.paultough.com/the-books/whatever-it-takes/extras/.

44. Donna Foote, "Building the Village: A Harlem Educator's Radical Program to Help Impoverished Children Succeed," Washington Post, October 12, 2008, http://www.washingtonpost.com/wp-dyn/content/story/2008/10/10/ST2008101001636.html.

45. "History: The Beginning of the Children's Zone."

46. Ibid.

47. Linda Perlstein, "The Transformer," New York Times Sunday Book Review, October 17, 2008, http://www.nytimes.com/2008/10/19/books/review/Perlstein-t.html?_r=0.

48. Hanson, "Assessing the Harlem Children's Zone."

49. "The Baby College," Harlem Children's Zone, http://hcz.org/our-programs/the-baby-college/.

50. Hanson, "Assessing the Harlem Children's Zone."

51. Ibid.

52. "History: The Beginning of the Children's Zone."

53. Chicago Policy Research Team, "Chicago Promise: A Policy Report on Reinventing the Harlem Children's Zone," University of Chicago, May 2009, i, http://cprt.uchicago.edu/0809/reports/CPRTFullReportChicagoPromise.pdf.

54. Hanson, "Assessing the Harlem Children's Zone."

55. "Harlem Gems," Harlem's Children Zone, http://www.hcz.org/our-programs/harlem-gems.

56. "History: The Beginning of the Children's Zone."

57. Tough, *A New Afterward*, 5–6.

58. "Harlem Children's Zone: A National Model for Breaking the Cycle of Poverty With Proven Success," Harlem Children's Zone, http://hcz.org/wp-content/uploads/2014/04/FY-2013-FactSheet.pdf.

59. Ibid.

60. See, e.g., Jean Piaget, *The Origins of Intelligence in Children* (New York: International University Press, 1952).

61. Jean Piaget, *The Language and Thought of the Child* (London: Routledge Classics, 1926).

62. Ibid.

63. Ibid.

64. Elena Bodrova and Deborah J. Leong, *Tools of the Mind: The Vygotskian Approach to Early Childhood Education* (Boston: Pearson 2007), 6.

65. Martha Torrence and John Chattin-McNichols, "Montessori Education Today," in Roopnarine and Johnson, *Approaches to Early Childhood Education*, 359, citing Maria Montessori, *The Absorbent Mind* (New York: Dell, 1967), 28.

66. Torrence and Chattin-McNichols, "Montessori Education Today," 359.

67. Ibid., 361.

68. Ibid.

69. Ibid., 361–62.

70. Ibid., 362.

71. Ibid., 362–63.

72. Ibid., 363.

73. Ibid.

74. Ibid., 363.

75. Ibid.

76. Ibid.

77. ibid., 365.

78. Ibid

79. Ibid., 357, citing D. Schapiro and B. Hellen, *Montessori Community Resource* (Minneapolis: Jola, 2011).

80. Torrence and Chattin-McNichols, "Montessori Education Today," 361.

81. Ibid.

82. Ibid., 370.

83. Ibid., 371.

84. Ibid., 359.

85. Ibid.

86. Ibid., 365.

87. Ibid.

88. Ibid., 366.

89. Ibid.

90. See, e.g., "Montessori Learning Materials," American Montessori Society, http://amshq.org/Montessori-Education/Introduction-to-Montessori/Montessori-Learning-Materials.

91. Torrence and Chattin-McNichols, "Montessori Education Today," 366, citing Maria Montessori, *From Childhood to Adolescence* (New York: Schocken Books, 1973).

92. Torrence and Chattin-McNichols, "Montessori Education Today," 366.

93. Ibid.

94. "Montessori Learning Materials."

95. Torrence and Chattin-McNichols, "Montessori Education Today," 367.

96. Ibid.

97. Ibid.

98. Ibid.

99. Ibid., 368.

100. Ibid.

101. Ibid.

102. Ibid., 369, *Montessori Education* (New York: American Montessori Society, 1994).

103. Torrence and Chattin-McNichols, "Montessori Education Today," 369.

104. Ibid.

105. Ibid., 375.

106. Ibid.

107. See, e.g., Bodrova and Leong, *Tools of the Mind*; Lev Vygotsky, *Mind in Society: The Development of Psychological Processes* (Boston: Harvard University Press, 1978); Lev Vygotsky, *Thought and Language* (Boston: MIT Press, 1986).

108. Bodrova and Leong, *Tools of the Mind*, at 67.

109. Vygotsky, *Mind in Society*, 88.

110. Ibid., 57.

111. Ibid.

112. Ibid.

113. Ibid.

114. Lev Vygotsky, "Development of Higher Mental Functions," in *Psychological Research in the USSR*, ed. A.N. Leontiev, A. Luria, and A. Sminov (Moscow: Progress, 1966), 43.

115. Vygotsky, *Thought and Language*, 251.

116. Ibid., 218.

117. Ibid., 255.

118. Ibid., 10.

119. Ibid., 11.

120. Ibid. (emphasis in original).

121. Ibid.

122. Ibid.

123. See generally Yuriy V. Karpov, *The Neo-Vygotsky Approach to Child Development* (Boston: Cambridge University Press, 2005); A. Kozulin, *Vygotsky's Psychology: A Biography of Ideas* (Boston: Cambridge University Press, 1990).

124. Elena Bodrova and Deborah J. Leong, "Tools of the Mind: The Vygotskian Approach to Early Childhood Education," in *Approaches to Early Childhood Education*, ed. Jaipaul L. Roopnarine and James E. Johnson (Boston: Pearson, 2013), 241.

125. Ibid.

126. Ibid., 242.

127. Ibid.

128. Ibid.

129. Ibid.

130. Ibid., citing Vygotsky, *Mind in Society*.

131. Ibid., 243, citing Yuriy V. Karpov, "L.S. Vygotsky as the Founder of a New Approach to Instruction," *School Psychology International* 16(2) (1995): 131–42.

132. Bodrova and Leong, "Tools of the Mind: The Vygotskian Approach," 243.

133. Ibid.

134. Ibid.

135. Ibid.

136. Ibid.

137. Ibid., 244, citing Lev Vygotsky, *The History of the Development of Higher Mental Functions*, trans. M.J. Hall (New York: Plenum Press, 1997), 106.

138. Ibid., citing Lev Vygotsky, "The Problem of the Cultural Development of the Child," in The Vygotsky Reader, ed. R. van der Veer and J. Valsiner (Cambridge: Blackwell, 1994).

139. Bodrova and Leong, "Tools of the Mind: The Vygotskian Approach," 244.

140. Ibid.

141. Ibid.

142. Ibid., 247.

143. Ibid., citing Karpov, *The Neo-Vygotsky Approach*.

144. Bodrova and Leong, "Tools of the Mind: The Vygotskian Approach," 247.

145. Ibid., citing D. Wood, J.C. Bruner, and G. Ross, "The Role of Tutoring in Problem Solving," *Journal of Child Psychology and Psychiatry* 17(2) (1976): 89–100.

146. Bodrova and Leong, "Tools of the Mind: The Vygotskian Approach," 247.

147. Ibid., 247–48, citing A. Zaporozhets, *Izbrannye psikhologicheskie trudy* (Moscow: Pedagogika, 1986).

148. Bodrova and Leong, "Tools of the Mind: The Vygotskian Approach," 248.

149. Ibid., 249–50.

150. Ibid., 250.

151. Ibid.

152. Ibid.

153. Ibid.

154. Ibid.

155. Ibid., 251.

156. Ibid.

157. Ibid.

158. Ibid.

159. Ibid., citing L.E. Berk, T.D. Mann, and A.T. Ogan, "Make-Believe Play: Wellspring for Development of Self-Regulation," in *Play-Learning: How Play Motivates and Enhances Cognitive and Social-Emotional Growth*, ed. Dorothy G. Singer, Roberta Michnick Golinkoff, and Kathryn A. Hirsh-Pasek (New York: Oxford University Press, 2006).

160. Bodrova and Leong, "Tools of the Mind: The Vygotskian Approach," 251.

161. Ibid., 252.

162. Ibid., 253, citing Bodrova and Leong, *Tools of the Mind.*
163. Bodrova and Leong, "Tools of the Mind: The Vygotskian Approach," 254.
164. Ibid.
165. Ibid.
166. Ibid.
167. Ibid.
168. Ibid.
169. Ibid.
170. Ibid., citing Vygotsky, *Higher Mental Functions*, 147.
171. Schweinhart and Weikart, "The HighScope Model," 217.
172. Ibid., 218–19.
173. Ibid., 218.
174. Ibid., 217.
175. Ibid., 219.
176. Ibid., 218.
177. Ibid., 219.
178. Ibid.
179. Ibid., 217–18.
180. Ibid., 221.
181. Ibid.
182. Ibid.
183. Ibid.
184. Ibid.
185. Ibid.
186. Ibid.
187. Ibid.
188. Ibid.
189. Ibid.
190. Ibid., 222.
191. Ibid.
192. Ibid.
193. Ibid.
194. Ibid.
195. Ibid.
196. Ibid.
197. Ibid., 222–23.
198. Ibid., 223.
199. Ibid., 218.
200. Ibid.
201. Ibid., 223.
202. Ibid.
203. Ibid., 225.
204. Ibid.
205. Ibid.
206. Ibid., 219.
207. Ibid., 219–220.
208. Ibid., 220.
209. Ibid.
210. Ibid.

211. Ibid.

212. Ibid.

213. Ibid.

214. Ibid.

215. Ibid., 221.

216. Ibid.

217. Ibid.

218. Ibid.

219. Ibid.

220. Lawrence J. Schweinhart et al., *The High/Scope Perry Preschool Study Through Age 40: Summary, Conclusions, and Frequently Asked Questions* (Ypsilanti, MI: High-Scope Press, 2011), http://www.highscope.org/file/Research/PerryProject/specialsummary_rev2011_02_2.pdf.

221. Ibid.

222. Ibid.

223. Ibid.

224. See Pia Hinckle, "The Best Schools in the World," Newsweek, December 2, 1991.

225. Rebecca S. New and Rebecca Kantor, "Reggio Emilia in the 21st Century: Enduring Commitments Amid New Challenges," in *Approaches to Early Childhood Education*, eds Jaipaul L. Roopnarine and James E. Johnson (New York: Pearson, 2013), 331.

226. See Emily Chertoff, "Reggio Emilia: From Postwar Italy to NYC's Toniest Preschools," The Atlantic, January 17, 2013, http://www.theatlantic.com/national/archive/2013/01/reggio-emilia-from-postwar-italy-to-nycs-toniest-preschools/267204/.

227. Lella Gandini, "History, Ideas, and Basic Principles: An Interview With Loris Malaguzzi," in *The Hundred Languages of Children*, ed. Carolyn Edwards, Lella Gandini, and George Forman (Santa Barbara, CA: Praeger, 2012), 35.

228. Rebecca S. New, "Reggio Emilia as Cultural Activity Theory in Practice," *Theory Into Practice* 46(1) (2007): 5, 6.

229. Ibid., 6.

230. Gandini, *Hundred Languages*, 36.

231. Ibid.

232. See Matthew Grabell, "Should More American Preschools Take a Lesson From Google? An Analysis of Reggio Emilia Preschools and their Impact on a Child's Life," *Loyola University Chicago Journal of Early Education Law and Policy* (2012), http://www.luc.edu/media/lucedu/law/centers/childlaw/earlyeducation/2012studentpapers/grabell.pdf.

233. Lillian G. Katz, "Impressions of Reggio Emilia Preschools," Young Children 47(11) (1990): 11.

234. Donna E. Davilla and Susan M. Koenig, "Bringing the Reggio Concept to American Educators," *Windows on the World* 51(18) (1998):18 (stating that so many American educators have been travelling to Northern Italy to get a better idea of why the Reggio Emilia schooling methodology has been so successful).

235. Carolyn Edwards, Lella Gandini, and George Forman, "Final Reflections and Guiding Strategies for Teaching," in *The Hundred Languages of Children*, ed. Carolyn Edwards, Lella Gandini, and George Forman (Santa Barbara, CA: Praeger, 2012), 367.

236. Ibid., 372.

237. New and Kantor, "Reggio Emilia in the 21st Century," 331; Valarie Mercilliott Hewett, "Examining the Reggio Emilia Approach to Early Childhood Education," *Early Childhood Education Journal* 29(95) (2001): 96–97 (expressing that some of the central

qualities in Reggio schools are that the "child [acts] as an active constructor of knowledge," "the child as a social being," "the child as a researcher," and "the child as having
rights").

238. New and Kantor, "Reggio Emilia in the 21st Century," 335.

239. Ibid.

240. Ibid.

241. Ibid. See also T. Filippini, "Introduction to the Reggio Approach" (paper presented
at the annual conference of the National Association for the Education of Young Children,
Washington, DC, November 1990).

242. New and Kantor, "Reggio Emilia in the 21st Century," citing C. Topal and L.
Gandini, *Beautiful Stuff: Learning With Found Materials* (St. Paul, MN: Redleaf Press,
1999), 335.

243. New and Kantor, "Reggio Emilia in the 21st Century," 335–36.

244. Ibid., 336.

245. Ibid.

246. Ibid.

247. Ibid.

248. Ibid.

249. Ibid.

250. Ibid.

251. Ibid.

252. Ibid.

253. Ibid., 336–37.

254. C.W. Topal and L. Gandini, *Beautiful Stuff: Learning With Found Materials* (St.
Paul, MN: Redleaf Press, 1999).

255. Daniel R. Scheinfield, Karen M. Haigh, and Sandra J.P. Scheinfeld, *We Are All
Explorers, Learning and Teaching With Reggio Principles in Urban Settings* (New York:
Teachers College Press, 2008), 71–74.

256. Loris Malaguzzi, "No Way. The Hundred Is There," translated by Lella Gandini,
in *The Hundred Languages of Children*, ed. Carolyn Edwards, Lella Gandini, and George
Forman (Santa Barbara, CA: Praeger, 2012), 3.

257. New and Kantor, "Reggio Emilia in the 21st Century," 338–39.

258. Lella Gandini, "History, Ideas, and Basic Principles: An Interview With Loris
Malaguzzi," in Edwards, Gandini, and Forman, *The Hundred Languages of Children*, 35.

259. New and Kantor, "Reggio Emilia in the 21st Century," 338–39.

260. Ibid. See also Nancy B. Hertzog, "Reflections and Impressions From Reggio
Emilia: 'It's Not About Art!,'" *Early Childhood Research & Practice* 3(1) (2001),
http://ecrp.uiuc.edu/v3n1/hertzog.html (describing the layout of a Reggio school
room).

261. New and Kantor, "Reggio Emilia in the 21st Century," 339, citing Lella Gandini,
L. Hill, L. Caldwell, and C. Schwall, In the Spirit of the Studio: Learning From the Atelier
of Reggio Emilia (New York: Teachers College Press, 2005).

262. Ibid., citing G. Forman and B. Fyfe, "Negotiated Learning Through Design, Documentation and Discourse," in *The Hundred Languages of Children: The Reggio Emilia
Approach—Advanced Reflections*, ed. Carolyn Edwards, Lella Gandini, and George Forman (Greenwich, CT: Ablex, 1998), 239–60.

263. New and Kantor, "Reggio Emilia in the 21st Century," 339.

264. Ibid., 338.

265. Ibid, 338, citing R. New, "Theory and Praxis in Reggio Emilia: They Know What They Are Doing, and Why," in Edwards, Gandini, and Forman, *Advanced Reflections*, 261–84; Carlina Rinaldi, "The Emergent Curriculum and Social Constructivism," in *The Hundred Languages of Children: The Reggio Emilia Approach*, ed. Carolyn Edwards, Lella Gandini, and George Forman (Norwood, NJ: Ablex, 1993), 101–11; Carlina Rinaldi, "Projected Curriculum Constructed Through Documentation—Progettazione: An Interview With Lella Gandini," in Edwards, Gandini, and Forman, *Advanced Reflections*, 113–25; and Carlina Rinaldi, *In Dialogue With Reggio Emilia: Listening, Researching, and Learning* (Contesting Early Childhood Series) (New York: Routledge, 2006).

266. New and Kantor, "Reggio Emilia in the 21st Century," 338.

267. Donna E. Davilla and Susan M. Koenig, "Bringing the Reggio Concept to American Educators," *Art Education* 51(18) (1998): 19.

268. Edwards, Gandini, and Forman, *Hundred Languages*, 369.

269. Margaret Inman Linn, "An American Educator Reflects on the Meaning of the Reggio Experience," *Phi Delta Kappan* 83(332) (2001): 333–34. See also Ivana Soncini, "The Inclusive Community," in Edwards, Gandini, and Forman, *Hundred Languages*, 187.

270. See ibid.

271. New and Kantor, "Reggio Emilia in the 21st Century," 340, citing L. Gandini and J. Goldhaber, "Two Reflections About Documentation," in *Bambini: The Italian Approach to Infant/Toddler Care*, ed. Lella Gandini and Carolyn Edwards (New York: Teachers College Press, 2001), 124–45; Rebecca S. New, "Culture, Child Development and Developmentally Appropriate Practices: Teachers as Collaborative Researchers," in *Diversity and Developmentally Appropriate Practices Challenges for Early Childhood Education*, ed. B. Mallory and Rebecca S. New (New York: Teachers College Press 1994); and Carlina Rinaldi, "The Teacher as Researcher," Innovations in Early Education: The International Reggio Exchange 10 (2) (2003): 1–4.

272. New and Kantor, "Reggio Emilia in the 21st Century," 340.

273. Ibid.

274. Ibid.

275. Rebecca S. New, "Reggio Emilia as Cultural Activity Theory in Practice," *Theory Into Practice* 46(1) (2007): 5, 8.

276. Ibid.

277. Ibid.

278. Ibid.

279. Ibid.

280. Ibid.

281. Loris Malaguzzi, Jorn Moestrup, and Karin Eskesen, *Conversations With Loris Malaguzzi* (Odense: Danish Reggio Emilia Network, 2009).

282. Scheinfield, Haigh, and Scheinfeld, *We Are All Explorers*, 60.

283. Ibid. Multiple perspectives are also facilitated by the flexibility and mobility of the environment.

284. Ibid.

285. Malaguzzi, "No Way. The Hundred Is There," 3.

286. Alice Wexler, "A Theory for Living: Walking With Reggio Emilia," *Art Education* 57(13) (2004): 13–16; see also Hewett, "Examining the Reggio Emilia Approach," 96–97.

287. Valarie Mercilliott Hewett, "Examining the Reggio Emilia Approach to Early Childhood Education," *Early Childhood Education Journal* 29(2) (2001): 96.

288. See Lella Gandini, Lynn Hill, Louise Cadwell, and Charles Schwall, In the *Spirit of the Studio: Learning From the Atelier of Reggio Emilia* (New York: Teachers College Press. 2005), 54.

289. Hewett, "Examining the Reggio Emilia Approach"; Wexler, "A Theory for Living," 13–16.

290. See Linn, "An American Educator Reflects," 333.

291. G. Dahlberg and P. Moss, "Introduction: Our Reggio Emilia," in C. Rinaldi, In *Dialogue With Reggio Emilia: Listening, Researching and Learning* (Abingdon: Routledge, 2007), 1–22, here 10.

Chapter Seven

The Proven Benefits of the Social Constructivist Approach

An investment in any early childhood program would produce benefits for young learners. In an era of scarce resources, however, it is essential to determine which particular approaches and pedagogies are best able to realize the benefits of early childhood education. Chapter 7 shows that the most effective early childhood education programs are those that are designed to develop in children the capacity to construct knowledge by building meaningful relationships.

The chapter first presents compelling evidence showing that early education programs that prioritize social constructivist practices are particularly able to achieve the precise educational, social, and economic benefits that realize a return on an investment of resources in early education.

The chapter then presents the most recent evidence from neuroscience and behavioral science that reveals precisely how and why the social constructivist approach to early childhood education produces particularly robust investment returns. Specifically, an early learning environment designed to develop in children the ability to construct knowledge through meaningful relationships strengthens their mirror neurons, inter-subjectivity, and executive function. Those capacities are directly linked to the success and well-being that bring remarkable investment returns to the child and to the nation.

THE SOCIAL CONSTRUCTIVIST APPROACH HAS BEEN PROVEN TO PRODUCE ROBUST EDUCATIONAL, SOCIAL, AND ECONOMIC BENEFITS

The social constructivist approach, which is exemplified by the early learning centers in Reggio Emilia, Italy, has been proven to produce particularly robust educational, economic, and social returns from an investment in early childhood education.

Overwhelming evidence compiled by James Heckman and others demonstrates that early childhood programs that develop the ability to engage in meaningful relationships are far more likely to produce educational, economic, and social benefits than are the programs that concentrate primarily on traditional academic achievement.

The longitudinal study of children enrolling in the HighScope Perry Preschool program produced data regarding the efficacy of various pedagogical approaches to early childhood education. The children in the treatment group who were given a high-quality early childhood education program were subdivided into three groups. Each group was given a different early childhood education delivery model:

- The "Direct Instruction" model, in which teachers initiated drill and practice activities designed to reward children for responding correctly to a predetermined set of tests to measure academic performance;
- The "Nursery School" model, in which teachers facilitated self-initiated play of students and introduced projects in a relatively unstructured, supportive environment; and
- The "HighScope" Perry model, in which teachers arranged the classroom and daily routine to enable active learning by children, who play and engage in their own activities in small and large groups and who are observed to determine whether they demonstrate key developmental indicators.

All aspects of the treatment group's early childhood education programs were identical, except for the delivery model. After one year of pre-K, the overall average IQ of children in all three groups rose 27 points, from a borderline level of 78 to a normal range level of 105. Ultimately the average IQ settled at 95, within the normal range. By age 23, however, the differences in the results of the three different early childhood education approaches became acute.

Children given the "Direct Instruction" model of early childhood education demonstrated no statistical advantage over children who were given the other two models. But children who received the "HighScope" model showed tremendous advantages over those children who received the "Direct Instruction" program.

Although the "Nursery School" group performed significantly better than the "Direct Instruction" group, the "HighScope" group had eight significant advantages over the "Direct Instruction" group, including fewer felony arrests, fewer arrests for property crimes, fewer years requiring treatment for emotional impairment or disturbance, fewer anger management issues, less teen misconduct, a higher percentage living with spouse, more who planned to graduate from college, and more who did volunteer work.[1]

By performing and refining sophisticated statistical regression analyses of a wealth of data, Professor Heckman has demonstrated that early childhood programs that are designed to develop so-called non-cognitive skills are likely to achieve the greatest socio-economic returns.[2] These critical skills are: (1) "the ability to work with others" and (2) "socio-emotional regulation," including perseverance.[3]

The Perry School and Abecedarian Projects demonstrate the critical significance of developing these skills. Although initial gains in IQ scores for the treatment group dissipated over time, the academic achievement scores of those children who developed these skills in an early childhood program continued to increase relative to the control group.

Professor Heckman concludes from this evidence—as well as from consistent evidence from other research—that the development of social and emotional competencies is critical to obtaining the academic, social, and economic benefits of a pre-K program. Among these competencies, "the ability to work with others" through meaningful relationships characterized by caring, cooperation, and communication is particularly critical to economic success and well-being.[4] He concludes that these relationship-building skills are important based on evidence that people who perform poorly on traditional standardized tests nonetheless do well in life if early interventions have developed those skills.

Professor Heckman likewise shows that people who perform well on traditional standardized tests nonetheless do poorly in life if they have not developed such relationship-building skills. Heckman's research therefore indicates that an early childhood education program designed merely to produce children who can demonstrate apparent competence in traditional "academic" skills will not achieve as much long-term economic, educational, and social benefit as a program designed to support children in their development of meaningful relationships.

Heckman's conclusion that relationship-building skills are more important to success than traditional academic skills is supported by the extraordinary work of Paul Tough. With the keen eye of a journalist, Mr. Tough has chronicled the lives of young people and the determinants of their economic and personal well-being.

In his book, *How Children Succeed: Grit, Curiosity, and the Hidden Power of Character,* Mr. Tough shows that qualities such as grit, persistence, conscientiousness, and self-control are crucial to success.[5] These qualities comprise what neuroscientists call "executive function." They all are developed through meaningful relationships in a child's early learning environment. Moreover, Tough reports that the quality of those relationships in the early environments of children who grow up in poverty are far more important to their educational, social, and economic well-being than the level of their intellectual stimulation.[6]

As both Tough and Heckman recognize, their research has profound pedagogical implications. Tough observes:

> The problem is that science isn't yet reflected in the way we run our schools. . . . And that's a big part of why so many low-income kids don't do well in school. We now know better than ever what kind of help they need to succeed in school. But very few schools are equipped to deliver that help.[7]

The evidence demonstrates that those early childhood education pedagogical methods that include an emphasis on social development and executive function produce significantly greater educational, economic, and social benefits than those that emphasize traditional, short-sighted measures of "academic" performance.

Differences in pre-K curricula can produce important differences in the academic, social, and economic success of children.[8] The skills of relationship-building and internal self-control all have "significant positive effects on earnings and the rate of returns to education."[9] The evidence is clear that these skills matter.[10]

The positive effects of early childhood interventions are "not attributable to IQ improvements of children, but rather to their success in boosting non-cognitive skills."[11] Enhanced relationship building and socio-emotional regulation promote learning, even as measured in achievement test scores.[12] In fact, between 30 and 40 percent of the variance in achievement test scores is attributable to these social skills and not intelligent quotient.[13]

A pre-K curriculum that promotes "social competency" therefore will positively alter life outcomes in the most significant way.[14] The Perry curriculum is designed to implement the social-constructivist principles of Lev Vygotsky, by which children are encouraged to engage with adults, peers, and their environment to construct their own knowledge.[15] The Perry curriculum stressed collaboration, the development of meaningful interpersonal relations, and interpersonal skills.[16]

The positive impact of the Perry project on life outcomes can be precisely tied to its emphasis on social-emotional skills. In particular, the Perry curriculum focused upon developing "executive function" and reducing "externalizing behavior," including socially disruptive interactions. The "HighScope" Perry students emerged from the program with significantly less propensity for socially destructive behavior than the control students. The Perry students also exhibited significantly less "externalizing behavior" than the control group students.

The fact that the Perry students exhibited significantly less "externalizing behavior" than the control students ultimately resulted in significant economic benefits from reduced anti-social and criminal behavior in adolescence and adulthood.[17] Reducing externalizing behavior in early childhood learning environments is precisely linked to a reduction in crime and involvement with the criminal justice system, as well as an increase in employment, wages, and wellness.[18] Similarly, student perseverance is precisely linked to labor market outcome through a reduction in unemployment.[19]

As Heckman concludes: "Success in life depends on personality traits that are not well captured by measures of cognition. Conscientiousness, perseverance, sociability, and curiosity matter."[20]

The Perry Preschool Program improved the lives of its students (and reduced the social costs of education, health, and crime) by changing their "personality traits in a lasting way."[21] The Perry program "substantially improved externalizing behaviors (aggressive, antisocial, and rule-breaking behaviors), which, in turn, improved a number of labor market outcomes and health behaviors and reduced criminal activities."[22] The program also significantly increased "academic motivation," particularly in girls.[23] Furthermore, "[e]nhanced personality skills promote learning, which, in turn, boosts achievement test scores."[24] As Heckman concludes: "a few hours of preschool at ages three and four with a curriculum that promotes social competency, planning, and organization can significantly and beneficially affect life outcomes."[25]

The ability to engage in meaningful relationships and to use executive function to facilitate focus and perseverance leads directly to positive educational achievement, labor market performance, and health.[26] Indeed, the evidence demonstrates that social-constructivist early childhood education programs have "improved the lives of [their] participants, demonstrating why it is problematic to focus curricula exclusively on improving cognitive test scores."[27]

In "Educational Effectiveness of a Vygotskian Approach to Preschool Education: a Randomized Trial," the National Institute for Early Education Research confirms that social-constructivist pre-K delivery models are particularly effective in producing dramatic economic, educational, and social benefits.[28] The Perry Model and the Reggio Emilia approach are consistent with Vygotsky's belief that child development is constructed through social relationships, in an environment that encourages children to be active participants with teachers in their own learning.[29]

According to the National Institute for Early Education Research, this approach produces "substantial positive effects on social behavior" relative to other early childhood education models.[30] These effects are linked to the development of self-regulation[31] and executive function.[32] Critical ingredients in executive function include cognitive flexibility, dedicated memory, and self-control.[33]

Independent studies using controlled randomized trials also have revealed that the social constructivist approach to early childhood produces significantly greater long-term benefits than the direct-instruction approach.[34] Children in social constructivist early childhood education environments far surpass those in direct instruction environments in skills critical to success in life, particularly collaboration, executive function, and perseverance. Moreover, children educated in social constructivist environments actually surpass their direct instruction peers on academic achievement tests measured over time.[35]

After reviewing the evidence comparing various models of early childhood education, Alfie Kohn goes so far as to conclude:

> The results are striking for their consistent message that a tightly structured, traditionally academic model for young children provides virtually no lasting benefits and proves to be potentially harmful in many respects.[36]

The conclusion that direct instruction or tightly structured academic models of early childhood education produce "no lasting benefits" for children is perhaps overstated. In the hands of a skilled educator, direct instruction may be used effectively within a social-constructivist environment to help inform the choices that children can make. Yet, what is clear from the evidence is that the long-term educational, economic, and social benefits of a social-constructivist *approach* to early childhood education significantly surpass those from a tightly structured direct instruction approach.[37]

Despite this overwhelming evidence, policy makers still may be tempted to push for programs that prioritize the direct instruction of traditional academic skills. Their temptation may be based on their assumption that children who do not acquire math and literacy skills at home "need" the direct instruction of those skills at school and are not "ready" for social constructivist approaches to education. Policy makers also may assume that social constructivist practices are more expensive than direct instruction. Both assumptions, however, are unfounded.

As the myriad studies and data sets show, the social constructivist approach has been proven to achieve remarkable results for all children, regardless of their race, ethnicity, or socio-economic status. In fact, in order to test the impact of the Reggio Emilia approach on children's learning outcomes,[38] researchers specifically examined data from 74 Reggio-inspired programs in diverse communities from across the United States.[39] Educational programs that are inspired by the Reggio approach rely on direct and authentic measures of student learning through documentation. They do not merely rely upon indirect and inauthentic standardized test scores. Nonetheless, some Reggio-inspired programs do collect child outcome data, largely because of government regulations.[40] The results of the research are clear and compelling: children in these programs, many of whom have significant educational risk factors, score better than or at least as well as their counterparts in programs that are not Reggio-inspired.[41]

For example, the Reggio Magnet School of the Arts in Avon, Connecticut, is one of 18 magnet schools formed in response to a court order to integrate Hartford.[42] Half of the school's students are from Hartford, and half live in the surrounding suburbs.[43] Forty-eight percent of the students come from families with extremely low socio-economic status and are eligible for free or reduced lunch.[44] The students' backgrounds are also diverse: 25.39 percent are Hispanic, 31.16 percent are white, and 39 percent are African American.[45]

In September 2011, 87 percent of all students, 81 percent of students on free and reduced lunch, and 75 percent of students from Hartford in the three-year-olds' classroom were rated proficient on the Peabody Picture Vocabulary Test.[46] In May 2012, that number reached 100 percent in all categories. In September, 49 percent of students in the four-year-olds' classroom (many of whom are new to the school) received a "basic" score (the lowest rating) on the Literacy Profile Card.[47] By January, that number was reduced to 0 percent, and by the close of the school year, 100 percent of the children reached proficiency.[48]

Another Reggio-inspired school serving a diverse population of children achieved similar measurable results. The Velma F. Thomas Early Childhood Center in Chicago, Illinois, serves 224 pre-K and kindergarten children, 72 percent of which are Hispanic, and 62 percent of which are Spanish speaking.[49] Ninety-seven percent come from low-income families and 16 percent have special needs.[50]

In third grade, public school students take the Illinois Standards Achievement Test (ISAT).[51] To date, two cohorts of alumni have taken the test. In 2010, 70 percent of the students scored at "meets" or "exceeds" with 25 percent at "exceeds."[52] In 2011, 74 percent scored at "meets" or "exceeds."[53] These scores are significantly better than those of other similarly situated low-income students in the state who attended schools that emphasized traditional academic skills and who did not have the advantage of attending a Reggio-inspired school.[54]

The available data indicate that the social constructivist approach, exemplified by the Reggio Emilia experience, is effective in supporting the learning of all children.[55] This is true in public and private elementary schools, public early childhood education programs, and Head Start classrooms.[56] The data from Reggio-inspired schools in cities like Chicago and Hartford demonstrate that this approach works well for all children, and particularly well for disadvantaged students.[57]

Nor is there any evidence that social constructivist practices are more expensive than other approaches to early childhood education. The materials in a social constructivist learning environment are beautiful, but they are also inexpensive. They are often natural or repurposed. The teachers are particularly adept at really listening to children and making visible the learning that takes place in the environment. But the cost of teaching professional educators to use best social constructivist practices is no greater than the cost of training them to use outmoded and disproven practices.

If the ability to develop meaningful relationships is a skill vital to socio-economic success and personal well-being, then early childhood programs should be structured to enable all children to construct those relationships. If knowledge is constructed through meaningful relationships, then early childhood education must be designed to empower all children to construct their own knowledge through their relationships with their teachers, peers, and environments.

RECENT DISCOVERIES IN COGNITIVE NEUROSCIENCE AND PSYCHOLOGY DEMONSTRATE HOW THE SOCIAL CONSTRUCTIVIST APPROACH PRODUCES PARTICULARLY ROBUST RETURNS ON AN INVESTMENT IN EARLY CHILDHOOD EDUCATION

By performing careful analyses of numerous data sets, Heckman and others have identified skills such as the ability to work with others, socio-emotional regulation, and perseverance as the key ingredients in lifelong success and well-being. As the most recent evidence from the field of cognitive neuroscience and psychology demonstrates, however, these ingredients are interrelated.

Relying on sophisticated research techniques including brain imaging, the world's foremost neuroscientists and psychologists have discovered that a child's cognitive process are significantly improved through meaningful relationships in the child's early learning environment.[58] Specifically, an early learning environment that enables a child to construct knowledge by building meaningful relationships produces particularly robust investment returns because it develops a child's mirror neurons, inter-subjectivity, healthy integration of mental processes, healthy attachment, well-being, and executive function.

Each of these transformations that take place in a child's brain bring tremendous benefits to the child and the community. The development of each of those cognitive processes is linked to the strength of a child's ability to work with others and executive function, the very qualities that result in robust educational, social, and economic benefits.

The Social Constructivist Approach Develops Mirror Neurons

Vygotsky's discovery that knowledge cannot be constructed without social relationships was way ahead of its time. With the help of imaging technology, the latest neuro-scientific research has validated Vygotsky's insights and demonstrated precisely how the brain constructs knowledge through social relationships.

In "From Neurons to Neighborhoods: The Science of Early Child Development,"[59] the National Academy of Sciences provides path-breaking insights into early childhood brain development. Those insights begin with the discovery of "mirror neurons." In the 1980s, neuroscientist Giacomo Rizzolatti, working at the University of Parma in Italy, discovered that particular neurons, labeled FS, in the premotor cortex of macaque monkeys fired when the monkeys reached for a peanut and when the monkeys observed the experimenter do the same activity. [60] In other words, performing an activity and watching the activity can have the same impact on the brain. In 1996, the researchers identified their discovery by the term "mirror neurons."[61]

The existence of these mirror neurons in animals led to their discovery in humans. Rizzolatti and Luciano Fadiga found that discrete muscles in the hands of humans twitched both when the individual and the experimenter were grasping for the same objects.[62] Magnetic Resonance Imaging has since confirmed the function of mirror neurons in humans. Although it is difficult to isolate the particular neurons in a human being that are equally activated by the act of doing and seeing, and there is some debate about the true significance of mirror neurons, neuroscientists have been able to identify specific regions in the frontal cortex and the parietal lobule of humans that fire equally when an individual performs an activity and when an individual observes another person doing the same activity.

Research also has revealed the step-by-step process by which all neurons, including mirror neurons, operate. An experience or internal motivation initially triggers activation of a particular set of neurons in a person's brain. Ions are transmitted from activated neuronal cell bodies to intermediary neurons and their final destinations via axon membranes. These longitudinal projections carry messages throughout the body in the form of electrical currents that have potential to trigger specific biological responses.

Signals are passed from neuron to adjacent neuron through synaptic spaces, wherein electrical currents from the terminal end of the activated neuron incite the release of chemical neurotransmitters that activate the next neuron in the chain. The transmission process continues until the electrical impulse is in position to elicit the originally intended response. Certain lines of transmission of neuronal message can be conditioned to function more readily when the neurons are repeatedly activated through recurring experiences, emotional arousal, and dedicated focus.[63]

In this way, a child's early experiences change the structure of the brain. As Dr. Daniel J. Siegel writes, "from our first days of life, our immature brain is also directly shaped by our interactions with the world, especially by our relationships."[64] These early relationships create repetitive neural firings that strengthen the synaptic connections between neurons. When neurons are activated together, the genes in their nuclei "express" themselves by producing proteins that in turn reshape and strengthen the synaptic connectors.[65] In addition, these early experiences generate myelin that dramatically increases the speed at which the electrical currents travel.

The development of the mind therefore is a *"relational"* process.[66] As Siegel demonstrates, "[e]nergy and information flow between and among people . . . [o]ur minds are created within relationships."[67] Reviewing all of the research regarding mirror neurons, Dr. Siegel concludes: "mirror neurons help us to understand the nature of culture and how our shared behaviors bind us together, mind to mind."[68] Human beings "first know [them] selves as reflected in the others."[69] Attachment with others is prior to, and necessary for, self-awareness. Therefore, "[d]evelopmentally and evolutionarily, our modern self-awareness" is based upon our human experience as social beings.

When a child internalizes the energy and information received through social interactions, that child begins the process of constructing knowledge.[70] The feelings and sensations that a child acquires in a relationship with others alter that child's "critical awareness, shaping how we reason and make decisions."[71] As Siegel concludes: "Relationships are woven into the fabric of our intense world. We come to know our own minds through our interactions with others."[72]

The fact that human brains react the same way when they are doing an activity as when they observe another person doing the same activity further led researchers to discover the neuroscientific basis for human emotions such as empathy. Christian Keysers and his colleagues have demonstrated that the same area of the somatosensory cortex reacted in the same way when individuals were lightly touched on the leg with a feather-duster device as when they watched pictures of someone else being touched in the same way.[73] From this research, Keysers concludes that the capacity for "tactile empathy" exists within the chemistry of the human brain. Similarly, a particular part of the brain called the "anterior insula" was equally activated when an individual experienced the emotion of disgust from inhaling noxious odors as when that individual observed another person appear to experience the same emotion of disgust.[74]

The next step in the research regarding mirror neurons was to determine how human beings respond to their perceptions of the feelings and intentions of others. The most recent research indicates that mirror neurons respond not only to the acts and emotions of others, but also to the motivations and intentions behind those acts and emotions. Marco Iacoboni and his colleagues found that mirror neurons in the premotor cortex react differently when the individual perceives different intentions behind the same activity.

Thus, the same act of a hand picking up a teacup triggers a stronger reaction when the observer perceives the intention behind the action to be taking a sip of tea from the cup rather than clearing the cup from a cluttered table.[75] According to Iacoboni, this research suggests that "neurons are important for understanding intentions as well as actions."[76] They help to explain empathy and the evolution of communication itself.[77]

As neuroscientist Vittorio Gallese at the University of Parma observes: the neural mechanism is "automatic"; human beings react naturally with empathy for the feelings of others and with an understanding of the intentions of others.[78] Gallese concludes from all of the latest neuroscience research: "It seems we're wired to see other people as similar to us, rather than different. At the root, as humans we identify the person we're facing as someone like ourselves."[79]

Moreover, mirror neurons are critical to human survival because they enable individuals to perceive the intentions of others and to respond to them appropriately.[80] Neuroscientist V.S. Ramachandram at the University of California, San Diego conducted early research regarding mirror neurons and has concluded that they are the "basis for civilization."[81] As he explains, "If I really and truly empathize with your pain, I need to experience it myself. That's what the mirror neurons are doing, allowing me to empathize with your pain."[82] Thus, they are "important in transmitting skills from generation to generation. I need to put myself in your shoes to observe what you are doing, and to mime it accurately. Mirror neurons are important in that."[83]

The human disposition to internalize the feelings and intentions of others is transmitted both genetically and socially through a cultural context.[84] Accordingly, leading psychologist V.S. Ramachandram has determined that the discovery of mirror neurons is one of the "single most important unpublicized stories of the decade."[85]

Significantly, the process of constructing knowledge about the intentions of others does not emanate from a logical thought process. Rather, human beings come to understand their environments and the intentions of others not by thinking, but by feeling.[86]

Individuals experience the intentions in others automatically. Evidence from research regarding mirror neurons therefore also calls into question the traditional dichotomy between reason and emotion. Language is formed from the natural desire of humans to mimic others, not from traditional logic or cognitive functions. The basis for human survival is not a purely rational apprehension of danger followed by a purely rational cost-benefit response. Rather, human survival depends on our innate capacity to feel the intentions of others, to internalize the intentions of others and to act in relationships with others.[87]

The research regarding mirror neurons also unpacks the social construction of language. The mirror neuron system is the basic foundation from which language evolved. As Vygotsky argued, and as the latest neuroscience confirms, language develops in a social relationship. One child observes another's child's behavior, internalizes that other child's feelings and intentions, and mimics those feelings, intentions, and behaviors through mirror neurons. The communication that takes place between them, which is fueled by mirror neurons, is language. That language is only possible through a social dynamic. Thus, the human capacity for language, and the human capacity for survival, are dependent on the human ability to internalize the feelings and intentions of others.

As Vygotsky demonstrated, and as neuroscience confirms, a child's initial act of grasping for an object becomes a communicative gesture to a caregiver who understands the child's intention is to want the object. The child then learns to communicate through hand gesturing.[88] This process is consistent with the mirror neuron explanation for speech development: "When an individual listens to verbal stimuli, there is an automatic activation of his speech-related motor centers."[89] What is special about speech sounds is their "capacity to evoke the motor representation of the heard sounds in the listener's motor cortex."[90]

Mirror neurons evolved to enable human beings to link gestures with sounds. Accordingly, "heard speech sounds produced not only a tendency to imitate the sound but also an understanding of the accompanying body-action gestures."[91] In a recent study at Arizona State University, researchers have found that mirror neurons also play a role in the learning of a second language."[92] Their work confirms that the mirror neuron system not only can support language acquisition, it can be shaped and strengthened through the process of language acquisition.[93]

The development of mirror neurons in an early learning environment enables children to build positive meaningful relationships throughout their lives. Additionally, an early childhood program designed to exercise these mirror neurons by supporting relationships thereby creates habits of mind and heart that are critical to life-long success and well-being.[94]

The Social Constructivist Approach Develops Inter-Subjectivity

Inter-subjectivity is the process by which mental activities, intentions, and emotions are transferred between individuals. Human inter-subjectivity is the instantaneous appreciation of the feelings and intentions of others. That appreciation is communicated through multiple forms of expression, including facial movements, body adjustments, hand gestures, and vocalizations.

The messages communicated by these expressions have evolved through generations and cultures. They give immediate cues about the feelings and intentions of others. The expressions have meaning to individuals only within the social context in which they are communicated. The evolution of the capacity to understand the thoughts, feelings, and intentions of others is critical to human survival, and critical to well-being in any particular social situation.

Inter-subjectivity grows through interpersonal relations in which children further develop their understanding of another person's thoughts and emotions. Inter-subjectivity is the essence of humanity. Children are born with the capacity to develop inter-subjectivity.[95] Overwhelming evidence of "the earliest orientations, preferences, and intentional actions of newborns . . . prove[s] that the newborn human is ready for, and needs, mutually regulated intersubjective" interactions.[96]

But a child's level of inter-subjectivity decrease in early learning environments that do not nurture inter-subjectivity. Conversely, a child's capacity for inter-subjectivity grows when the child interacts with individuals who sincerely appreciate the child's capacity for inter-subjectivity.[97]

Language provides a short cut to inter-subjectivity by allowing individuals to store and carry common meanings and mental perceptions. But language is not the basis for interpersonal relationships. The opposite is true; language develops after social relationships are formed through inter-subjectivity. The meaning of letters and words is acquired by repeating or imitating dynamic exchanges between the child and companions in which they share intentions and feelings.[98]

As Colwyn Trevarthen observes, empirical evidence of human inter-subjectivity undercuts a strong current in the Western philosophic tradition that presumes that individuals are naturally overwhelmed by their self-serving emotions that must be regulated by conventional rewards and punishments:

> The evidence that infants learn by emotional referencing to evaluate experiences through attunement with motives of familiar companions, for whom they have, and from whom they receive, affectionate regard, proves that it is the sense of individuality in society that is the derived state of mind, developed in contrast to more fundamental intersubjective needs and obligations.[99]

In exercising their natural disposition toward inter-subjectivity, individuals find great joy; they realize what they have in common with others.[100]

The evolutionary development that allowed human beings to become the dominant species was the ability to engage in inter-subjective communication that facilitated levels of cooperation, as opposed to competition, that exceed those of any other primates. Unlike chimpanzees, human children are "motivated to cooperate for the sake of cooperation"; have the capacity to engage in "altruism and cooperation"; and are able to "exchange complementary roles" with others.[101] Inter-subjectivity thus has a "ubiquitous role that permeates all other mental functions and makes us uniquely human."[102] By building a child's capacity for inter-subjectivity, a social constructivist learning program enables the child to recognize, respect and respond to the thoughts, feelings, and intentions of others. The child acquires the tools to engage in the kind of meaningful relationships that are vital to success and well-being.

The Social Constructivist Approach Develops the Healthy Integration of Cognitive Processes

Daniel J. Siegel has found that "We come into the world wired to make connections with one another, and the subsequent neural shaping of our brain, the very foundation of our sense of self, is built upon these intimate exchanges between the infant and the caregiver. In the early years, this interpersonal regulation is essential for survival, but throughout our lives we continue to need such connections for a sense of vitality and well-being."[103]

According to Dr. Siegel, meaningful early childhood relationships transform the prefrontal cortex in the brain, thereby integrating the cognitive processes that are essential to success and well-being, including: (1) bodily regulation; (2) attuned communication; (3) emotional balance; (4) response flexibility; (5) fear modulation; (6) empathy; (7) insight; (8) moral awareness; and (9) intuition.[104]

The meaningful relationships supported in a social constructivist early learning environment also develop this healthy "integration." In its broadest sense, integration is the bringing together of different components into a single system. As Siegel writes: "In a relationship, integration entails each person being respected for his or her autonomy and differentiated self, while at the same time being linked to others in emphatic communication."[105]

Such a relationship develops a healthy brain. Siegel demonstrates that well-being and higher-order mental processing skills require an integrated mind, one in which apparently disparate components of mental processes such as thoughts and feelings, logic, and intuition are linked to each other through extremely active synaptic connections. These connections are vital to coherent cognitive functioning, self-regulating emphatic relationships, resilience, health, and well-being.[106]

The path breaking research of Nobel Prize–winning psychologist Daniel Kahneman confirms that the importance of developing a healthy integration of cognitive process. Kahneman demonstrates that the process of thinking cannot be segregated into traditional "cognitive" abilities like literacy and math and other abilities such as intuition, emotion, and empathy.[107]

Kahneman's evidence challenges the presumption that human behavior is the product of purely rational, cost-benefit decision making.[108] With his colleague Amos Tversky, Professor Kahneman discovered that most people do not actually make decisions that are consistent with maximizing their own expected utility. He created a "map of bounded rationality, by exploring the systematic biases that separate the beliefs that people have and the choices that they make from the optimal beliefs and choices assumed in rational agent models."[109]

As Kahneman explains: "We show that people are not adequately characterized as fully rational by a definition of rationality which is completely unrealistic. This is the definition of rationality in standard decision theory."[110]

According to Kahneman, the choices that individuals make are bounded by their social contexts, frames, or environments. Humans are prone to many cognitive biases or heuristics that distort their judgment. These heuristics produce decisions that cannot be separated from their social context and cannot fully be explained by classical models of pure rational choice or subjective utility.[111] For instance, individuals display a bias toward loss aversion; they feel the pain of a loss much more acutely than the pleasure of an equivalent gain. As such, their decisions reflect a "status quo bias" and "an endowment effect" which leads them to over-value what they have and to refrain from making many value-maximizing transactions. Contrary to the model of the rational decision-maker, Kahneman proved that the objects of choice are assessed by individuals through an emotional and intuitive psychological process.

As Kahneman also shows, the complexity of human thought and action can be understood by envisioning two systems operating simultaneously in the brain. System 1 drives the brain's first response; it is the mind's quick, automatic, intuitive, and mostly unconscious, associative response to stimuli. System 2 is the slow, deliberate, conscious, calculating, analytical, laborious, and seemingly rational mode of cognition.

The rapid judgments and reactions directed by System 1 are indispensable to human survival; but they are also influenced by biases and mistakes. System 1 generates an effortless response to a choice. Yet, when an appropriate response is not readily accessible, System 1 produces a response to a different choice, one that is only "associatively" related to the actual choice presented.[112] Kahneman also performed many experiments and observations, which demonstrate that the rapid associations and intuitions produced by System 1 usually overwhelm and therefore skew the supposed objective deliberations of System 2. As a consequence, individual choices are more likely to reflect predictable intuitions than purely rational calculations.

The "calculating mind" has commonly been thought to be the home of the kind of cognition measured by standardized achievement tests. Yet Kahneman proves that that calculating mind is highly influenced by social context and emotions such as empathy. Indeed, the skills that often are perceived to be non-cognitive (such as the ability to develop meaningful relationships) cannot be separated from the thinking process; they are the leading drivers of cognition itself.[113]

Social constructivist early childhood education programs are designed to support these social-emotional skills. As Kahneman's research confirms, by strengthening a child's ability to develop meaningful relationships, social constructivist early childhood education programs also strengthen a child's cognition.

In this sense, a meaningful relationship assumes that each of the participants in the relationship is a sentient human being. Yet, such relationships also can be developed between individuals when they experience materials in their environment.

David Hawkins writes brilliantly about the relationship that forms between a child, a teacher and such materials. The relationship is formed from respect.[114] When a teacher explores an object with a child, the teacher has made possible a "relation between the child and 'It.'"[115] The material is "a basis for communication with the teacher on a new level, and with new dignity."[116] The "child comes alive for the teacher as well as the teacher for the child."[117] The materials present a common theme for their engagement; "they are involved together in the world."[118]

The relationships that a child forms with teachers, peers, and materials allow the child to develop the indispensable "capacity for synthesis, for building a stable framework within which many episodes of experience can be put together coherently."[119] The child's ability to explore new relationships, to differentiate those relationships, and to integrate them into the child's evolving sense of reality of the world is vital to that child's well-being.[120] As Hawkins shows, a child's critical "synthetic achievements in exploratory learning" grow not only "in relation" to teachers and other caregivers, but also "in relation" to the child's "surrounding physical environment."[121]

Not surprisingly, the latest research regarding the acquisition of literacy indicates that children learn to read by building relationships with the "inanimate" material presented in a book.[122] Indeed, profound writers have recognized that a relationship develops between the author of a book and the reader, a relationship that transcends the words on a page.[123]

Reading is one way in which a child continues the process of making meaning by integrating new information into known information, detecting similarities and differences amid patterns.[124] Reading does not take place without a relationship between the author, the reader and the text, in a "sociocultural context." By supporting the development in children of the capacity to build meaningful relationships, social constructivist programs facilitate the healthy integration of mental processes that is indispensable to learning.

The Social Constructivist Approach Develops Healthy Attachment Relationships

Cognitive abilities are intertwined with all other human motivational constructs, including attachment. Meaningful attachment relationships are based upon contingent communication. The quality, intensity, and timing of an educator's signals to a child support the "development of many domains, including social, emotional, and cognitive functioning."[125] A relationship built upon reflective communication enables children to assess their own process of constructing knowledge, which helps them to refine those particular learning strategies that are successful for them.[126]

Early attachment experiences also alter the chemicals in the brain that develop the nervous system's capacity to support emotional resilience. Social interactions and attachments that are perceived to be positive support emotional resilience, while those that are negative "diminish emotional resilience in children and compromise their ability to adjust to stressful events in the future."[127] The lack of a healthy primary attachment relationship can have an immediate detrimental effect on inter-subjective understanding.[128] A child who develops unrepaired patterns of insecure or traumatic attachment has difficulty understanding, respecting, and responding to the thoughts, feelings, and intentions of others.[129] Security of attachment on the other hand allows a child to develop a healthy sense of self and resilience—the ability to overcome effects of negative consequences or experiences.[130]

Children who experience reciprocal responsiveness in early learning environments associated with a secure attachment are more likely to exhibit control over their behavior, resulting in a decreased risk of externalizing behaviors.[131]

By building or rebuilding a child's capacity for attachment, a social constructivist learning environment therefore develops the child's socio-emotional control and perseverance in the face of negative events and challenges. Children who experience an early learning environment associated with a secure attachment are also more likely to exhibit control over their behavior, resulting in a decreased risk of externalizing behaviors.[132]

The security in feeling that a disruption in the relationship will be repaired allows a child to develop grit, resiliency, and perseverance in the face of life's inevitable hardships. If a relationship includes profound communication of both negative and positive emotions, the child will learn that he will not be abandoned during a period of emotional pain or loss, and will not be isolated in his feelings of joy.

The attachment relationships experienced by children in their early learning environments are critical to their ability to develop what Paul Tough calls "grit." Put simply, the quality of "grit" is the ability to persevere or "stick to" a problem or an experience even in the face of hardship or struggle. A child who was "stuck to" by parents, peers, or educators in an early learning environment is more likely to "stick to" challenges later in life. As Dan Siegel concludes: "interactive forms of emotional communication may be at the core of how interpersonal relationships help to shape the ongoing emotional and social development of the growing mind of the child."[133]

In fact, the forms of attachment that are supported in a social constructivist learning environment develop in children habits of mind and heart that are vital to their life long success and well-being.

First, meaningful attachment relationships in an early learning environment enable children to develop habits of sharing and amplifying positive emotional states (such as joy and elation) and sharing and comforting negative states (such as fear and sadness).[134]

Second, meaningful relationships enable children to develop habits of collaboration, empathy, and emotional communication.[135]

Third, meaningful relationships enable children to develop habits of contingent communication in which the verbal and nonverbal signals of a peer or educator are precisely responsive to the child's. The mind of the child is joined with another person at a basic level of emotion, and each person feels emotionally connected to the other.

Fourth, meaningful relationships enable children to develop habits of reflective dialogue. Each participant feels comfortable sharing their own mental processes, including thoughts, emotions, memories, beliefs, and ideas.

Fifth, meaningful relationships enable children to develop habits of re-establishing relationships when they inevitably become interrupted or disrupted.

Sixth, meaningful relationships enable children to develop habits of joining together with others to co-construct their knowledge about the world by sharing coherent stories about the past, present, and future.

Seventh, meaningful relationships enable children to develop the habits of perseverance and self-regulation when confronted with challenging experiences and emotions. In a meaningful relationship, the emotional connection survives pain and difficult feelings. It is enduring and reliable.[136]

Eighth, meaningful relationships enable children to develop habits of providing and receiving emotional warmth steadfastly and predictably provided over an extended period of time.[137]

Finally, a relationship built upon reflective communication enables children to assess their own process of constructing knowledge, which helps them to refine those particular learning strategies that are successful for them.

The Social Constructivist Approach Develops Habits of Well-Being

The field of hedonic psychology provides remarkable new data regarding the social determinants of happiness and well-being.[138] The overwhelming evidence is that the single most important factor in fostering happiness and well-being is the quality of a person's relationships. Children who have developed the ability to form and maintain meaningful relationships are happy and healthy adults. They are significantly happier and healthier than their peers who do not have such meaningful relationships.[139]

Moreover, although there is a connection between the ability to form meaningful relationships and economic success, those children who have formed meaningful relationships are even happier and healthier than their wealthier peers who have not formed those relationships.

In "A Survey Method for Characterizing Daily Experience: The Day Reconstruction Method," Daniel Kahneman and his colleagues present their transformative research regarding the determinants of happiness and well-being. The evidence indicates that individuals experience the greatest degree of happiness from their social relationships.[140] People report greater levels of happiness from their relationships with friends than any other activity.[141] Although relationships with friends bring the greatest level of enjoyment, relationships with spouses and family also bring relatively strong feelings of happiness and satisfaction.

Significantly, income and even education level have "little impact on the enjoyment of a regular day."[142] In fact, positive affect ratings are associated with all kinds of meaningful relationships. The data reveal that "substantial differences in household income have a modest influence on enjoyment, . . . which shrinks to marginal statistical significance under controls."[143] Although extremely low levels of household income can create stresses of subsistence that greatly diminish happiness, levels of wealth above subsistence have no statistically significant connection to happiness.

Every reliable study conducted after Professor Kahneman presented his research has confirmed that the most significant determinant of happiness—whether measured as momentary feelings, reflective thoughts or life satisfaction—is the quality of a person's relationships.[144] In fact, the evidence shows that "very happy people" differ from unhappy or modestly happy people in the level of their "fulsome and satisfying interpersonal lives."[145]

The quality of relationships also is connected to physical well-being, health, and wellness. Meaningful relationships increase immunity to disease and infection, lower the risk of heart disease, and reduce the degree of cognitive decline through the aging process.[146] Indeed, the absence of meaningful relationships is as deleterious to health as obesity or smoking.[147] It is not surprising therefore that James Heckman, in *Giving Kids a Fair Chance (A Strategy That Works)*,[148] presents irrefutable evidence that early childhood programs that develop in children the capacity to build meaningful relationships actually produce significant health advantages, including a reduction in obesity, blood pressure, and hypertension.

Accordingly, the acquisition in early childhood of the ability to form meaningful relationships is not only vital to happiness and well-being, it also reduces the personal and social costs of ill health.

The Social Constructivist Approach Develops Executive Function

An early childhood learning environment that prioritizes relationship building skills not only develops mirror neurons, inter-subjectivity, attachment, cognitive integration, happiness, health, and well-being, it also fosters executive function. The concept of "executive function" typically includes three types of capacities: working memory, cognitive flexibility, and inhibitory control.[149] These capacities enable individuals to make plans, stay focused, and control impulses.[150] Children are born with the potential to perform these critical skills, but they are developed in early learning environments in which children construct their knowledge through meaningful relationships.

Working memory is the ability to collect and manage information in the mind for short periods of time so that the information can be immediately used.[151] Cognitive flexibility is the ability to adjust mental strategies to meet changing circumstances, including the ability to try different approaches to solving problems, resolving conflict, and overcoming obstacles.[152] Inhibitory control is the capacity to master impulses, resist temptations, and avoid distractions. In its absence, people act entirely on their immediate feelings, lose focus and attention, and pursue instant gratification.

Children who do not develop their executive function in early childhood "have a very hard time managing the routine tasks of daily life."[153] As Paul Tough has observed, and as the latest economic and neuroscientific research confirms, executive function provides an important "link between early school achievement and social, emotional and moral development."[154]

Which approaches to early childhood education are best able to develop executive function? There is overwhelming evidence that social constructivist programs that develop in children the capacity to build meaningful relationships thereby also develop their executive function.[155] Children who receive an early childhood education based on the social constructivist approach show significant improvement in executive function capacities compared with children who receive an early childhood education focused on traditional academic skills.[156]

Moreover, children who experience an early childhood education curriculum based on early literacy and math skills emerged with far less skill in attention and impulse control than the children who experienced an early learning environment dedicated to developing executive function.[157] In fact, because the development of executive function is critical to cognitive flexibility, the ability of a child to control impulsivity contributes significantly to long-term academic achievement.[158]

The healthy growth of executive function depends on the proper development of particular regions of the child's brain.[159] Early learning environments can have a dramatic impact on the development of these regions and the fluidity of interconnections between them.[160]

The mental process associated with executive function is connected to brain structures that manage a child's response to stress.[161] A child whose brain has developed executive function in early learning environments is better able to manage stress throughout life.[162]

Executive function also provides the foundation for traditional academic success: "Children with stronger working memory, inhibitors and attentional skills also have been found to make larger gains on tests of early math, language, literacy development during the preschool years than their peers with weaker executive function skills."[163] Executive function is particularly predictive of future academic success in math and reading among children from "economically disadvantaged" families.[164] Children who do not grow executive function skills not only have difficulty in school, they also display significantly more confrontational and aggressive externalizing behaviors as adults.[165]

Although children have an innate genetic predisposition toward executive function, they do not simply acquire executive function through the mere passage of time. Children do not just "outgrow" their inabilities to focus, control impulses, or adjust to challenging circumstances. Rather, early learning experiences are crucial to the development of executive function.[166]

Early childhood education programs that enable children to develop meaningful, positive relationships are particularly effective in supporting the growth of executive function. As the Harvard Graduate School of Education has concluded: "A young child's environment of relationships plays an important role in the development of executive capacities."[167] The learning environment must provide opportunities for children to engage in "social play."[168]

Through cooperative relationships with peers, children necessarily exercise their executive function muscles. They must control their own impulses and emotions, they must collect and manipulate information, they must eliminate distractions and focus on a shared objective, and they must be flexible in response to any problems or obstacles they encounter. A child who learns to engage in constructive social relationships thereby also learns habits of mind that are vital to demonstrating traditional academic achievement: dedicated memory, cognitive activity, focus, and self-control.

Executive function is also promoted in an environment in which children have meaningful, positive relationships with educators. Such educators will understand the child's progress in developing executive capabilities and will present scaffolding opportunities to help the child in practicing their executive function skills until the child is able to perform them without assistance.

A meaningful, positive relationship between the child and the educator is the foundation that allows the child to take risks that will ultimately result in the child's ability to exercise executive function independently. Where that relationship exists, the educator is attuned to the underlying reasons that a child may not have yet developed executive capabilities and will be able to support the child in strengthening those capabilities.

An educator who instead punishes the child for exhibiting an inability to exercise executive function actually exacerbates the cause of that inability. Punishment or threats of punishment increase the stress levels in the child that make control more difficult. In addition, when an educator punishes a child for displaying a symptom of inadequate attachment or integration, the educator actually frustrates the creation of a relationship with the child that might replicate, repair, or replace healthy primary attachment and integration.

A meaningful, positive relationship between teacher and child requires attuned and sustained communication even during periods when the child is expressing uncomfortable emotions. The teacher who dismisses the child's behavior by punishing the behavior without being attentive to the emotional cause effectively abandons the child, reinforcing a pattern of relationships that are antithetical to learning and well-being.

Similarly, a teacher who responds to a child's struggles with executive function by requiring the child to "sit still and learn" traditional math or literacy skills is only further frustrating that child's efforts to develop executive function. A child who is still developing a working memory, cognitive flexibility, and self-control does not benefit from lesson plans likely to frustrate or inhibit the expression of those functions. Conversely, when a teacher supports a child's development of executive function by attending to the relational issues at play, the teacher also simultaneously develops the child's capacity to engage in genuine literacy and mathematics.

After reviewing all of the evidence, therefore, the Harvard Graduate School of Education concludes: "Early education policies that emphasize literacy instruction alone are missing an important opportunity to increase their effectiveness by including attention to the development of executive function skills."[169] Early childhood education programs that are designed to develop executive function, by contrast, not only improve student performance in traditional academic subjects, they establish an indispensable foundation for success and well-being throughout life.

The early childhood education programs that are best able to achieve a robust return on an investment of resources, therefore, are those designed to develop in children the capacity to build meaningful, positive relationships. Rigorous economic analyses of such programs have demonstrated their particular efficacy for all children, regardless of race, ethnicity, or socioeconomic status.

Recent advances in neuroscience, neurobiology, and hedonic psychology show why. When an early learning environment helps children to develop meaningful relationships, it thereby strengthens their mirror neurons, inter-subjectivity, integration of cognitive processes, and capacity for attachment. These capacities in turn build a child's ability to collaborate with others and to engage in executive function. The ability to collaborate with others and engage in executive function also is linked to personal success, health, and well-being. Early childhood programs that develop these capacities in children reduce the social costs of externalizing behavior and produce robust returns on an investment.

NOTES

1. See Lawrence J. Schweinhart and David P. Weikart, *Lasting Differences: The High-Scope Preschool Model Comparison Study Through Age 23* (Ypsilanti, MI: HighScope Press, 1997); Schweinhart et al., *Lifetime Effects: Through Age 40*; Schweinhart and Weikart, "The HighScope Model," 228-231.

2. See James J. Heckman and Yona Rubinstein, "The Importance of Noncognitive Skills: Lessons from the G.E.D. Testing Program," *American Economics Review* 91(2) (2001): 145–49, http://jenni.uchicago.edu/papers/Heckman_Rubinstein_AER_2001_91_2.pdf ("Much of the effectiveness of early childhood interventions comes in boosting noncognitive skills.").

3. Heckman, "Schools, Skills and Synapses," 10. See also Les Borghans, Bas ter Weel, and Bruce A. Weinberg, "Interpersonal Styles and Labor Market Outcomes" (working paper, National Bureau of Economic Research, January 2007), http://www.nber.org/papers/w12846.pdf. See also John F. Tomer, "Adverse Childhood Experiences, Poverty, and Inequality: Toward an Understanding of the Connections and the Cures," *World Economic Review* 3: 20–36 (2014).

4. Ibid.

5. Paul Tough, *How Children Succeed: Grit, Curiosity, and the Hidden Power of Character* (London: Random House, 2013).

6. "About Paul: Q&A," www.paultough.com/about-paul/qa/.

7. Ibid.

8. W. Steven Barnett et al., "Educational Effects of the Tools of the Mind Curriculum: A Randomized Trial," *Early Childhood Research Quarterly* 23 (2008): 299–313.

9. Heckman and Raut, "Intergenerational Long-Term Effects," 22.

10. Ibid., 30.

11. James J. Heckman, Jora Stixrud, and Sergio Urzua, "The Effects of Cognitive and Noncognitive Abilities on Labor Market Outcomes and Social Behavior" (working paper, National Bureau of Economic Research, 2006), 5, http://www.nber.org/papers/w12006.pdf.

12. Heckman, Pinto, and Savelyev, "Understanding the Mechanisms."

13. Lex Borghans et al., "Identification Problems in Personality Psychology," *Personality and Individual Differences*, 51(3) (2011), 315–20, http://www.ncbi.nlm.nih.gov/pmc/articles/PMC3126096/; Lex Borghans et al., "The Economics and Psychology of Personality Traits," *The Journal of Human Resources* 43 (2000), 972–1050, http://www.roa.nl/cv/borghans/pdf/JHR%202008b.pdf.

14. Heckman, Pinto, and Savelyev, "Understanding the Mechanisms," 2053.

15. See, e.g., Heckman, Pinto, and Savelyev, "Understanding the Mechanisms," 2058.

16. Ibid.

17. Ibid., 2053–73.

18. Ibid., 2073.

19. Ibid., 2053.

20. James J. Heckman and Tim Kautz, "Hard Evidence on Soft Skills," NBER Working Paper Series (2012), 3.

21. Ibid., 6.

22. Heckman, Pinto, and Savelyev, "Understanding the Mechanisms," 2053.

23. Ibid.

24. Ibid., 2056.

25. Ibid., 2080.

26. Heckman and Kautz, "Hard Evidence on Soft Skills," 18–19.

27. Ibid., 38.

28. Barnett et al., "Educational Effects," 299–313. See also Brent W. Roberts et al., "The Power of Personality: The Comparative Validity of Personality Traits, Socioeconomic Status, and Cognitive Ability for Predicting Important Life Outcomes," *Perspectives in Psychological Sciences* 2(4) (2007): 313–45; J.A. Durlak et al., "The Impact of Student's Social and Emotional Learning: A Meta-Analysis of School-Based Universal Interventions," *Child Development* 82(1) (2011): 405–32.

29. Heckman and Kautz, "Hard Evidence on Soft Skills," 35. See also Laura E. Berk and Adam Winsler, *Scaffolding Children's Learning: Vygotsky and Early Childhood Education* (National Association for the Education of Young Children, 1995).

30. Barnett et al., "Educational Effects," 299–313. See also Adele Diamond et al., "Preschoool Program Improves Cognitive Control," *Science* 318(5855) (November 2007): 1387–88.

31. Heckman and Kautz, "Hard Evidence on Soft Skills," 32.

32. Diamond et al., "Preschool Program Improves Cognitive Control," 1387–88.

33. Barnett, "Effectiveness of Early Educational Intervention," 35.

34. Alfie Kohn, "Appendix A, The Hard Evidence: Early Childhood Education: The Case Against Direct Instruction of Academic Skills," in *The Schools Our Children Deserve* (Boston: Houghton Mifflin, 2009).

35. Ibid., 4.

36. Ibid., 5.

37. See, e.g., Jeanne E. Montie, Zongping Xiang, and Lawrence Schweinhart, "Preschool Experience in 10 Countries: Cognitive and Language Performance at Age 7," *Early Childhood Research Quarterly* 21 (2005): 313–31; Elizabeth Bonawitz et al., "The Double-Edged Sword of Pedagogy: Instruction Limits Spontaneous Exploration and Discovery," *Cognition* 120(3) (2011): 322–30, http://www.ncbi.nlm.nih.gov/pmc/articles/PMC3369499/.

38. Ben Mardell and Rachel Carbonara, "A Research Project on the Reggio Emilia Approach and Children's Learning Outcomes," *Innovations in Education* (Summer 2013): 6.

39. Ibid., 7.

40. Ibid.

41. Ibid., 8.

42. Ibid., 12.

43. Ibid.

44. Ibid.

45. Ibid., citing School Digger/Reggio Magnet School of the Arts website, http://www.schooldigger.com/go/CT/schools/0070001516/school.aspx.

46. Mardell and Carbonara, "A Research Project," 12.

47. Ibid.

48. Ibid., citing J. Di Pietro Smith personal communication, May 20, 2012.

49. Mardell and Carbonara, "A Research Project," 12.

50. Ibid., citing Chicago Public Schools/Velma F. Thomas Early Childhood Center website.

51. Mardell and Carbonara, "A Research Project," 13.

52. Ibid.

53. Ibid., citing Chicago Public Schools/Velma F. Thomas Early Childhood Center website.

54. Mardell and Carbonara, "A Research Project," 13.

55. Ibid., 16.

56. Ibid.

57. Ibid.

58. B. D. Perry and A. Jackson, "Long and winding road: From neuroscience to policy, program and practice," *In Sight: Victorian Council of Social Services Journal* 9: 4–8 (2014).

59. Committee on Integrating the Science of Early Childhood Development, *From Neurons to Neighborhoods: The Science of Early Childhood Development,* ed. Jack P. Shonkoff and Deborah A. Phillips (Washington, DC: National Academy Press 2000).

60. Lea Winerman, "The Mind's Mirror," *American Psychological Association* 36(9) (October 2005): 48.

61. V. Gallese, "Action Recognition in the Premotor Cortex," *Brain* 119 (1996): 593–609.

62. L. Fadiga et al., "Motor Facilitation During Action Observation: A Magnetic Stimulation Study," *Journal of Neurophysiology* 73(6) (1995): 2608–11, http://jn.physiology.org/content/jn/73/6/2608.full.pdf.

63. Daniel J. Siegel, *Mindsight: The New Science of Personal Transformation* (New York: Bantam Books, 2011), 40.

64. Ibid., 41.

65. Ibid., 42.

66. Ibid., 55.

67. Ibid.

68. Ibid., 60.

69. Ibid., 62.

70. Ibid.

71. Ibid., 63.

72. Ibid.

73. Christian Keysers et al., "A Touching Sight: SII/PV Activation During the Observation and Experience of Touch," *Neuron* 42 (2004): 335–46.

74. Bruno Wicker et al., "Both of Us Disgusted in *My* Insula: The Common Neural Basis of Seeing and Feeling Disgust," *Neuron* 40(3) (2003): 655–64.

75. Marco Iacoboni et al., "Grasping the Intentions of Others With One's Own Mirror Neuron System," *PloS Biology* 3 (3) (2005): e79. See also Marco Iacoboni, *Mirroring People: The Science of Empathy and How We Connect With Others* (New York: Picador, 2009).

76. Ibid.

77. See Winerman, "The Mind's Mirror," 48.

78. Ibid., 45.

79. Ibid.

80. Ibid.

81. Vilayanur S. Ramachandram, *The Tell Tale Brain: A Neuroscientist's Quest for What Makes Us Human* (New York: W.W. Norton, 2010).

82. Jason March, "Do Mirror Neurons Give Us Empathy?," *The Greater Good*, March 29, 2012, http://greatergood.berkeley.edu/article/item/do_mirror_neurons_give_empathy.

83. Ibid.

84. Ibid.

85. Ramachandram, *The Tell Tale Brain*.

86. Ibid.

87. See Giacomo Rizzolatti and Laila Craighero, "The Mirror Neuron System," *Annual Review of Neuroscience* 27 (2004), 169–92, http://psych.colorado.edu/~kimlab/Rizzolatti.annurev.neuro.2004.pdf.

88. See Giacomo Rizzolatti and Michael A. Arbib, "Language Within Our Grasp," *Trends in Neuroscience* 21 (1998): 188–94, http://isites.harvard.edu/fs/docs/icb.topic151491.files/rizzolati-arbib.pdf; Vygotsky, *Thought and Language*.

89. Giacomo Rizzolatti and Laila Craighero, "Language and Mirror Neurons," in *The Oxford Handbook of Psycholinguistics*, ed. Gareth Gaskell (Oxford Library of Psychology: 2007), 782.

90. Ibid.

91. Ibid., 783. See also Maxim I. Stamenov and Vittorio Gallese, eds., *Mirror Neurons and the Evolution of Brain and Languag* (Amsterdam: Benjamins, 2002).

92. Noah Zarr, Ryan Ferguson, and Arthur M. Glenberg, "Language Comprehension Warps the Mirror Neuron System," *Frontiers in Human Neuroscience* 7(870) (December 2013).

93. Ibid.

94. There is some debate about mirror neurons: some have noted that there is no conclusive proof that humans have mirror neurons and question whether this they are the neurological explanation for empathy in humans. See, e.g., Sharon Begley, "The Trouble with Mirror Neurons," *Mindful* (June 2004), http://www.mindful.org/mindful-magazine/begley-mirror-neurons.

95. Giannis Kugiumutzakis, "Neonatal Imitation in the Intersubjective Companion Space," in *Intersubjective Communication and Emotion in Early Ontogeny*, ed. Stein Braten (Cambridge: Cambridge University Press, 1998).

96. Colwyn Trevarthen, "Intersubjectivity," *MIT Encyclopedia of Cognitive Science*, http://ai.ato.ms/MITECS/Entry/trevarthen1.html.

97. Kenneth Kaye, *The Mental and Social Life of Babies* (Chicago: University of Chicago Press, 1992); H. Papousek and M. Papousek, "Intuitive Parenting: A Dialectic Counterpart to the Infant's Integrative Compliance," in *Handbook of Infant Development*, ed. J.D. Osofsky (New York: Wiley, 1987), 669–720.

98. Jerome Bruner, *Child's Talk: Learning to Use Language* (New York: Norton, 1983).

99. Trevarthen, "Intersubjectivity." See also C. Trevarthen and K. Aitkin, "Infant Intersubjectivity: Research Theory and Clinical Applications," *Journal of Child Psychology and Psychiatry* 42(1) (2001): 3–48.

100. John Barresi and Chris Moore, "The Neuroscience of Social Understanding," in *The Shared Mind: Perspectives on Intersubjectivity*, ed. Jordan Zlatev et al. (Amsterdam: Benjamins, 2008), 39–66.

101. Ibid., 422–23.

102. Ibid., 416.

103. Siegel, *Mindsight*, 10.

104. Ibid., 26.

105. Ibid.

106. Ibid.

107. See e.g., Daniel Kahneman, *Thinking, Fast and Slow* (New York: Farrar, Straus and Giroux, 2011).

108. See generally Richard Posner, *Economic Analysis of Law* (New York: Aspen, 2010); Gary S. Becker, *The Economic Approach to Human Behavior* (Chicago: University of Chicago Press, 1978), 3–14.

109. Daniel Kahneman, "Maps of Bounded Rationality: Psychology for Behavioral Economics," *American Economic Review* 93(5) (2003): 1449.

110. See Daniel Kahneman, "Keynote Address at Loyola University Chicago School of Law," October 5, 2012. Transcript on file at the office of the Loyola University Chicago Law Journal. See also Daniel Kahneman and Amos Tversky, "Prospect Theory: An Analysis of Decision Under Risk," *Econometrica*, 47(2) (March 1979): 263–92, http://pages.uoregon.edu/harbaugh/Readings/GBE/Risk/Kahneman%201979%20E,%20 Prospect%20Theory.pdf.

111. Nicholas C. Barberis, "Thirty Years of Prospect Theory in Economics: A Review and Assessment," *Journal of Economic Perspectives* 27(1) (Winter 2013), 173–96, http:// pubs.aeaweb.org/doi/pdfplus/10.1257/jep.27.1.173.

112. See Carey K. Morewedge and Daniel Kahneman, "Associative Processes in Intuitive Judgment," *Trends in Cognitive Sciences* 14(10) (October 2010): 435–40.

113. See, e.g., Daniel Pink, *A Whole New Mind: Why Right-Brainers Will Rule the Future* (New York: Riverhead Books, 2006).

114. David Hawkins, "I, Thou and It," in *The Informed Vision: Essays on Learning and Human Nature* (New York: Agathon Press, 2002), 56–57.

115. Ibid., 57.

116. Ibid.

117. Ibid.

118. Ibid.

119. Ibid., 59.

120. Ibid.

121. Ibid., 60.

122. See, e.g. Laura Pardo, "What Every Teacher Needs to Know About Comprehension," *International Reading Association* 58 (2004), 276, http://www.learner.org/work shops/teachreading35/pdf/teachers_know_comprehension.pdf.

123. See e.g. Ronald Sharp, *Friendship and Literature: Spirit and Form* (Durham: Duke University Press, 1986); W.C. Booth, "The Way I Loved George Eliot: Friendship With Books as a Neglected Critical Metaphor," *Kenyon Review* 2 (1980): 4, 5. See also Michael Kaufman, "The Value of Friendship in Law and Literature," *Fordham Law Review* 60 (1992): 645, 659, http://ir.lawnet.fordham.edu/cgi/viewcontent. cgi?article=2961&context=flr.

124. Pardo, "What Every Teacher Needs to Know," 276.

125. Ibid., 50.

126. Ibid., 426.

127. Ibid., 42.

128. Ibid., 428.

129. Ibid., 429.

130. Ibid.

131. S. Guttmann-Steinmetz and J.A. Cromwell, "Attachment and Externalizing Disorders: A Developmental Psychopathology Perspective," *Journal of the American Academy of Child & Adolescent Psychiatry* 45(4) (2006).

132. Ibid.

133. Ibid., 50.

134. Daniel Siegel, *The Developing Mind: Towards a Neurobiology of Interpersonal Experience* (New York: Guilford Press, 1999).

135. Ibid., 40–50. See also Maia Szalavitz and Bruce D. Perry, *Born of Love: Why Empathy Is Essential—and Endangered* (New York: HarperCollins 2010).

136. Siegel, *The Developing Mind*, 50.

137. Maria Robinson, *From Birth to One: The Years of Opportunity* (Buckingham: Open University Press, 2003).

138. See Jonathan Masur, John Bronsteen, and Christopher Buccafusco, "Welfare as Happiness," *Georgetown Law Journal* 98 (2010): 1583, 1586.

139. Mark D. Holder and Ben Coleman, "The Contribution of Social Relationships to Children's Happiness," *Journal of Happiness Studies* 10 (2007): 329–49 (multiple dimensions of social relations contributed to the happiness of children).

140. Daniel Kahneman et al., "A Survey Method for Characterizing Daily Life Experience: The Day Reconstruction Method," *Science* 306(5702) (2004): 1776–80.

141. Ibid., 1777.

142. Ibid., 1778.

143. Ibid.

144. See, e.g., Ed Diener and Robert Biswas-Diener, *Happiness: Unlocking the Mysteries of Psychological Wealth* (Malden, MA: Wiley-Blackwell, 2008); Martin E.P. Seligman, *Flourish: A Visionary New Understanding of Happiness and Well-Being* (New York: Free Press, 2011).

145. Ed Diener and Martin E.P. Seligman, "Very Happy People," *Psychological Science* 13(1) (January 2002).

146. See, e.g., Sally S. Dickerson and Peggy M. Zoccola, "Towards a Biology of Social Support," in *The Oxford Handbook of Positive Psychology*, ed. Shane J. Lopez and C.R. Snyder (New York: Oxford University Press, 2009).

147. Ibid.

148. James J. Heckman, *Giving Kids a Fair Chance (A Strategy That Works)* (Cambridge, Massachusetts: MIT Press/Boston Review Books, 2014).

149. National Scientific Council on the Developing Child and National Forum on Early Childhood Policy and Programs, "Building the Brain's 'Air Traffic Control' System: How Early Experiences Shape the Development of Executive Function" (working paper no. 11, Harvard University Center on the Developing Child, 2011).

150. Ibid., 1.

151. Ibid.

152. Ibid.

153. Ibid., 3.

154. Ibid., 5. See also Paul Tough, *How Children Succeed: Grit, Curiosity, and the Hidden Power of Character* (London: Random House, 2013).

155. "Building the Brain's 'Air Traffic Control' System," 5.

156. Ibid., 10, citing W. Steven Barnett, et al., "Educational Effects of the Tools of the Mind Curriculum: A Randomized Trial," *Early Childhood Research Quarterly* 23 (2008), 299–313.

157. "Building the Brain's 'Air Traffic Control' System," 10.

158. Ibid. See also Greg J. Duncan et al., "School Readiness and Later Achievement," *Developmental Psychology* 43(6) (2007): 1428-1446.

159. "Building the Brain's 'Air Traffic Control' System," 10.

160. Ibid.

161. Ibid.

162. Ibid.

163. Ibid., 5.

164. Ibid., See also Janet A. Welsh et al., "The Development of Cognitive Skills and Gains in Academic School Readiness Programs for Children from Low-income Families," *Journal of Educational Psychology* 102(1) (2010): 43-53 (2010).

165. Ibid., 5.

166. Ibid., 6.

167. Ibid., 6.

168. Ibid.

169. Ibid., 11.

Section 3

STRATEGIES FOR EXPANDING, DEVELOPING, AND DESIGNING EARLY CHILDHOOD LEARNING COMMUNITIES THAT CONSTRUCT KNOWLEDGE THROUGH MEANINGFUL RELATIONSHIPS

In this final section, the book provides implementation strategies. Chapter 8 offers legal, political, economic, and comprehensive roadmaps for increasing access to early childhood programs for all three- and four-year-olds in America. Chapter 9 then suggests specific steps that providers of early childhood education programs can take to create a learning environment in which children develop the capacity to construct knowledge by building meaningful relationships. The book concludes with chapter 10 by making visible the profound and joyful learning that can take place in such an environment.

Chapter Eight

Legal, Political, Economic, and Comprehensive Strategies for Expanding Access

Chapter 8 provides the legal, political, economic, and comprehensive strategies for expanding access to early childhood education programs.

LEGAL STRATEGIES FOR EXPANDING ACCESS TO EARLY CHILDHOOD EDUCATION PROGRAMS

Viable Legal Challenges

As described in Chapter 3, there are at least four kinds of viable legal challenges that can be raised to a government's failure to provide sufficient access to early childhood programs: (1) a claim that the failure infringes upon the federal constitution's right to be free from the absolute deprivation of a minimally adequate education; (2) a claim that the failure violates a state constitution's obligation to provide an equitable, adequate, thorough, or efficient educational system; (3) a claim that expanding access to early childhood education programs is an appropriate remedy for the failure to provide equitable or adequate resources for children enrolled in the state's education system; and (4) a claim that the failure has a disparate impact on children who members of minority groups, in violation of a state's civil or human rights statute.

Federal Constitutional Arguments

Plaintiffs can allege that a lack of access to early childhood education constitutes an absolute deprivation of a minimally adequate education. Because the U.S. Constitution supports a right to such access, a finding that the failure to provide access to early childhood programs infringes upon this constitutional right has the potential to increase access to early childhood programs significantly.

State Constitutional Arguments Based on Adequacy, Equity, Efficiency, and Thoroughness

In the majority of the cases, the courts have recognized that the failure to provide sufficient education funding violates the state's constitutional guarantees. Depending on the state, those guarantees may include the right to adequate, equitable, efficient, or thorough education funding. In those jurisdictions, plaintiffs can allege that a lack of access to early childhood education programs violates those guarantees under the state constitution.

State Constitutional Arguments Based on Proper Judicial Remedies

Plaintiffs also should allege a claim that expanding access to early childhood education programs is an appropriate remedy for the failure to provide equitable or adequate resources for children enrolled in the state's education system. Although plaintiffs have filed and won dozens of adequate funding lawsuits in forty-five states, they have not always included expanded access to early childhood education in their requests for relief.[1]

As *Abbott* and *Hoke* both demonstrate, however, plaintiffs should include such a remedy in any litigation challenging education funding. Those decisions make clear that the issue of whether children are entitled to access to early childhood education programs does not depend on the age at which school attendance is mandated but whether the state is preparing those children to enter school with the ability to avail themselves of the opportunity to obtain a sound education.

In *Abbott V*, plaintiffs succeeded in obtaining a judgment from the New Jersey Supreme Court that ordered the state to provide full-day kindergarten and half-day early childhood education programs for three- and four-year-olds as a remedy for the state's failure to provide school-age children in the Abbott districts with a thorough and efficient education. The New Jersey Supreme Court relied on empirical evidence regarding the benefits of pre-kindergarten education programs. Accordingly, such evidence should be included in any complaint alleging this cause of action.

The importance of providing an evidentiary foundation for the remedy of increased access to early childhood education is further highlighted by *Hoke*. In that litigation, the North Carolina Supreme Court initially found that a judicially imposed remedy of expanding access to early childhood education for "at risk" four-year-olds was premature.[2] The Court deferred to the state legislature to determine how best to meet the needs of those children.

The legislature then concluded that the most effective way to insure that the state's "at risk" four-year-olds received a constitutionally required "sound basic education" was to provide them with early childhood education programs. After taking some steps to develop those programs, however, the legislature capped enrollment because of fiscal constraints.

When the issue returned to the North Carolina courts, they ultimately ordered the legislature to provide the remedy of enhanced access to early childhood education for all at risk four-year-olds.[3] The courts reasoned that the legislature already had demonstrated its acceptance of the benefits of providing early childhood education, but had failed in its attempt to do so.

Based on this reasoning, litigants seeking increased access to early childhood education programs as a remedy for a state's failure to provide an adequate or equitable public education should include in their pleadings evidence of the remedial benefits of those programs, evidence of the legislature's previous recognition of those remedial benefits, and evidence that the provision of those benefits would be necessary to remedy the proven violation.

State Statutory Arguments

Plaintiffs wishing to challenge the quality or availability of their state's pre-kindergarten education system can argue that the education system violates their state's particular civil rights or human rights statutes. Here, plaintiffs need not prove that a state intentionally denies to minority children access to early childhood education programs, only that the state's failure to provide access to those programs has a disparate impact on particular groups of minority children.

A model template of a complaint that makes these arguments in the early childhood education context is presented in Appendix A.

Overcoming Arguments Opposing the Legal Case for Access to Early Childhood Education

Litigants are likely to get four responses in opposition to legal arguments for increasing access to early childhood education programs: (1) a separation of powers argument that legislatures, not courts, should determine whether early childhood education programs are offered; (2) a social science argument that the evidence does not justify a right to early childhood education; (3) a slippery slope argument that recognizing a right to access to early childhood education would require recognizing a right to education "from the cradle to college"; and (4) a political argument that providing increased access to early childhood education programs would supplant the family.[4]

Separation of Powers

The first objection is that the legislatures, not the courts, should be determining whether early childhood education programs are offered. In school funding cases, however, the overwhelming majority of courts already have concluded that language in state constitutions that creates an affirmative right to education requires interpretation and implementation to give context to these rights.[5] These courts have recognized that the judiciary has the primary responsibility to determine whether a legislative regime or a governmental program violates the federal or state constitution. Similarly, litigants in early childhood education cases can properly seek judicial review of early childhood programs that violate constitutional obligations.[6]

Moreover, courts already have indicated their willingness to assess the inputs and outputs necessary to define an adequate education. They certainly are competent to include early childhood education as a part of this analysis.[7] The fact that legislatures in most of the states have already committed to providing early childhood education indicates that those legislatures already believe that these programs are not ineffective or inefficient.[8] As such, a court would not be creating an entirely new program, but relying on legislative judgments embedded in pre-existing, legislatively created programs.[9]

Social Science Evidence

A second objection is that the evidence regarding the benefits of early childhood education is not yet strong enough to justify a judicial finding regarding those benefits. State courts, however, have already rendered opinions specifically finding that an investment in early childhood education programs produces robust educational, social, and economic benefits.[10]

Moreover, courts commonly rely upon expert witnesses who offer opinions on complex social scientific issues, even if those opinions are not based upon a "reasonable certainty."[11] Judges in fact often make factual findings based on less than a "reasonable certainty." But the evidence of the economic, social, and educational benefits of early childhood education programs for all children is much stronger than even a "reasonable certainty."[12]

As demonstrated throughout this book, the social science evidence regarding the benefits of early childhood education is exceptionally strong.[13] There is no credible study or source of data that seriously questions those benefits. Those few studies that purport to call into question the link between early childhood education and robust economic, social, and educational benefits have been proven to be deeply flawed.[14] In fact, the evidence is undeniable that an investment in early childhood education yields significant returns.

The Slippery Slope

As James Ryan has observed, a court decision recognizing a right to early childhood education might be questioned on the ground that it also would require recognizing a right to neo-natal care or to college.[15] The judicial recognition of a right to pre-kindergarten education, however, would not logically obligate the courts to recognize such additional rights.[16]

The right to early childhood education for three- and four-year-olds is narrowly tailored to the state's existing obligation to provide a free primary education. The state constitutions in virtually every state already require the states to provide such a primary education for all children in the state.[17] As the *Abbott* and *Hoke* courts reasoned, adequate and equitable access to that pre-existing, state-mandated system of public schools is dependent on adequate and equitable access to pre-kindergarten programs.[18]

Moreover, by mandating in IDEA that the states provide early childhood special education services for all three- and four-year-olds with educational disabilities, Congress also has recognized the tight nexus between educational services for children at those ages and the free appropriate public education services that those children must receive when they enter a public school district's elementary classrooms. While there are undoubtedly very strong public policy reasons to increase access to neo-natal care, therefore, the logic of the judicial recognition of a legal right to access to early childhood education would not inevitably lead to the judicial recognition of any such additional legal rights.

The Myth That Early Childhood Education Supplants the Family

Opponents of the expansion of access to early childhood programs may assert that it represents a government takeover of family relationships. The expansion of access to early childhood programs, however, does not and cannot interfere with the fundamental liberty of parents and guardians to direct the upbringing of their children. Rather, that expansion merely provides families with a range of additional choices regarding the upbringing of their children.

Increasing the availability of early childhood programs increases the choices available to all families with young children. Furthermore, early childhood education programs do not supplant the family. To the contrary, the most effective early childhood programs provide tremendous resources and support for the family.[19]

The Use of Litigation to Initiate Policymaking

A court order recognizing a right of access to early childhood education programs is just the beginning of the provision of access. Translating a court order into effective legislation requires continued advocacy and collaboration.[20] At the same time, even unsuccessful litigation may lead to legislative action.[21] In Arkansas, for example, the legislature increased early childhood education spending even after the Supreme Court ruled that the state constitution did not guarantee access.[22] And, the *Abbott* and *Hoke* litigation in New Jersey and North Carolina are further evidence of the interplay between the judicial and legislative branches of government. Even litigation that appears to be unsuccessful can ultimately:

- Raise the salience of an issue;
- Force legislators to take a position; and
- Help foster and inspire a political movement.[23]

POLITICAL STRATEGIES FOR EXPANDING ACCESS TO EARLY CHILDHOOD EDUCATION PROGRAMS

This section presents national, state, local, and comprehensive political strategies for increasing access to early childhood education programs.

National Executive and Legislative Strategies

In February 2013, the President made a commitment to universal early childhood education:

> Study after study shows that the sooner a child begins learning, the better he or she does down the road. But today, fewer than 3 in 10 four-year-olds are enrolled in a high-quality preschool program. Most middle-class parents can't afford a few hundred bucks a week for a private preschool. And for poor kids who need help the most, this lack of access to preschool education can shadow them for the rest of their lives. So tonight, I propose working with states to make high-quality preschool available to every single child in America. . . .
>
> Every dollar we invest in high-quality early childhood education can save more than seven dollars later on—by boosting graduation rates, reducing teen pregnancy, even reducing violent crime. In states that make it a priority to educate our youngest children, like Georgia or Oklahoma, studies show students grow up more likely to read and do math at grade level, graduate high school, hold a job, form more stable families of their own. We know this works. So let's

do what works and make sure none of our children start the race of life already behind. Let's give our kids that chance.

Immediately following this address, the President set forth his plan for early childhood education programs for all Americans. In that plan, he emphasized that early childhood education programs can help level the playing field for children from lower-income families and can help students stay on track and engaged in the early elementary grades.[24] The plan also recognized that children who attend early childhood education programs are more likely to do well in school, find good jobs, and succeed in their careers.[25] The plan noted that the benefits of these programs were not solely for the children alone. Taxpayers also receive a high average return on investment, with savings in areas like improved educational outcomes, increased labor productivity, and a reduction in crime.[26]

One year later, in his January 2014 State of the Union, the President reiterated this commitment by stating: "Research shows that one of the best investments we can make in a child's life is high-quality early education. . . . [T]hirty states have raised pre-K funding on their own. They know we can't wait."

The administration proposed several investments that work to expand access to early childhood programs, including developing partnerships with states to provide voluntary, full-day early childhood education programs for four-year-olds from low-income families.[27] In an effort to increase access to high-quality pre-K programs, the administration proposed to provide states with $75 billion in matching funds over the next ten years.[28]

The national effort to increase access to early childhood education has been advanced to various degrees through three legislative initiatives: the Appropriations Act of 2014, Race to the Top, and the Strong Start for Children Act.

Appropriations Act of 2014

The Consolidated Appropriations Act of 2014 restored funding to early childhood education programs that were previously cut due to sequestration. The Appropriations Act also provided new, additional funding to Head Start for the Early Head Start programs to allow them to partner with local child care providers to provide more high-quality programs to more low-income infants and toddlers.

Race to the Top

The Administration provided additional funding for early childhood education programs for low-income families through the Department of Education's Race to the Top Preschool Development Grants. These grants encourage states to develop, improve, or increase access to early childhood education programs for children in low- to moderate-income families.[29]

Strong Start for Children Act

Although it may ultimately fail to garner sufficient support, the Strong Start for Children Act provides a model of national legislation that would expand access to high-quality early childhood education for low-income families. The Act addresses several components of early childhood education, including funding, quality, and implementation.

The Act calls for the federal government, states, and local communities to partner in order to offer more high-quality early childhood education programs to children at 200 percent of the poverty line. States that do not yet offer full day, full year, high-quality early childhood education programs would be able to receive development funds in order to help them become eligible for larger grants.

The Strong Start for Children Act defines high-quality early childhood education programs as those with high staff qualifications, comparable compensation, and critically important professional development and training for teachers. Early childhood education teachers must have a bachelor's degree and their salaries must be comparable to those of other K-12 teacher salaries. Programs must be full day, have small class sizes, and meet children's comprehensive cognitive, social-emotional, and physical development needs. Additionally, programs must provide other wrap-around services, such as nutrition, health, and social services, and programs to educate and engage parents.[30]

State Strategies

Mirroring the national focus on increasing access to early childhood education programs, many states have been considering creating and funding universal pre-K programs. States like Oklahoma, Florida, New York, Indiana, and California have been particularly active in advocating universal pre-K programs for four-year-old children.[31]

Across the country, 40 states offer a total of 52 state-funded pre-K programs, along with a program in the District of Columbia. As defined by NIEER, a state early childhood education program is one that is funded, controlled, and directed by the state; services children who are usually three or four years of age; and focuses on early childhood education as distinct from the state's system for subsidized child care. Of these programs, 32 have an income requirement, limiting eligibility to low- and middle-income families.

State-funded pre-K programs have doubled the percentage of children served over the past decade. But state-by-state funding for pre-K programs recently decreased by over half a billion dollars, resulting in a decrease in pre-K enrollment.

As of 2012, Florida and Oklahoma lead other states in four-year-old enrollment, both serving more than 70 percent of their four-year-old population. Although state pre-K programs primarily tend to enroll only four-year-olds, some states, including the District of Columbia, have programs for three-year-olds. Washington, DC, leads the other states with its three-year-old enrollment, serving over 50 percent of three-year-olds in the district.[32]

Most state-funded pre-K programs either require or depend on local or federal funds to operate pre-K programs. Some states incorporate pre-K costs through the same funding formula as their K-12 schools, and several states previously used funding from the American Recovery and Reinvestment Act (ARRA) to prevent cuts to pre-K funding in 2011.[33]

There are several states that have long-recognized the benefits of increased access to early childhood education programs. Their experiences provide lessons for all states trying to develop greater access to those programs.

- **California:** California was one of the first states in the country to develop a state-funded early childhood education program, introducing its State Preschool Program (SPP) in 1965. This program is limited to children who are receiving protective services and are at risk for abuse, neglect, or family violence. In 2007, the state established the Pre-kindergarten and Family Literacy Program (PKFLP) that offered families that were at 70 percent or below the state's median income full and half-day services with a focus on childhood literacy. After a 2008 bill, the state streamlined funding for its multiple early childhood education programs and consolidated the programs into the California State Early Preschool Program (CSPP), the largest state-funded early childhood education program in the country.[34] The CSPP also provides services to families with incomes substantially below the state median income, or to families who exceed the income requirement but have children that receive protective services or are at risk of abuse, exploitation, or neglect. The CSPP provides services to local education agencies, faith-based and private childcare centers, Head Start programs, and other public agencies. California also won a Race to the Top Early Learning Challenge grant, which it used to develop a quality rating system to measure a pre-K program's success, children's school readiness, teacher quality, and environment quality.

- **Michigan:** Michigan established the Michigan School Readiness Program (MSRP) in 1985. The program, also known as the Great Start Readiness Program (GSRP), only includes families with incomes below 300 percent of the federal poverty line, with a few exceptions for families that have risk factors for educational disadvantages. In 2011, the state increased teaching requirements to require teachers to have teaching certifications. The state spends about $4,422 per child enrolled, according to 2012 data. The GSRP only enrolls four-year-olds; there is not a program for three-year-olds.[35]

- **Mississippi:** In 2008, Mississippi developed "Mississippi Building Blocks," an expansive private-funding pilot program designed to improve early childhood education and to help increase the state's children's school readiness. The investment provides existing childcare centers with scholarships to train teachers, provides them with on-site, classroom-based mentors, helps them develop research-based literacy curriculum, provides programs with business advice, and provides programs with up to $3,000 in classroom supplies. The Building Blocks program, a $6 million investment, is largely privately funded by business owners, philanthropists, corporate sponsors, and foundations. While the Building Blocks program provides early learning centers with additional monetary support, it does not cover the cost of a child's tuition to attend the program. Unlike every other state in the South, Mississippi also does not fund pre-kindergarten.[36] In 2013, however, Mississippi established a small pre-K program as part of a larger group of education reforms. The "Early Learning Collaborative Act" establishes a collaborative delivery model for a state-funded pre-K programs, including Head Start programs, licensed childcare facilities, licensed private, parochial, and public school pre-kindergarten programs.[37] Among other items, the Act requires participating programs to employ teachers with at least a bachelor's degree (assistant teachers need only have associate's degrees), provide teachers with at least fifteen hours of annual professional development, including early literacy focused professional development, use state-adopted comprehensive early learning standards, implement research-based curriculum designed to prepare students to be school-ready, and adopt small teacher-student ratios.

- **Georgia:** Georgia created the nation's first universal pre-kindergarten program for four-year-olds in 1995. The program, which was operated by the state's Department of Early Care and Learning, includes Head Start Schools, private child care centers, faith-based organizations, state colleges and universities, and military facilities. The program serves over 81,000 children from all income levels. All of the programs must abide by Georgia's "Bright from the Start" Pre-K Operating Guidelines, which require facilities to align standards with the Georgia Early Learning standards from birth through age three, and are monitored by a statewide assessment system. The state also sets class size and teacher-student ratio limits and requires its lead teachers to have at least a bachelor's degree.[38]

- **Oklahoma:** In 1998, Oklahoma became the second state to offer free, voluntary early childhood education programs for the state's four-year-olds. As of 2012, the program is offered in 99 percent of the state's school districts. The program is funded through the state's school funding formula, which is based on the age of the child and the length of the program day. In addition to public school settings, districts can also subcontract with other community programs, child care centers, and Head Start settings, allowing districts to place public school teachers in those alternate settings. Students instructed in the alternate settings are still considered public school students. In 2011, Oklahoma again focused on pre-K education when its legislature passed a bill to require all students to be reading on grade level by the end of the third grade.[39]

- **West Virginia:** In 2002, West Virginia passed legislation to implement a universal pre-K program for the state's four-year-olds and three-year-olds with Individualized Education Plans. To maximize resources, the state collaborated with community partners, such as community centers and Head Start. The program is funded through the state's funding formula, and, as enrollment increases, so will funding.[40]

- **New York:** New York's Universal Prekindergarten (UPK) program, which started providing services in 1998, aims to provide all four-year-olds in the state with pre-K; however, the state has not yet met this goal due to fiscal constraints. The state operates a lottery system to determine enrollment. UPK teachers in nonpublic settings must meet the same requirements as teachers in public settings. Teachers hired after 1978 must have a bachelor's degree in either early childhood education or a related field and must obtain early childhood certification, or teachers must have a master's of arts and a valid teaching license or early childhood certificate. New York also implemented high-quality pre-kindergarten learning standards aligned with the Common Core in September 2011.[41]

Local Strategies

- **New York City**: In New York City, Mayor Bill de Blasio developed a plan to offer pre-K to all four-year-olds by raising taxes for high-income residents.[42] Pursuant to that plan, the city already has enrolled more than 50,000 four-year-olds in early childhood education programs. Many of those children otherwise would not have had access to any pre-kindergarten education. Significantly, the city has determined that the most effective approach to early childhood education for all children requires training professional educators to employ the social constructivist practices exemplified by the early learning centers of Reggio Emilia: "Under the stewardship of Carmen Fariña, the schools chancellor, who has spoken frequently about her commitment to joyful learning, more and more poor children will theoretically be taught as the city's affluent children are, which is to say according to the principles of immersive, play-based, often self-directed and project-driven learning."[43]

- **San Antonio**: In San Antonio, Mayor Julian Castro persuaded voters to approve an eighth of a cent sales tax increase to expand pre-K in 2012.[44] This plan expands early childhood education programs to more than 22,000 four-year-olds over the next eight years. In pushing for his plan, Mayor Castro stressed the importance of a well-educated workforce for the future economic growth of the city, which helped to get the city's business community on board.[45] To win over taxpayers, city officials calculated the tax would cost the median household only $7.81 per year.[46] The program garnered further political support by reserving 10 percent of the preschool slots for families who earn too much to qualify for free tuition.[47] Finally, the program required the involvement of parents whose children attend the early childhood education programs to help counter critics who argued parents should be doing more.[48]

Universal and Targeted Strategies

One issue faced by policy makers is whether efforts to expand access to early childhood education should be limited to targeted populations or should be universal. While there are benefits to each approach, National Institute for Early Education Research (NIEER) persuasively concludes:

> Most public support for preschool education targets children in poverty or low-income families. This is supported by evidence that shows high returns for public investments in the education of these young children. Unfortunately, there are several problems with this approach in practice. First, programs are trying

to target a status that changes fairly frequently with a service that must be provided consistently over a sustained time. The result is a failure to successfully serve much of the target population. Second, benefits to children's learning and development extend up the income ladder far beyond poverty. If the goal is to prevent the majority of school failure and dropout, this cannot be accomplished by ignoring the middle class.[49]

Moreover, NIEER's research demonstrates the significant advantages of a universal approach:

Obviously, the most effective approach would be to offer preschool programs to all children. A preschool program for all children would cost the public more, but the added benefits from serving more children could more than justify the added costs. In addition to reaching previously underserved disadvantaged children, newly served children from families that are not currently eligible also would benefit in ways that can contribute to the public good, such as increased school readiness and achievement. These families benefit from the enhanced educational opportunities their children receive even if they already had access to some preschool education or childcare. For many middle-income families "preschool participation" does not mean high-quality education. They simply cannot afford high quality. Parents who need long hours of child care to stay afloat financially can face an especially difficult trade-off between quality and hours.[50]

STRATEGIES FOR AUTHENTICALLY ASSESSING EARLY CHILDHOOD EDUCATION PROGRAMS

When states implement and fund early childhood programs for their three- and four-year-olds, they also inevitably develop quality controls or certification standards for programs that receive their funds.

Several states have adopted quality-rating systems for licensed early childhood education programs in order to increase the availability of information regarding the quality of each program. States like North Carolina have implemented a one- to five-star-rating system to help parents and policy makers gauge the effectiveness of the state's programs. To reach the highest rating of five stars, programs must allow trained, university-based observers to evaluate the programs using the Early Childhood Environment Rating Scale (E-CERS).[51]

The E-CERS is one of four child-focused environment scales, and it evaluates a program's abilities to provide high-quality care environments for children. The E-CERS assesses 43 items organized into 7 sub-categories. These categories examine a program's physical spaces, basic care of children, activities, interactions, and structure, while also assessing children's language-reasoning and surveying parents and staff.[52]

Like other environment rating scales, the E-CERS was developed to evaluate the "process quality" for children. Process quality refers to children's experiences within a child care setting, including interactions, materials, and activities. The quality of the interactions in the educational environment, which is best measured through observation, has proven to be a better predictor of child outcomes than class-size ratios, group size, cost of care, and type of care.[53]

States that would like to achieve a robust return on their investment in expanding access to early childhood programs may wish to consider a range of authentic assessment tools that document the learning relationships within the educational environment. There are three potential sources of guidelines for assessment.

NIEER Benchmarks

States could use the NIEER quality benchmarks as a method of measuring the basic structural ingredients of an early childhood education program, including quantitative inputs like class size and teacher training and professional development.

NAEYC Certification and Standards

The National Association for the Education of Young Children (NAEYC), an organization that promotes excellence in early childhood education, has created standards that provide an excellent foundation for assessing whether a state program is using best practices. In order to promote effective, healthy, and safe environments, NAEYC recommends that states license facilities that operate early childhood education programs.[54]

NAEYC further provides useful guidelines for early childhood education teacher preparation and professional development programs, and offers two types of accreditation: Early Childhood Associate Degree Accreditation (ECADA) and NAEYC recognition of the National Council for Accreditation for Teacher Education (NCATE) for baccalaureate and graduate degrees that lead to initial or advanced licensure.[55]

NAEYC also recommends that early childhood education programs meet the following Early Childhood Program Standards:

1. **Relationships:** The program promotes positive relationships among all children and adults to encourage each child's sense of individual worth

and belonging as part of a community and to foster each child's ability to contribute as a responsible community member.

2. **Curriculum:** The program implements a curriculum that is consistent with its goals for children and promotes learning and development in each of the following areas: social, emotional, physical, language, and cognitive.

3. **Teaching:** The program uses developmentally, culturally, and linguistically appropriate and effective teaching approaches that enhance each child's learning and development in the context of the program's curriculum goals.

4. **Assessment of Child Progress:** The program is informed by ongoing systematic, formal, and informal assessment approaches to provide information on children's learning and development. These assessments occur within the context of reciprocal communications with families and with sensitivity to the cultural contexts in which children develop. Assessment results are used to benefit children by informing sound decisions about children, teaching, and program improvement.

5. **Health:** The program promotes the nutrition and health of children and protects children and staff from illness and injury.

6. **Teachers:** The program employs and supports a teaching staff that has the educational qualifications, knowledge, and professional commitment necessary to promote children's learning and development and to support families' diverse needs and interests.

7. **Families:** The program establishes and maintains collaborative relationships with each child's family to foster children's development in all settings. These relationships are sensitive to family composition, language, and culture.

8. **Community Relationships:** The program establishes relationships with and uses the resources of the children's communities to support the achievement of program goals.

9. **Physical Environment:** The program has a safe and healthful environment that provides appropriate and well-maintained indoor and outdoor physical environments. The environment includes facilities, equipment, and materials to facilitate child and staff learning and development.

10. **Leadership and Management:** The program effectively implements policies, procedures, and systems that support stable staff and strong personnel, fiscal, and program management so all children, families, and staff have high-quality experiences.

Reggio Emilia

A truly Reggio-inspired social constructivist early learning program will readily satisfy these important NAEYC standards, as well as the NIEER benchmarks. Furthermore, a Reggio-inspired social constructivist learning environment will significantly exceed the NAEYC and NIEER standards. A state or city could determine if a program has created a Reggio-inspired social constructivist learning environment by observing whether that environment reflects the following truly "democratic" qualities:

Documentation deepens and makes visible individual and community learning
Emergent and negotiated curriculum
Multiple representations are valued
One hundred languages of children are expressed and supported
Collaboration is modeled and encouraged
Research about learning is performed by teachers, families, and students
Atelier integrates creative expression into all learning
Time for exploration is not artificially limited
Image of the child as a curious, competent, and caring citizen guides all learning
Community is developed from meaningful relationships inside and outside of the school

A state could develop a funding system that not only insures ample funds for programs that meet the NIEER and NAEYC standards, but also rewards programs in which highly trained educators are given the professional autonomy to develop learning environments in which children are encouraged to construct knowledge through meaningful relationships. The state would thereby incentivize social constructivist practices, and would also insure the highest rate of return on the investment of its scarce resources.

ECONOMIC STRATEGIES FOR EXPANDING ACCESS TO EARLY CHILDHOOD EDUCATION PROGRAMS

Full funding of early childhood education programs for all four-year-olds would require an additional annual expense of $24 billion, full funding of early childhood education programs for all three-year-olds would require an additional $28 billion, and full funding to provide outstanding early childhood education programs for all three- and four-year-olds would require a total additional annual expenditure of public funds of $52 billion.

Because these amounts are based on the assumption that all children would be enrolled in publicly funded programs and, in fact, many children would undoubtedly attend private pre-K programs, these estimates of the total additional funds needed to provide access to early childhood education programs for all three- and four-year-olds are significantly inflated. The actual expenditures would likely be less than these estimates.

Even these over-estimated expenditures comprise only about 8 percent of the total amount of the approximately $600 billion of public funds spent each year on the education of all elementary and secondary school children.[56] The amount required to educate all three- and four-year-olds in America is far less than one percent of the entire federal budget.[57]

This begs the question, then, as to how to fund early childhood education programs that would educate all of the nation's three- and four-year-old children. Public funding streams can include both federal and state investment sources. Private funding streams include social impact bonds. All funding streams produce robust investment returns.

Public Investments With Robust Returns

Federal and state investment sources can contribute modest amounts of funds to achieve the goal of providing outstanding early childhood education programs to all of the nation's children.

Federal Investment Sources

An increase in the federal tax on cigarettes by $0.94 would generate about $78 billion over the course of 10 years and pay for early childhood education for all three- and four-year-olds in America.[58] Other actual and potential sources of federal funding include community development block grants, Race to the Top Early Learning Challenge Grants, and funding available through Temporary Assistance to Needy Families.

Community Development Block Grants

In 1974, the U.S. Department of Housing and Urban Development created the Community Development Block Grant (CDBG) to provide states with resources to be used on a wide range of unique community development needs. The CBDG is a flexible program that provides communities annual grants to ensure affordable housing, create jobs, and provide services to the most vulnerable people in communities. The grant is allocated between states and local jurisdictions, depending on the size of their urban or metropolitan cities, requiring at least 70 percent of the CDBG funds to be used for activities that benefit low- and moderate-income persons.[59]

Race to the Top—Early Learning Challenge Grants

States may also apply for the Race to the Top—Early Learning Challenge Grant to help fund pre-K. The grant is designed to increase access to high-quality early learning programs for children with high needs. In 2013, six states were awarded the $280 million grant—Georgia, Kentucky, Michigan, New Jersey, Pennsylvania, and Vermont. The Grant is jointly administered by the U.S. Department of Education and the Department of Health and Human Services. Along with 14 previously existing grantees that shared a $500 million grant, 20 states across the country have access to more resources to support their early childhood education programs.

Temporary Assistance to Needy Families

Some states may be able to use Temporary Assistance to Needy Families (TANF) funds to help pay for early childhood education, but only if they are not offering universal, free early childhood education.

States have broad discretion in terms of what services and benefits it can offer to its communities via TANF funds, and can use their funds in combination with state and federal funds. TANF funds must be used in any manner that is "reasonably calculated" to accomplish at least one of the TANF purposes, which include providing assistance to needy families so children can be cared for in their own homes or in the homes of their relatives, to promote job preparation, work, and marriage in order to end parents' dependence on government benefits, to prevent and reduce pregnancies out-of-wedlock, and to encourage the formation and maintenance of two-parent families.[60]

States and local governments may not use TANF grants to pay for services normally provided to the public, such as fire and police programs, prisons, and traditional K-12 schooling. States that do not generally provide a universal and free early childhood education program may use federal TANF funds for that purpose.[61]

State Investment Sources

In a period of shrinking budgets and fiscal pressures, the states generally have reduced the funds allocated to early childhood education. They should be doing the opposite. As all of the economic evidence indicates, an investment in early childhood education programs saves costs, generates revenue, and yields robust returns. Such an investment is particularly necessary during periods of economic distress.[62] States that wish to pursue prudent investments in early childhood education may take advantage of alternative funding strategies, including adding early childhood education programs to the state school funding formula and creating Title I-supported early childhood education programs.

Adding Pre-K to State Funding Formulas

States' school funding formulas set the number of dollars to be allocated per student in the state for K-12 public schools. Generally, school districts have some flexibility in determining how state education funding formula dollars are to be spent, unless the legislature reserves certain funding for certain programs. Formulas are complex and varied across the country, but usually funds are generated from federal, state, and local funds. State funds most often are generated by property taxes; although some states use other sources, such as lottery ticket sales or other taxes. In order to ensure a consistent and stable funding source, states may incorporate early childhood education funding into their education funding formula.

By incorporating early childhood education funding within states' "foundation levels" of education funding formulas, early childhood education programs will likely experience more political and fiscal support, as foundation levels are usually well received within the political community. Additionally, including pre-kindergarten as a requirement for school funding will force states to create an "adequate" or "thorough and efficient" system of pre-kindergarten education and allow states to determine the precise amount of funding necessary to develop effective early childhood education programs. As states determine how much money to allocate to certain aspects of programs, they will adduce evidence of the particular benefits of social constructivist practices and further support those practices. States like Iowa, Oklahoma, and West Virginia have incorporated funding for four-year-olds into their general school funding formulas.

Other states use certain supplemental funds for early childhood education. Such funds, known as categorical grants, provide localities with funding that must be used specifically for pre-kindergarten purposes. Other states have a per-pupil rate for pre-K in their funding formula but supplement the funds with categorical grants for specific groups of students, such as English Language Learners or economically disadvantaged students.[63]

Title I-Supported Pre-K Programs

States with local education agencies that receive Title I funds may use those funds to operate or support a pre-kindergarten program. Any local education agency (LEA) that receives Title I funds may use a portion, or all, of those funds to operate an early childhood education program that complies with Title I requirements. LEAs may use all of the funds to operate a program for eligible children, or they may use a part of the funds to operate a program for eligible children in the district as a whole or in a portion of the district (i.e., use funds only for pre-K children who live in a specific Title I school attendance area). Alternatively, an LEA may use Title I funds to support eligible children enrolled in other early childhood education programs, like Head Start.[64]

For LEAs operating a school-wide program, all pre-K children residing in the attendance area of that school are eligible to participate in the Title I early childhood education program.[65] For LEAs providing a targeted assistance program, children who are residing in the attendance area of the school operating the program and who are identified as most at risk of failing to meet academic achievement standards are eligible to participate.[66] Only children who are identified as at risk of failing to meet the academic achievement standards are eligible for a district-wide LEA early childhood education program.

Private Investments in Social Impact or Social Benefit Bonds With Robust Returns

Another viable funding stream comes through that of private investments in social impact or social benefit bonds. Social impact or social benefit bonds are tools used to improve public services' outcomes, specifically those in disadvantaged populations, without burdening taxpayers. Social impact bonds, also known as "pay for success" programs, allow the government to pay for certain services, contingent on the success achieved by such services. Social impact bonds pay the public sector for their initial financing if the public sector reaches agreed upon measurable outcomes.[67]

In social impact bond agreements, the investor pays an external organization if the organization achieves specific agreed-upon measurable goals. If the organization reaches its goals, the government repays the organization's original investors. However, if the organization fails, the investors do not get repaid the government's funds, and the government is not responsible for any of the organization's debts.[68]

In the fall of 2013, Utah received a social impact bond from Goldman Sachs and J.B. Pritzker to expand one of the state's early childhood education programs by 450–600 students, with the goal of reducing the need for costly special education services later in the students' academic careers. In this case, the investors will make money if the district meets its goals, but will lose money if the district fails.

To identify students who are more likely to need special education services in the future, Utah's students are tested at the beginning of the program. Students will be tested again later, and, for every student that scores at grade level, investors are paid back an amount equal to the avoided special education services cost. When the loan is completely paid, any additional money saved is split between the district and investors until students complete the sixth grade.[69]

These Investments Would Benefit All Children

The expenditure of these funds would benefit all children. There is a significant problem of access to early childhood education programs in America. A majority of both African American four-year-olds and Latino or Hispanic children do not attend any such program.[70] Expanding early childhood education programs to all four-year-olds would provide access to about 900,000 African American and Latino children who would not otherwise receive any pre-K education.[71]

But expanding access would produce substantial educational, social, and economic benefits for all children, regardless of their race, ethnicity, or socioeconomic status. The investment of state and federal funds would provide robust returns to the community as a whole.

DEVELOPING PUBLIC-PRIVATE PARTNERSHIPS TO EXPAND ACCESS TO EARLY CHILDHOOD EDUCATION PROGRAMS

Another way to expand access to early childhood education programs is to develop public-private partnerships. From a legal standpoint, there is no question that a school district can lawfully allow a non-district provider of early childhood education programs to use its school facilities. A public school district may allow its property and facilities to be used or shared by non-district organizations. The district clearly has the power to partner with private and even religious providers of early childhood education.

From an economic standpoint, a school district's facilities typically are its most valuable resource. Where a district allows a private provider of pre-K education to use or share its facilities, it may receive a direct economic benefit by charging the provider for its use of those facilities.

Yet, when a public school enables a private provider of early childhood education to use its facilities, it also reaps a more significant economic benefit. The children served by that private program will likely attend the district's schools when they reach kindergarten or first grade. By virtue of having a pre-K education, those children will not need as many district resources as they otherwise would have needed. The district's special education costs, health care costs, grade retention costs, and remediation costs will be substantially reduced.

From a political standpoint, the school district may want to present itself as an important part of the whole community. Consequently, the district may consider its physical assets to be those of the community at large. The district may even position its schools as the "hub of the community." Accordingly, another way in which a community can expand access to early childhood education programs—while reaping additional, community-wide benefits—is to create public-private partnerships.

Methods by Which a School District Can Lawfully Structure a Partnership With a Private Entity

There are at least three ways in which a school district can lawfully structure a partnership with non-district providers of early childhood. First, the district may create and promulgate a policy governing the use of its facilities. Second, the district may forge intergovernmental agreements that allow other public taxing bodies to use district facilities to provide early learning environments, in return for monetary or nonmonetary consideration. Third, the district may enter leases or license agreements between the district and third-party users of its facilities.

Create and Promulgate a Community Use Policy

One way a district can partner with a non-district early childhood provider is to create and promulgate what is known as a "community use policy." The language of a public school district's community use policy can be used to facilitate partnerships between the district and non-district providers of early childhood education.

The policy language must preserve the district's control over the quality of the providers who use its facilities while insuring that the district does not unlawfully discriminate among users. One common method of reconciling these interests involves a priority schedule. The district's policy may provide, for example, that its facilities will be available first to the district and, only if the district is not utilizing the facilities, second to other governmental bodies and third to other potential users. An example of a Community Use Policy that would facilitate the community's use of district facilities to provide early childhood education programs is in Appendix B.

Forge Intergovernmental Agreements

Another way that a school district can partner with a non-district entity is to forge an intergovernmental agreement. School districts often adopt policies or practices that involve allowing other governmental bodies priority over the use of their facilities when they are not being used for district purposes.

For instance, the city's elected officials (i.e., the mayor and city council) may wish to use a school for their public meetings, or a secondary school district may wish to use a primary school district's facilities, or perhaps the park district may wish to use the school's facilities for its recreational programs. These governmental units generally have the power to tax the school district's constituents. These bodies also are elected by some, if not all, of these constituents. Accordingly, some school districts believe that the district's assets are the community's assets and should be used cooperatively by the governmental agencies that serve the community.

In addition, to the extent that such governmental bodies already tax the community, some districts feel that to charge other governmental bodies significant fees for the use of district facilities is tantamount to a double tax on the community.

Suppose, for example, an elementary school district charges the community's secondary school district a rental fee for the use of an auditorium for a high school play. The taxpayers already are taxed by the high school district and by the elementary school district. When the high school district is charged a fee by the elementary school district, that fee is arguably an additional tax on the high school district (and its constituents) by the elementary school district. Alternatively, the community may view such rental fees as an efficient "value-maximizing" exchange of assets between two taxing bodies, each of which is separately entrusted to maximize the value of its resources.

A school district that wants to expand into pre-K education, or to contract with private early education providers, or to support a Head Start program, may attempt to find space for the program by entering into an intergovernmental agreement with another governmental entity such as the park district. These intergovernmental contracts tend to be based on in-kind consideration or below-market consideration.

The typical intergovernmental agreement can be divided into the following basic sections: the recitals and incorporation of recitals; the term and termination clause; the exchange of consideration, including maintenance and use provisions; risk allocation in the context of indemnity and insurance; incorporation and/or preservation of prior agreements; nondiscrimination; and signature. Appendix C provides examples of each of these sections.

Enter Into Lease or License Agreements

If a school district ultimately decides to allow a non-district organization (not governed by an intergovernmental agreement) to use its facilities, the district will have to enter a lease or licensing agreement. These contracts often have the following sections: (1) recitals; (2) incorporation of recitals; (3) relationship among the parties; (4) supervision of the facilities; (5) payment terms; (6) utilities fees; (7) custodial services; (8) penalties for alteration of the premises or damage to the premises; (9) validity of occupant's licenses and permits; (10) subletting; (11) insurance; (12) nondiscrimination; (13) indemnification; (14) termination; (15) removal rights; (16) use of school district's name; (17) governing law; and (18) acceptable uses of the facilities.

An example of a license agreement that can be used by a public school district to allow a private early childhood education provider to use the school's facilities is present in Appendix D.

Examples of Public-Private Partnerships That Have Been Successfully Employed to Expand Access

Several states and districts have used public-private partnerships to fund their early childhood education programs. In a public-private partnership, a government agency enters into an agreement with a private sector organization to provide a public service.

In the context of early childhood education, a school district may contribute to a private provider financial support, certified teachers, training, professional development, materials, supplies, and equipment.[72] A school district may have resources that can enhance program delivery.[73] Additionally, a school district may be able to provide to a private provider guidance on personnel, payroll, and policy decisions, and administrative functions.[74] The private provider may contribute space, "wrap around care," advertising to the community, wellness screenings, and additional resources.[75]

In order to be successful, the participants in a public-private partnership should build a relationship based upon mutual respect, develop a shared data base and directory, identify gaps in service delivery, clarify expectations upon entrance to kindergarten, and communicate to the public the value of this investment.[76]

The following are examples of successful partnerships:

Educare

Educare provides an exceptional model of a highly successful public-private partnership. Educare is a state-of-the-art school early childhood education program that is open full-day and full-year and serves at-risk children from birth to five years old. The first site opened in Chicago in 2000 by the Ounce of Prevention Fund, an early childhood advocacy group that operates home-visiting, Head Start, and Early Head Start programs. In Educare learning environments throughout the country, children receive an array of early childhood services—everything the research suggests is effective—under one roof. Educare facilities are supported by anchor philanthropists, foundations, the school superintendent, and other local and community partners.[77]

Educare serves at-risk children and helps them enter kindergarten close to the national average on vocabulary, social-emotional skills, and other indicators of school readiness.[78] Even more than that, Educare's effects do not diminish over time—Chicago graduates in third grade experienced less grade retention and fewer special education placements and maintained their early gains in math and reading.[79] Research from the Frank Porter Graham Child Development Institute at the University of North Carolina found that low-income children who enroll in Educare as infants or toddlers enter kindergarten with the same skills as their middle-income peers.[80]

Furthermore, Educare helps families become advocates for their children in school and their daily lives—more than two-thirds of Educare graduates' parents were rated "actively involved" by elementary school teachers.[81] Diana Rauner, president of the Ounce of Prevention Fund, considers the Educare network "a two-generation program": "[a] key goal is to empower parents to advocate for themselves and their children: to demand that quality continue once their kids get to elementary school and beyond, and to encourage others in their communities to do the same."[82]

The private sector, Head Start and Early Head Start, families, community leaders, and local school districts are brought together in each Educare school.[83] Each Educare School allows leaders to experience firsthand what high-quality early education looks like for the most at-risk children, causing these leaders to become voices that help catalyze policy change and spark new investments in early childhood education.[84]

Vermont

In 2007, Vermont passed a law that encourages public-private partnerships in its provision of three- and four-year-old early childhood education programs. Under this program, the state provides towns with funding to support early childhood programs. The towns may provide those programs through public school districts or by contracting with private providers. State funding is provided for up to half of the three- and four-year-olds' school that reside in a school district.[85] The local taxpayers can contribute the remainder.

Vermont's Act 62 defined public funded pre-K as a 6–10 hour a week program for three- to five-year-olds that lasts at least 35 weeks a year. Pre-K can be held in center-based child care programs, home-based child care programs, private early childhood education programs, and in public schools. Participating school districts can partner with community care and education programs as well.

Like other programs that exist throughout the country, Vermont's law requires these public-private programs to meet educator and curriculum standards and restricts public funding to only 10 hours per week per child. Vermont stresses that early childhood education is a local decision, so Act 62 also requires community input when a new early childhood education program is opened.[86]

North Carolina

North Carolina created its "Smart Start" program in 1993 as a way to better prepare children for school. This public-private partnership works with all of the state's counties to provide resources to create a high-quality, comprehensive, accountable system for the care and education of children. The program partners with private child care programs to increase their accessibility to more four-year-olds throughout the state and to improve the quality of their programs.[87] Smart Start also manages a large portion of the state's pre-K program, called NC Pre-K. NC Pre-K provides early childhood education for eligible four-year-olds.

Alaska

Alaska's "Best Beginnings" program, developed in 2006, facilitates public-private investments in early childhood education. The Best Beginnings program brings together seven communities throughout the state to develop public-private partnerships to promote effective and efficient early childhood education programs and services. The program is funded by the state and local donations.[88]

The Collaboration for Early Childhood and the Community Family Center in Illinois

The Collaboration for Early Childhood (CEC) and the Community Family Center (CFC) in Illinois are excellent examples of successful public-private partnerships. Both organizations are dedicated to bringing together a community's outstanding public and private early childhood education providers to meet the needs of young learners. Their objective is to ensure that every child arrives at kindergarten safe, healthy, ready to succeed and eager to learn, and that families receive the support they need.

The CEC comprises more than 60 active partners including the Village, township, Park District, Library, health clinics, social service agencies, child care centers, and early childhood providers. Funded by governmental units, foundations, and individual donors, the CEC has an integrated early childhood system that provides early detection screenings, parent information and support, professional development, and public early childhood education coordination.

Similarly, the CFC brings together public and private early childhood education providers, family services organizations, public school districts, and local governmental agencies to provide a full range of early education services to children and families throughout the community. The organizations create tremendous synergies in their support for children and their families by sharing facilities, services, and best practices.

The CEC and the CFC also have developed a shared mission and a sense of interdependency.[89] The visionary educators, policy makers, and collaborators in these programs have identified and articulated a community-wide need, and then addressed that need by building relationships around their shared purpose.[90] Finally, both the CEC and the CFC have established governance structures that assure the maintenance of strong relationships and a fair and inclusive process.[91]

THE COMPREHENSIVE IMPLEMENTATION STRATEGY: SUPPORTING TEACHERS AND RECONCILING POLICY DEBATES ABOUT ACCOUNTABILITY AND PRIVATIZATION

Federal, state, and local policy makers should focus on a comprehensive approach in which they implement policies that transcend the debates about "accountability" and "privatization." They can do this by providing teachers in public, private, or charter schools the professional training and professional development to create Reggio-inspired social constructivist learning environments. These teachers should be held accountable through a range of authentic assessment tools, including documentation.

Finland provides a particularly compelling model for policy makers seeking to expand access to early childhood educational opportunities. In *Finnish Lessons: What Can the World Learn from Educational Change in Finland?* (2011), Pasi Sahlberg describes how Finland transformed its educational system into a paragon of excellence and equity—during a period of tremendous economic distress.

As a result of its national reform initiatives, "Finland is one of the world's leaders in the academic performance of its secondary school students. . . . This performance is remarkably consistent across schools. Finnish schools seem to serve all students well, regardless of family background, socio-economic status or ability. . . . The strength of the educational performance of Finland is its consistent high level of student learning, equitably distributed across schools throughout the country."[92]

According to virtually every international indicator of educational quality, Finland now "has one of the most educated citizenries in the world, provides educational opportunities in an egalitarian manner, and makes efficient use of resources."[93]

In particular, data and surveys from the Organization for Economic Cooperation and Development, Trends in International Mathematics and Sciences Study, and the Program for International Student Assessment show that Finnish students excel in educational performance over all assessed domains, including math, literacy, and science. In the Global Index of Cognitive Skills and Educational Attainment, which compares performance on international education tests, literacy, and graduation rates for students from 40 industrialized countries, Finland ranks at or near the top and well ahead of the United States.[94]

Moreover, Finland has accomplished this remarkable level of student learning in an extremely cost-efficient manner. Although virtually all of Finland's expenditures for education derive from public funds, its total educational expenditures are only 5.6 percent of its gross domestic product.[95] That percentage is less than the average spent by the other highest-performing countries and substantially less than America's rate of 7.6 percent of gross domestic product. Significantly, the cumulative cost of educating a student from ages 6 to 15 in Finland is approximately 60 percent of the cost of educating such a student in the United States.[96]

What are the particular educational reforms that have led to Finland's remarkable success? Educators from all over the world have studied the Finnish experience and have settled on five critical ingredients:

1. Equal educational opportunities are available for all, including early childhood education resources.[97]
2. Teaching is a revered and highly valued profession to which the best and brightest students aspire.
3. Parents, students, and political figures trust teachers and school administrators and give them professional freedom to develop and adjust their skills to meet student needs.

4. The political forces surrounding education maintain a stable vision of education as a public service and defer to the professional judgments of educators to implement that vision.
5. The nation has not fallen prey to the fallacious educational "accountability" movement rooted in externally imposed, high-stakes standardized tests.

Among these characteristics, "research and experience suggests that one factor trumps all others: the daily contributions of excellent teachers."[98] The development of an excellent and equitable national system of early childhood education starts with improving teacher education. The Finnish experience "shows that it is more important to ensure that teachers' work in schools is based on professional dignity and social respect. . . . Teachers' work should strike a balance between classroom teaching and collaboration with other professionals in school."[99]

As Sahlberg and virtually all serious education experts throughout the world who have studied Finland have concluded, "[a]ll of the factors that are behind the Finnish success seem to be the opposite of what is taking place in the United States."[100] Finland has rejected the American strategies of test-based accountability, standardization, privatization, charter schools, school closings, and belittling teachers and their unions. Instead of pursuing these policies, Finland has achieved its remarkable educational improvement by investing public funds wisely in a system that trains and trusts its professional educators to teach all of its children to develop habits of mind vital to their future.

Reliance on Finland as a guide to educational reform in the United States has been criticized on the grounds that Finland is a relatively small country with a homogeneous population. Yet the reforms that have driven Finland's success have been employed with similar results throughout the world. In *The Learning Curve*, the Economist Intelligence Unit analyzed data from over 50 countries to determine the strength of correlation between education reforms and nationwide student outcomes.

Data reveal lessons for early education policy makers in the United States. Five strategies are indispensable to effective early childhood education programs: (1) a long-term investment and a sustained system-wide approach; (2) support for the value of education for all children within the surrounding culture; (3) collaboration with—not control by—parents and care givers; (4) instructional practices and goals designed to teach children skills and habits of mind they will need for the future, not the past; and (5) a systemic commitment to respecting and valuing early childhood educators as professionals.

In particular, the report found: "There is no substitute for good teachers. . . . Successful school systems have a number of things in common: they find culturally effective ways to attract the best people to the profession; they provide relevant, ongoing training; they give teachers a status similar to that of other respected professions; and the system sets clear goals and expectations but also lets teachers get on with meeting these."[101] The remarkably diverse group of countries that have achieved educational excellence all share Finland's commitment to valuing teachers as professionals and to granting them the autonomy to collaborate with their colleagues in educating their students according to their professional judgment.

NOTES

1. Michael A. Rebell and Molly A. Hunter, "The Right to Preschool in Education Adequacy Litigations," National Access Network, Teachers College, Columbia University, October 2006, http://www.schoolfunding.info/resource_center/issuebriefs/preschool.pdf.

2. *Hoke County Bd. v. State of North Carolina*, 599 S.E. 365 (M.C. 2004).

3. *Hoke County Bd. of Educ. v. State of North Carolina*, No. COA 11-1545 (Aug. 21, 2012).

4. James E. Ryan, "A Constitutional Right to Preschool," *California Law Review* 94(1) (2006): 84. See also James J. Heckman, "The Case for Investing in Disadvantaged Young Children: Remarks at the White House Conference on December 16, 2011," http://heckmanequation.org/content/resource/remarks-white-house-early-learning-challenge-announcement.

5. Ryan, "A Constitutional Right to Preschool," 85.

6. Ibid.

7. Ibid., 86.

8. Ibid.

9. Ibid.

10. See, e.g., *Raymond Abbott et al. v. Burke*, 153 N.J. 400 (1990).

11. See, e.g., Federal Rule of Evidence 702; *United States v. Mornan*, 413 F.3d 372 (3d Cir. 2005); Robert M. Lloyd, "The Reasonable Certainty Requirement in Lost Profits Litigation: What It Really Means" (working paper, University of Tennessee, November 2010), 6.

12. Ryan, "A Constitutional Right to Preschool," 87.

13. Ibid.

14. Heckman, "The Case for Investing."

15. Ryan, "A Constitutional Right to Preschool," 88.

16. Ibid., 89.

17. Ibid.

18. Ibid.

19. See Heckman, "The Case for Investing."

20. Ryan, "A Constitutional Right to Preschool," 97.

21. Ibid.

22. Ibid. See also *Lake View School District No. 25 v. Huckabee*, No. 01-836, 2004 WL 1406270 (Arkansas, June 18, 2004).

23. Ryan, "A Constitutional Right to Preschool," 97. Michael J. Klarman, *From Jim Crow to Civil Rights: The Supreme Court and Racial Equality* (New York: Oxford University Press, 2004), 463–64; Michael McCann, *Rights at Work: Pay Equity Reform and the Politics of Legal Mobilization* (Chicago: University of Chicago, 1994).

24. The White House: Office of the Press Secretary, "Fact Sheet President Obama's Plan for Early Education for All Americans," February 13, 2013, http://www.whitehouse.gov/the-press-office/2013/02/13/fact-sheet-president-obama-s-plan-early-education-all-americans.

25. Ibid.

26. Ibid.

27. U.S. Department of Education, "Early Learning: America's Middle Class Promise Begins Early," http://www.ed.gov/early-learning.

28. W.S. Barnett et al., *The State of Preschool 2012: State Preschool Yearbook* (New Brunswick, NJ: National Institute for Early Education Research, 2012), http://nieer.org/sites/nieer/files/yearbook2012.pdf.

29. U.S. Department of Education, "Early Learning."

30. First Five Years Fund, "Strong Start for Children Act," ffyf.org. See also Committee on Education and the Workforce, http://edworkforce.house.gov.

31. Barnett et al., *The State of Preschool 2012*.

32. Ibid.

33. Ibid.

34. California Department of Education, "Child Care and Development Programs," http://www.cde.ca.gov/sp/cd/op/cdprograms.asp.

35. Barnett et al., *The State of Preschool 2012*.

36. Barnett et al., *The State of Preschool 2012*.

37. Mississippi Senate Bill 2395, http://billstatus.ls.state.ms.us/2013/pdf/history/SB/SB2395.xml.

38. Barnett et al., *The State of Preschool 2012*.

39. Ibid.

40. West Virginia Board of Education, "West Virginia's Universal Access to a Quality Early Education System: Policy 2525," 2013–2014, http://apps.sos.wv.gov/adlaw/csr/readfile.aspx?DocId=25885&Format=PDF.

41. Barnett et al., *The State of Preschool 2012*.

42. Adrienne Lu, "Elected Officials Embrace Preschool, But Funding Is the Catch," *The Pew Charitable Trusts*, February 28, 2014, www.pewtrusts.org/en/research-and-analysis/blogs/stateline/2014/02/28/elected-officials-embrace-preschool-but-funding-is-the-catch.

43. See Ginia Bellafante, "Guiding Guided Play," *New York Times*, September 7, 2014, 26.

44. Lu, "Elected Officials Embrace Preschool."

45. Ibid.

46. Ibid.

47. Ibid.

48. Ibid.

49. W. Steven Barnett, "Benefits and Costs of Early Childhood Education," *Children Legal Rights Journal* 7 (2007): 14–15. See also W.S. Barnett et al., *The State of Preschool 2013: State Preschool Yearbook* (New Brunswick, NJ: National Institute for Early Education Research, 2013).

50. See W.S. Barnett and Donald J. Yarosz, "Who Goes to Preschool and Why Does it Matter?," *National Institute for Early Education Research* 15 (November 2007), http://nieer.org/resources/policybriefs/15.pdf.

51. Debra J. Ackerman and W. Steven Barnett, "Increasing the Effectiveness of Preschool Programs," *National Institute for Early Education Research* 11 (July 2006), http://nieer.org/resources/policybriefs/11.pdf, citing D. Cassidy, L. Hestenes, S. Mims, and S. Hestenes, *The North Carolina Rated License: A Three-Year Summary of Assessed Facilities (Executive Summary)* (Greensboro, North Carolina: University of North Carolina, 2003).

52. Ackerman and Barnett, "Increasing the Effectiveness."

53. Richard M. Clifford and Stephanie S. Reszka, "Reliability and Validity of the Early Childhood Education Scale" (working paper, FPG Child Development Institute, University of North Carolina at Chapel-Hill, January 2010): 2, http://www.ersi.info/PDF/ReliabilityEcers.pdf.

54. National Association for the Education of Young Children, "Licensing and Public Regulation of Early Childhood Programs: A Position Statement of the National Association for the Education of Young Children" (Washington, DC: National Association for the Education of Young Children, 1997): 8, https://www.naeyc.org/files/naeyc/file/positions/PSLIC98.PDF.

55. National Association for the Education of Young Children. "NAEYC Standards for Early Childhood Professional Preparation Programs" (Washington, DC: National Association for the Education of Young Children, 2009): 3, http://www.naeyc.org/files/naeyc/files/2009%20Professional%20Prep%20stdsRevised%204_12.pdf.

56. *Digest of Education Statistics* (Washington, DC: U.S. Department of Education National Center for Education Statistics, 2013), Table 205, http://nces.ed.gov/programs/digest/d12/tables/dt12_205.asp.

57. *Fast Facts* (Washington, DC: U.S. Department of Education National Center for Education Statistics, 2014), http://nces.ed.gov/fastfacts/display.asp?id=372.

58. B. Goad, "Public Health Group Backs Obama's 94-Cent Cigarette Tax Hike," *The Hill*, http://thehill.com/regulation/administration/324417-groups-back-obamas-94-cent-cigarette-tax-hike-to-fund-early-childhood-education.

59. U.S. Department of Housing and Urban Development, "State Administered CDBG," http://portal.hud.gov/hudportal/HUD?src=/program_offices/comm_planning/communitydevelopment/programs/stateadmin.

60. 45 CFR 260.20

61. Office of Child Care: An Office of the Administration for Children & Families, "Using TANF to Fund Childhood Education," April 14, 2005, http://www.acf.hhs.gov/programs/occ/resource/program-instruction-tanf-acf-pi-2005-01.

62. James J. Heckman, "Invest in Early Childhood Development: Reduce Deficits, Strengthen the Economy," December 7, 2014, http://heckmanequation.org/content/resource/invest-early-childhood-development-reduce-deficits-strengthen-economy. See also James J. Heckman, "Letter to National Commission on Fiscal Responsibility and Budget Reform," http://heckmanequation.org/content/resource/letter-national-commission-fiscal-responsibility-and-reform; Conor Desmond, "Illinois's Future is the Children: Why Funding Early Childhood Education Will Not Only Push Illinois' Economy to the Top but Will Play a Role in Paying Down Our Debt," *Loyola University Chicago Journal of Early Education Law and Policy* (2014), http://www.luc.edu/law/centers/childlaw/institutes/child_education/early_education/index.html.

63. Ellen Boylan and Shad White, "Formula for Success: Adding High-Quality Pre-K to State School Funding Formulas," The Pew Center on the States, May 2010, 10, http://www.edlawcenter.org/assets/files/pdfs/School%20Funding/AddingPre-KToFundingFormulas(2).pdf.

64. ESEA§ 1115(b)(1)(A)(ii); 34 C.F.R. §77.1

65. ESEA §1114(a)(2)(A)(i).

66. ESEA §1115(b)(1)(B).

67. "International Development: What If You Could Invest in Development?," *Social Finance*, http://www.socialfinance.org.uk/work/developmentimpactbonds.

68. Kristina Costa, "Fact Sheet: Social Impact Bonds in the United States," Center for American Progress, February 12, 2014, http://www.americanprogress.org/issues/economy/report/2014/02/12/84003/fact-sheet-social-impact-bonds-in-the-united-states/.

69. "Calculating Social Impact Bonds," *Education Week* 32(37), http://www.edweek.org/ew/section/multimedia/social-impact-calculator.html.

70. 2013 Kids Count Data Book, "National Key Indicators by Race and Hispanic Origin," (2013), 15, http://datacenter.kidscount.org/files/2013kidscountdatabook.pdf; 2013 Kids Count Data Book, "Child Population by Race" (2013). See also National Center for Education Statistics, Preschool: First Findings Early Childhood Longitudinal Study, Birth Cohort (2007).

71. See United States Census, State and County Quick Facts (2014); "Child Population by Race" (the U.S. population is approximately 316 million; 14 percent are African American and 24 percent are Hispanic or Latino).

72. Patte Barth, "Invest in Pre-K: Win Valuable Prizes" (presentation at Loyola University Chicago School of Law Early Childhood Education Symposium, Chicago, Illinois, March 15, 2013), http://www.luc.edu/law/centers/childlaw/institutes/child_education/symposium.html.

73. Maureen Hager, "Implementing the Vision: Strategies for Creating Lawful, High-Quality, and Cost-Effective Early Childhood Collaborations" (presentation at Loyola University Chicago School of Law Early Childhood Education Symposium, Chicago, Illinois, March 15, 2013), http://www.luc.edu/law/centers/childlaw/institutes/child_education/symposium.html.

74. Ibid.

75. Barth, "Invest in Pre-K."

76. Hager, "Implementing the Vision."

77. Sarah Mead, "Why Are These Kids So Short? An Introduction to Early Childhood Education" (presentation at Loyola University Chicago School of Law Early Childhood Education Symposium, Chicago, Illinois, March 15, 2013), http://www.luc.edu/law/centers/childlaw/institutes/child_education/symposium.html.

78. Educare, "Change the First Five Years, Change Everything."

79. Ibid.

80. Educare, "Demonstrating Results."

81. "Change the First Five Years, Change Everything."

82. Sara Neufeld, "The Power of Pre-K: Model Early Ed Program in Chicago Lifts Entire Family," in *In Plain Sight: Poverty in America*, November 23, 2013, http://www.nbcnews.com/_news/2013/11/23/21537069-the-power-of-pre-k-model-early-ed-program-in-chicago-lifts-entire-family.

83. "Change the First Five Years, Change Everything."

84. Ibid.

85. See "Act 62 of 2007," Vermont Agency of Education, http://education.vermont.gov/early-education/pre-kindergarten.

86. Ibid.

87. See "Smart Start & The North Carolina Partnership for Children, Inc.," http://www.smartstart.org/category/smart-start-information/about-smart-start

88. See "Best Beginnings: Alaska's Early Childhood Investment," http://www.bestbeginningsalaska.org/what-we-do/early-childhood-partnerships

89. Carolyn Newberry Schwartz, "Implementing the Vision: Strategies for Creating Lawful, High-Quality, and Cost-Effective Early Childhood Collaborations" (presentation at Loyola University Chicago School of Law Early Childhood Education Symposium, Chicago, Illinois, March 15, 2013), http://www.luc.edu/law/centers/childlaw/institutes/child_education/symposium.html.

90. Ibid.

91. See, e.g., http://collab4kids.org/ and http://communityfamilycenter.org/cfc/. See also Schwartz, "Implementing the Vision."

92. Pasi Sahlberg and Paul Michael Garcia, *Finnish Lessons: What Can the World Learn From Educational Change in Finland?* (New York: Teachers College Press, 2012), 55.

93. Ibid., 1.

94. *The Learning Curve* (Boston: Pearson 2012), Chart 9.

95. Ibid., 57.

96. Ibid., 58.

97. Although compulsory education in Finland does not begin until age seven, Finland fully supports and subsidizes a variety of early childhood education opportunities for all of its children.

98. Sahlberg and Garcia, *Finnish Lessons,* 70.

99. Ibid.

100. Ibid., 11.

101. See *The Learning Curve,* 1.

Chapter Nine

Strategies for Developing a Social Constructivist Early Learning Environment

The social construction of knowledge in early childhood requires an emphasis on the development of meaningful relationships in the educational environment. Those relationships are best formed in an educational setting in which children are encouraged to engage in role-playing, pursue shared activities, express their learning through multiple media and materials, and develop habits of literacy, mathematics, and science together with their peers. This chapter presents stories from such a setting, and displays how relationships have been built and knowledge has been constructed by three- and four-year-old children in early childhood education programs in the city of Chicago.[1]

ROLE-PLAYING

If the goal of early childhood education is to enable children to construct knowledge and meaning in their lives, then the educational environment must encourage the development of meaningful social relationships.[2] Children construct knowledge primarily through play. In the context of education, the concept of play often is disparaged as the opposite of "work." Policy makers may be tempted to argue that play takes away valuable instruction time that could be spent delivering academic or cognitive skills. When children are at play, it is often suggested, they are not learning their letters and their numbers.

The perception of play, however, is uninformed and unfounded. Play is an indispensable ingredient in a child's cognitive and social development.[3] In particular, role-playing among children develops their higher mental functions. When children engage in role-playing, they necessarily create an imaginary situation, place themselves in another person's mindset, act out another person's imagined feelings and intentions, and perform in accordance with standards of behavior appropriate to their role.[4]

Each aspect of role-playing advances a child's mental processes and creates vital habits of mind and heart. Children who create an imaginary situation must mediate their perception, focus their attention, exercise their deliberate memory, and solve problems through logical thinking.[5]

Strong empirical evidence has since confirmed Vygotsky's findings. Children are able to remember more items or words in a role-play setting than otherwise.[6] They also are able to focus and pay attention for more sustained periods of time during dramatic play.[7] The evidence also indicates that children develop their "executive function" during play. They practice and learn critical habits of self-regulation.

Children who role-play a restaurant scene, for example, are able to remember and follow a recipe, take their appropriate physical place in the scene, patiently wait until the meal is completed, and even patiently wait until it is their turn to be served. In the play situation, the children recognize that the meal may not start with ice cream, and will wait until it is time to have dessert. They may even "act" as if they are too impatient to wait for ice cream by pretending to cry or whine. But the child is in control of his or her own behavior and is able to compel himself to stop pretending to cry or whine.

By practicing the art of self-control, the child develops the skill, confidence, and self-awareness to exercise self-control in the "real world."[8] In addition, Vygotsky found that children actually experience great joy when they practice self-regulation in their role-playing. Although they must refrain from doing something that the rules of their role forbid, they discover "maximum pleasure" in their display of willpower.[9]

Because children are on the verge of developing critical skills of self-regulation and mental processes during their pre-K years, "group play has a unique role and cannot be replaced by any other activity."[10] Moreover, careful observation and documentation of the learning that occurs during play is a much more reliable predictor of a child's future success and well-being than a snapshot assessment of the child's "academic" performance.[11] During play, the teacher can observe the child's development in real time. The child's mental functions are emerging in the course of the play. The teacher can therefore follow the child's developmental path and fully appreciate how the child learns.[12]

The power of imaginative play to strengthen executive functioning and cognitive skills is evident in the following documentation. A teacher reflects on an emergent theatrical experience:

We started by gathering in a circle for "story time." I proceeded to read the story out loud inviting them to see the images (of the image-less story) in their heads. The students were able to anticipate what was going to happen next, showing great interest in the story.

After we were done reading the story, I encouraged the students to stand up (within the boundaries of the green rug) and to show me with their bodies the story as I re-read it out loud.

The children transformed from egg, to caterpillar, to chrysalis, and finally to butterfly.

The children immediately knew that caterpillars crawled on their bellies . . . a chrysalis is initially very still (Abigail and Mateo found great stillness and silence in this stage) . . . and butterflies flutter in the wind and travel from flower to flower feeding on nectar (Charlotte sucked on the nectar as if through a straw, while Jasmine and Eli licked the "flowers" as a lollypop).

It was so interesting to see how Charlotte, Jasmine, and Damian knew what the word "quivering" meant as I read out loud "the chrysalis quivered," trembling slightly in their imaginary cocoons.

The next day, the class started to mount their production on stage (an elevated corner of our classroom) in small groups:

The children physicalized the four stages in a butterfly's transformation, utilizing silks as their very own chrysalis and wings. I was quite impressed with the children as they navigated the very small stage as caterpillars and butterflies without bumping into each other (respecting each other's personal space . . . another very important lesson).

On the third day—performance day—all of the children were terribly excited to get on stage and show their classmates their "acting chops":

To make things a little bit more interesting we told them we would record their performance (on our iPad) and display it on our monitor at the end of the day (this REALLY got them hyped!).

It was wonderful to see how the children had retained the story . . . they not only knew what came next but seamlessly transitioned from "stage" to "stage" (as evident on our videos). The children were able to fill the "stage space" in a respectful way, always being mindful of each other's personal space . . . always allowing themselves and the other ensemble members a chance to shine.

Although children can engage in role-playing by themselves, the act of role-playing with others also requires them to develop inter-subjectivity—the essential ability to perceive and respond to another person's feelings and intentions.[13] The ability to put yourself in someone else's shoes is critical to success and well-being. It enables children to collaborate and to negotiate with others in satisfying ways.

According to Vygotsky, a child develops the mental tools necessary for self-regulation through a role-playing social process. The child acquires the tools to master his or her own behavior from the outside in, by internalizing the language of others. For example, children will learn to govern their impulse to touch dangerous objects by first receiving a message about their dangers from others or from their own experience, but then will internalize the message and be able to communicate to themselves to refrain from the behavior without being told or having to revisit the negative experience.[14]

By incorporating into their own mental processes the language of their experiences, children construct the tools they need to master their own behavior.[15] The development of mental tools needed for self-regulation and executive function begins in social interactions, and then, after they are internalized, can be used by the child in new situations.

Meaningful social relationships formed through play and role-playing are also indispensable to the development of higher mental functions. Vygotsky identifies four kinds of higher mental functions:

1. Mediated perception;
2. Focused attention;
3. Deliberate memory; and
4. Logical thinking.

Human beings use "mediated perception" to distinguish characteristics of people or materials and to categorize them based on differences and similarities. Focused attention is the ability to filter many stimuli and to concentrate on a particular stimulus. Deliberate memory is the tool of placing prior experiences into a meaningful context that will enable the individual to recall that experience. Logical thinking is the ability to exercise the mental and behavioral strategies necessary to solve problems.

Each of these higher mental functions requires a process by which a child internalizes social behaviors. External behaviors "grow into the mind" of the child.[16] For example, when a child interacts with another child, both children recognize that they are similar and different from each other. From the discovery of difference in a social relationship, each child then begins to internalize the process by which perceptions are categorized as similar or different. The internalization of that process becomes the higher mental function of "mediated perception."

When children interact with others and express their recognition of different people or different things, they develop strategies for mathematics. When children play a game of "duck-duck-goose," they express external counting strategies. They communicate to the group their perception of different beings. The social process of matching each separate being with a sound like "duck" is an external counting strategy. The child then internalizes that counting strategy by silently adding items in the child's head. Children may even vocalize counting numbers quietly to themselves as a strategy to facilitate the internalization process. Once the internalization is complete, the child has constructed higher mental functions. As Vygotsky concludes: "Social relations, real relations of people, stand behind all the higher mental functions and their relations."[17]

As the butterfly performance demonstrates, role-playing also leads directly to literacy. The "act of separating object and ideas is also preparation for the transition to writing, where the word looks nothing like the object it stands for."[18] As Vygotsky concludes: "the fact of creating an imaginary situation can be regarded as a means of developing abstract thought."[19]

Play thus creates the foundation for abstract thought. When a child imagines that a block is a truck, the child understands that a real object can represent another object, or another idea. The single block can then "stand for" the number 1, and another block can "stand for" the number 2. The child learns to count by imagining that the object represents an abstract idea like a number.

Play also creates a "zone of proximal development." Play enables the child to develop "skills that are on the edge of emergence."[20] When a child engages in play, "the child is always behaving beyond his age . . . in play he is, as it were, a head above himself."[21] The zone is a "distance between the actual developmental level as determined by independent problem solving and the level of potential development as determined by problem solving under adult guidance or in collaboration with more capable peers."[22] When the distance between collaboration problem solving and the child's internalizations of independent strategies for problem solving is "proximate," the opportunity for learning and development opens up. At that point—in that zone—a more knowledgeable teacher or peer can collaborate with the child so that "what the child is able to do in collaboration today, he will be able to do independently tomorrow."[23]

Accordingly, play develops in children those very habits of mind and heart that Howard Gardner has found to be indispensable to their future success: a disciplined mind because they become an expert in a particular situation; a synthesizing mind because they gather, organize, and communicate information for other role players; a creating mind because they must imagine and produce a novel dramatic situation; a respectful mind because they must understand the perspectives and motivations of the people whose roles they are acting out as well as the other role players; and an ethical mind because they must fully internalize the standards of behavior required for their particular role.[24]

SHARED ACTIVITIES

Because learning occurs in social relationships, an environment that facilitates shared activities is particularly conducive to learning. Shared projects encourage the construction of knowledge. They also require the child to develop processes for communicating with others through multiple means of expression, including written and spoken language. In a shared project, children also assist each other, which in turn allows them to practice their mental processes. The communication of mental functions among individuals perpetuates the dynamic process by which knowledge is constructed together externally and then internalized by each child independently.

In this early childhood learning environment, the teacher describes how her classroom uses blocks to construct knowledge together:

> *The children are just discovering the potential in the heavy hollow blocks and in the unit blocks to create imaginary worlds of their own. As they build, they experiment with size, shape, symmetry, proportion, height, weight, length, balance, gravity, angle and probably 100 other concepts that escape me at this minute. As teachers, one of our jobs is to articulate what they are doing, so that they have the words they need to reflect with others on what they have accomplished (e.g., "I notice you've built a ramp and that the cylinder rolls down the ramp."). Our observations get increasingly complex over time (e.g., "I see that the cylinder slides down when it is on its side on the ramp, but it rolls when turned around on the ramp."). We also allow ourselves to wonder aloud as to the possibilities yet uncovered (e.g., "I wonder if this cylinder on this ramp will roll faster or slower than this cylinder on this ramp? How could we find out?").*
>
> *But beyond making more visible the mathematical and scientific learning inherent in block building, I'd like to focus on social learning. More specifically, I'd like to look at how this kind of play presents opportunities for children to learn about relative power in the classroom.*

In this early childhood learning environment, the teacher encouraged the children to join in a shared project that emerged naturally from their own sense of empathy. The teacher then documented the profound learning that took place in the process:

Today the children built a house for Puppy . . . this always seems to be a popular idea with our class. Puppy is the stuffed animal who began the year by whispering important questions in my ear that many children were also wondering (e.g., What if I need to go to the bathroom? What if I miss my mommy?). Puppy is very loved. A few children began by taking a few heavy hollow blocks from the gathering space. Others introduced unit blocks into the design, and still others discovered that the angled blocks/ ramps caused other blocks, and children, to slide or roll down. As you might guess, even 6 children in one small area caused a bit of congestion. So here, in no particular order, are thoughts and questions about relation- ships that a nearby teacher might have observed children grappling with:

I brought that block in the room. It is my block.
He brought that block in the room, but it is touching my block so I can move it.
I wish I had a block like that. I wonder if I can use it. I wonder if I need to wait my turn.
I put blocks on top of that block so this is my building.
I really want to sit on that block and slide down. Do I need to ask the per- son who placed it here? Do I need to ask the group?
She just slid down and now it's my turn.
They are sliding down and breaking Puppy's house.
I was here first and I don't want anyone to slide.
I don't know why he is crying. I just wanted to build Puppy's house a dif- ferent way.

In sum, questions of ownership and possession abound. It would all be so simple if first was always right, but we learn in JK that sometimes the first person to engage in an activity that becomes collaborative needs to "flex" to include others. We learn that the reward for flexing is friend- ship. And we learn that sometimes, the most outgoing personalities need to listen to the softer voices. We learn that sometimes a question cannot be answered simply by what most children want . . . or by the most adamant voices. Think about the last time YOU worked on a common activity with 6 other people. And then pause and think about all that our children are learning about power in their community: How they feel when they are not

> *able to exercise their free will? How it feels when another child gets their way? How it feels when their wish is different from the wish of the many? How it feels when their wish isn't ok with the teacher? These are important questions of how power is distributed throughout a community, how it's used and misused, how it's transferred, how it's balanced, and how it multiplies. Is it any wonder that our children are exhausted at 11:45?*

The same early childhood education teacher reflects on how her students communicated with each other to solve a problem in the block corner, soon after the block exploration above, but still during the early days of the school year:

> *I happened to be in the corner of the room that houses the brick blocks, large brightly colored cardboard blocks designed to look like bricks. I noticed that one child (Ryan) had begun to build a structure. I was called away from this corner by a child for a few minutes and when I returned found that a commotion was underway. It seemed to me that a second structure was under construction by a group of 4 children working together. They told me that they were making "a house for Puppy." It looked to me like Puppy was inside this structure, and it was becoming more and more elaborate as each of the four children added to his/her vision (it included a telephone and other "housekeeping" items).*
>
> *Ryan appeared to be out of sorts when I returned, struggling to find the words for the injustice he was feeling. There were loud words spoken, "That's mine!" and his frustration was apparent from his body language. I watched as a girl (Sophie) quietly took a brick from his structure and used it to expand Puppy's house. Another girl (Layla) followed this lead, and Ryan's structure dwindled. He became more and more agitated.*
>
> *I situated myself within reach of both structures, sat down to be on the children's level, and announced "we seem to have a problem." "I wonder if someone could explain what is happening." Ryan immediately poured out words that suggested to me that he was not ok with the plan of the other four children to dismantle his structure. I asked the children in the group what they thought the problem was and they told me simply that they needed more bricks for puppy's house.*
>
> *At that point, I stated the problem clearly for the five children. "We seem to have different plans for these bricks. Do you think we can find a*

compromise?" I remember wondering as I said this whether they knew the meaning of compromise.

Almost immediately, Sophie walked toward Ryan to return the brick she had taken. I thanked her but together we reached the conclusion that this didn't rebuild his structure or give him enough bricks to build it again.

Layla suggested, "Let's get more bricks!" But together we looked at the shelves where they had been and concluded that there were no more bricks.

Yet another child, Eli, suggested that they take turns with the bricks. But the sense of urgency around building both structures was such that neither Ryan nor the small group building Puppy's house was inclined to walk away and wait for a turn.

I turned to Ryan, who had been very quiet and seemed to me to be recovering from the injustice he'd experienced, and asked him if he had any ideas. Without hesitation he asked "build something together?" We looked at one another and everyone nodded. Within seconds the group of 5 was building a bigger and better house for Puppy. And Ryan, the child who had originally been so unsettled, had rebounded from feeling wronged, and seemed to me to feel rightfully proud of having been the child who offered the compromise accepted by the group.

I love sharing stories like this because it shows the power of small group work to provide opportunities for:

* *problem-solving*
* *listening to one another*
* *collaboration*

And, this story shows how small group learning necessarily incorporates individual learning within domains. In this case, those building were gaining hands-on experience with the mathematical concepts of symmetry, balance, weight and height while they built. They were also telling a story about Puppy, an early literacy skill.

Of course, none of this learning would have been possible without teachers in the room to be a grounding presence where activity amongst 19 children was occurring, and to ask questions designed to support children in listening to one another and in expressing their own thoughts.

ENCOURAGING MULTIPLE EXPRESSIONS OF LEARNING THROUGH MEDIA AND MATERIALS

A social constructivist learning environment should also include beautiful natural and repurposed materials. Children should be encouraged to interact with those materials, which become media for communicating their learning. In some learning environments, there is sufficient space to create a studio in which children communicate their ideas through multiple forms of artistic expression. But, even in the absence of sufficient space for a studio, a learning center can encourage children to engage in an array of artistic expressions by integrating media and materials throughout the environment.

For instance, Alice and Bruce may be introduced to a new material such as clay. Neither has any understanding of the material or its qualities. Alice begins by placing her thumb into the clay. She observes that her thumb has created an indentation in the clay. Already, she has learned something about both her thumb and the clay. Her external relationship with the clay has become internalized and has shaped her knowledge of herself and her environment. But in a social relationship with Bruce, Alice then will be disposed to share her discovery with him. She will communicate her new knowledge to him, perhaps by showing him the indented clay. This social act alone will allow Alice to revisit the process by which she acquired knowledge of her relationship with the clay, which, in turn, will support her own learning.

In her effort to communicate her knowledge to Bruce, Alice also will make her learning visible to both of them. She is developing language. At first, she may communicate only by showing Bruce the already-indented clay. But, when Bruce communicates his curiosity (perhaps only with a nonverbal facial expression), about how the clay became indented, Alice will be inclined to "show" him how the clay became indented by repeating the activity. As Vygotsky suggested, and as the latest neuroscience research confirms, this collaboration process actually reshapes the mental processes within both Alice and Bruce. Their relationship has constructed their knowledge. Therefore, their knowledge has been co-constructed.

Together, they will assist each other in developing their higher mental functions. Alice helps Bruce to mediate his perception. She makes visible to him her own learning. Her model is an external "mediator" that will assist him in categorizing the textures of the clay, and even establishing a cause and effect context for the differences in their materials.[25] At the same time, this interaction helps both Alice and Bruce to focus their attention on their shared expression. Alice learns to attend deliberatively to communicating with Bruce her indented clay; she is attuned to the precise message that she is trying to convey. She will have to disregard objects or noises or events that compete for her attention. Bruce as well will have to train his attention on his interaction with Alice and his effort to replicate her model.

The act of sharing this experience through multiple forms of communication also helps both Alice and Bruce to exercise their higher mental functions of deliberate memory. Alice and Bruce will be better able to remember the recipe for creating indented clay if they communicate that recipe to each other. The act of recalling and representing the process by communicating it to others develops in memory. But more importantly, the relationship presents a context for the process that is critical to the child's capacity to engage in *deliberate* acts of recall. The recipe for clay indentation in the minds of children becomes inseparable from the social context in which they found joy together in shaping their environment. The recipe will be deliberately recalled whenever each of them constructs knowledge in the future.

The shared expression also creates a foundation for logical thinking. Alice and Bruce have developed behavioral strategies for designing solutions to problems. They have internalized the joy and value of collaborating to accomplish a shared goal, the process of communicating to achieve that goal, and the causal relationship between their behavior and its consequences in changing their environment.

In one early childhood learning environment, a teacher documented how ideas flow from one child to another, only to be picked up and executed in a totally unique way:

Eight children had the opportunity to explore the clay today (two groups of four). Because we chose to set the clay table in the middle of the room, many other children observed those engaged with the clay, and gathered ideas for their future work with clay.

Audrey: I am making some meatballs.
Kyle: It's like play dough! (to Mary) How did you make a sailboat?
Connor: I'm making something else. A surprise!
Maria: You push down on the floor. You can't have it too skinny, so get another piece and make it fatter. Then stick it to your boat.
Connor: I got ideas from Mary!
Kyle: Hey, you were right! Hers (sailboat) is a little deep and mine isn't.
Connor: I added some eyes and a little smile.
Audrey: I'm making all the little pieces into a big piece.
Maria: A snowman! (3 balls)
Enrique: . . . a snake!

As Vygotsky found, and as these learning relationships show, the origins of speech, language, and literacy are social. Language emerges only from shared activities. Public speech is communication with others, while "private speech" is self-directed and not designed for others. Children acquire public speech before private speech. They first develop the ability to use speech in social situations to communicate with others. After the child is able to use speech to communicate with others, the child then internalizes the public speech into private, self-regulating speech. Accordingly, a social exchange is the necessary predicate for all language.

When the child internalizes speech, the child's thinking becomes inseparable from language. A child's vocalizations are an indispensable part of the child's mental functions, and of the child's process of problem solving.[26] "Children become capable of thinking as they talk."[27] In fact, children process stimuli in their minds by speaking with themselves. A child's "private speech" is designed to be understood only by that child. In creating their private language, however, the child already has a natural, intuitive sense that there is an internal audience for the speech.

The very act of thinking is dynamic, expressive, and social. A child constructs knowledge by first participating in a social relationship, and then by expressing a social relationship in his or her own mind. Because children develop thought and language in social relationships, those relationships also are indispensable to making meaning. As Vygotsky showed, a "child constructs meaning through shared activity."[28]

In the following documentation, a teacher reflects on how learning is socially constructed in her classroom:

Anika's mom and Evan's mom came to class to share a little about Diwali, a holiday that is celebrated in India and other countries. The moms, and children Evan, Anika, and Ellie, dressed in traditional Indian clothes, and they brought a silk scarf for the teacher to wear. They also brought battery-powered tea lights to disperse throughout the room, and materials to create rangoli (symmetrical designs inspired by nature).

Teacher: How do lights make you feel?
Avery: (with a smile) Good.
Benjamin: Jewelry is called Bindi and it goes on your forehead.
Caden: My mom came from India.
Max: My dad came from Boston.
Gianna: The lights make me feel beautiful. My mama is from Argentina.

We talked about the rangoli . . .
Teacher: What does symmetrical mean?
Thomas: Everything on the same side is the same on the other side.

Overheard at the painting table . . .
Avery: My mom is from Ireland.
Max: My mom is from Kansas City.
Hannah: Where they grew up? Michigan. You have to drive your car there.

Where should we display our rangoli? (made on transparent contact paper
with colored sand)
Harper: On a wall.
Alex: On a ceiling.
Ellie: On a wall.
Avery: It looks like stained glass.
Teacher: What would happen if we hung it in the window?
Everyone: Oooooo . . . look!

Such shared expressive activities also provide the foundation for self-regu-lation.[29] Children must first seek to regulate other children in social situations before they are able to regulate themselves. If they are given a standard of behavior from an authority figure, children will practice the standard by ap-plying it to others. When the teacher, for example, says to the class that each child should take only one snack, the children often will rehearse the rule by applying it to violators. After they apply the rule to others, they become able to internalize the rule and apply it to themselves. The application of stan-dards of social behavior to peers is a necessary precursor to self-regulation. Children construct their own executive functions through social relationships.

A teacher therefore should try to design various kinds of shared activities be-tween peers with and without similar abilities and dispositions, and for discrete and complex projects. The interactions can even be imaginary. The teacher, for example, might ask students to help three-year-olds in a different school or in a different city understand their own environment by drawing a map.

THE SOCIAL CONSTRUCTION OF LITERACY

In this context, it becomes clear that literacy is also bound up with social relationships. Written speech makes thinking more explicit to others through a shared language. But the child already has learned to use language to construct knowledge and to communicate that knowledge to others. The formulation of written letters is a culturally conventional way of communicating thoughts to others. It is not the end or the beginning of literacy. Rather, letter formation is just one way in which the child uses language to develop the social relationships which are vital to the construction of knowledge and meaning. In criticizing teaching children reading and writing only as a mechanical skill, Vygotsky recognized:

> the teaching [of reading and writing to pre-K children] should be organized in such a way that reading and writing are necessary for something. If they are used only to write official greetings to the staff or whatever the teacher thinks up (and clearly suggests to them), then the exercise will be purely mechanical and may soon bore the child. . . . Reading and writing must be something the child needs. Here we have the most vivid example of the basic contradiction that appears in teaching of writing not only in Montessori's school but in most other schools as well, namely, that writing is taught as motor skill and not as complex cultural activity.[30]

In this early childhood education program within a large, diverse city, a teacher uses a blog to begin a discussion about how she introduced her children to writing instruments within the context of "cultural" activities that were meaningful to the children:

> *For example, a group of children busy in the kitchen began to create menus and to take orders from others. We gave one or two clipboards and pencils and encouraged them to write their menus and take orders. They inspired one another to do the same, and before long we were seeing many intentional lists, left to right squiggly lines, letters in combination, and we saw children reading their own writing to others.*
>
> *Another group of children built a house for Puppy. They asked if Puppy could come to his house, and I used the opportunity to ask them to make invitations for Puppy. They happily obliged, and we shared their invitations with Puppy and with one another at whole group time. I held up each invitation at group time and asked the author of it to come up and read it to the group. Each child recognized his/her own invitation, smiled broadly with pride, and read it aloud. I assured the children that they would soon see their invitations in their portfolios.*
>
> *Their invitations may have become important to us as evidence of the children's emerging literacy, but they began as important to the child for expressing something meaningful within their social world.*

Last week, we began to work with small groups of children in the gathering space, writing lines and curves. We introduced lines and curves of various lengths/sizes, and then asked the children to draw their own. They became deeply engaged in their work and in referencing one another's work.

In the near future, we plan to give each child a small unlined notebook to record messages. It is our hope that this notebook will go back and forth between home and school with meaningful messages written by your child shared between home and school. We will share more about this in time. For now, we ask you to look for opportunities in your everyday routines to engage with your child with writing materials. For example, in a restaurant, pull out a piece of paper and pen and draw a grid of dots and take turns connecting the dots into squares. Ask your child to draw lines (short, long, longer), and curves (big, little), and lines and curves in relation to one another (on top, on the side, under). Draw circles and squares and triangles. Together, seek out shapes in your environment and draw them. These are the little steps with these materials and with concepts that will support your child's emerging literacy.

Social relationships provide a "meaningful social context for learning, language, writing and reading."[31] The social context makes learning literacy both meaningful and enjoyable.[32] The child finds joy in the interaction with a caregiver or a teacher. From that relationship, the child constructs knowledge that can then be communicated with another person. The "shared activity of reading to someone else" is a much more effective learning tool than performing a reading task in isolation.[33]

Placing literacy within a social context is beautifully illustrated by this dialogue that occurred in one early childhood learning environment:

One of the children chose a library book this week titled Brush of the Gods *by Lenore Look with illustrations by Meilo So. This beautiful book tells the story of a young child (Daozi) who became a calligrapher. The story recounts his challenges and experiences, and culminates with the people understanding that "this man is no ordinary painter. He holds the brush of the gods!" It is based on the true story of the artist Wu Daozi who lived sometime around the year 700. A short excerpt:*

One day, Daozi painted a butterfly so exquisite and delicate that he couldn't take his eyes off it. The longer he admired it, the more real it looked. Then a wing moved, just a little, when the wind blew. "What?" said Daozi. He leaned closer. And suddenly, the butterfly rose and floated away like burnt paper above a fire.

The teacher tickled the children's hands with the paintbrush, so that they would understand the lightness of Daozi's touch. We talked about what it means to have "flying sleeves." (As an aside, I find that we have reason to talk about a metaphor at least once every day. It is a powerful learning tool.) At the end of the book, Daozi paints a beautiful mural of "paradise." He added a doorway to walk through, and Daozi walked into the painting and disappeared. The legend says that he lived always in the painting and never died.

We asked the children: What is paradise? Several children had ideas, and Marco said "where everything is beautiful."

We all shared memories of places that are paradise. Several children said "my house" or "my home."

The children posed their own questions and reflected:
Addison: Do you think we could walk into the painting and meet Daozi there?
Samuel: If we put signs there he might come out. If we do science. I had a volcano kit, and I tried it out and it sometimes works. If it doesn't work, you could always try again.
Teacher: We have a theory, an idea. My theory is that we will draw a door and be able to walk through it. We could try it.
Mason: You would need a magic paintbrush.
Teacher: If we go through that painting what would you want to tell Daozi?
Caroline: Your paintings are beautiful.
Drew: What if Daozi doesn't know how to paint cups and water and we're thirsty?
Evangeline: What about our food?
Teacher: There's a house with a kitchen.
Addison: I would ask "Do you know why your paintings are magic?"

> *Hailey: I know another beautiful place . . . the Dominican Republic. There are flowers and palm trees, a balcony and no snow.*
> *Mason: Maybe we can turn invisible.*
>
> *We talked about magic, and some of us shared that we believe in magic.*

THE SOCIAL CONSTRUCTION OF MATHEMATICS

Children construct their own knowledge through relationships that shape and reshape the structure of their brains. As such, children learn math by creating and recreating mathematical relationships in their minds. Young children are fully capable of constructing these relationships. The child must represent and express relationships through concrete interactions with materials (placing objects into groups) or through artistic expressions (drawing pictures of objects and placing them into categories). Children who are encouraged to express their thinking by interacting with materials or by representing their thoughts artistically construct meaning for the concepts and operations involved in a traditional math problem.

The children in the following early learning environment, for example, demonstrate how they share strategies, follow through, and share what they learned with each other when answering their class Puppy's question about how many stairs there were up to P.E. class:

> *We didn't know but we each guessed, with estimates ranging from 11 to well over 100. I asked if anyone had any ideas how we could find out how many steps there are. The children had many ideas: "We could count them." "We could count by 10s." "We could count by 2s." "We could step on them and count them." "We could draw a line for each step and then count the lines."*
>
> *In groups of four or five, we took our usual varied routes to and from P.E. Each child took a clipboard and pen. We really did not know what to expect but, as usual, your children dazzled us with their thinking, their planning, and their ability to follow through. I'd like to underline that this exercise was not really about learning how many steps there are. It was more about (1) helping Puppy, and (2) sharing strategies for arriving at desired information.*
>
> *As teachers, we were looking for the processes and the strategies. Would they stop on each stair? Would they point? Would they wait to count at the landing? Would they collaborate?*

Various strategies were observed and shared later in whole group:
- *I'm making a line for each step and then counting lines.*
- *Counting aloud by self*
- *Counting with a friend*
- *Counting quietly*
- *Counting really loudly, to drown out other voices*
- *Tally marks the length of the page. Confusing the marks for climbing up with those for climbing down.*
- *Tally marks starting in the center of the page to right, then the second time from the left side of the page to the right*
- *Drawing a circle or "dot" for each step. Starting by putting the circles across the center of the page. The second time from left to right in a line. When asked why the child used dots, the response was "because it helps me." This kind of metacognitive thinking is what we hope to inspire and support!*
- *Writing out numbers for the steps . . . all the way to 22. Because he was writing up in the air with a pen, his ink ran dry and he couldn't be sure how many he counted the first time. The second time he adjusted his pen downwards and counted to 23.*
- *Quiet . . . numbers in his head.*
- *"I counted with lines!" Very careful and precise with eyes down on the stairs, not on the paper.*
- *Very vocal. loud voice. He counted more and more quickly.*
- *Loved explaining how he counted. He talked about how the lines he drew helped him keep track of how many stairs there were. He tried writing numbers to five. Went back to marks.*
- *Child appeared deep in thought, as if counting sapped her physical energy.*
- *"I made stairs!" (child drew a zig-zag)*
- *Counted clearly to 18 on her way down. There were 18 stairs.*
- *"I counted 1,2,3,4,5,6,7,8. (with joy!) Look how many there are!" She drew a circle for each stair.*

Not surprisingly, the children counted different numbers of stairs on the way up and on the way down. They each counted different numbers in both directions. Clearly this exercise was not about accuracy but about sharing strategies, following through, and sharing what they learned with one another.

David Hawkins provides tremendous insight into why this kind of early mathematics education is particularly powerful. He argues that it should not be driven by computation, traditional arithmetic, or pointless rigor.[34] Instead, children should be encouraged to perceive discrete objects through all of their senses. They must be free to act on their natural impulse to take things apart, separate them, and put them back together.

In doing so, children will develop mental habits or strategies for interacting with their environment. They will soon label and count in the context of pursuing their natural curiosities. Once the separating (subtracting and dividing), recombining (adding and multiplying) habits have been constructed, children will soon reflect on their own strategies and recognize that they have used labels (numbers) to help them in their interactions with materials. The numbers can be transported to help the child with other pursuits.

When the child reflects on the quality or essence of a "number," the child reaches a level of abstraction or universe that may be more joyous than the early, playful interactions with the concrete materials. But children will not stop at that. They will be naturally driven to test and to try to overcome the limits of "numbers." What is the highest number? They will also invent new "numbers," or counting strategies. A very large amount of items is called a "sandbox full."

The exploration of mathematics cannot be limited to what is traditionally labeled math. Rather, as Hawkins demonstrates, "the curriculum discussions overlap in all childhood praxis of learning."[35] In fact, "the subject of mathematics is potentially the whole of experiences."[36] What distinguishes math from other disciplines is not the substance or the product of the enterprise, but the style of the inquiry. According to Hawkins, the "style" is "schematization"—"a searching out and delineation of structure which have already been consolidated within the minds of the searchers."[37] The "essential art of mathematics . . . is that of investigating hypothetical states of things through the disciplines of schematization."[38]

When the child develops the discipline of schematization, the child becomes his or her own teacher. Hawkins writes that the ultimate goal of any educational system should be to develop in our young learners their ability to educate themselves.[39] The most "conspicuous and valuable product" of education is the "child's ability to educate himself."[40]

The ultimate educational accomplishment is the attainment of a sense of objectivity or reality: "a stable, reliable vision of the world without losing [the] capacity for fantasy."[41] Hawkins writes that "one of the most important accomplishments of a human being" is the "capacity for synthesis, for building a stable framework within which many episodes of experience can be put together coherently."[42]

Children achieve this highest level of education through relationships. Some children will construct this highest level of meaning in relationships with caregivers or peers, but other children construct meaning in relationships with materials.[43] Hawkins recognizes that the child is capable of engaging with both the "social" environment and the "inanimate" environment "with far fresher eyes than ours."[44]

If educators can provide the child with a "rich" environment that encourages the child's explorations with other persons and materials, manmade and natural, an extraordinary "bond" develops between the child and the world that is indispensable to learning and well-being.[45] As Richard Louv documented in *Last Child in the Woods*, there is accumulating research to link the mental, physical, and spiritual health of children directly with nature. He warned that "[o]ur society is teaching young people to avoid direct experience in nature. That lesson is delivered in schools, families, even organizations devoted to the outdoors, and codified into the legal and regulatory structures of many of our communities."[46] Since publication of this highly influential book in 2005, many more educators have sought to expand learning beyond their classroom walls, encouraging young children to enter into meaningful explorations with their natural world.

While there is no replacement for exploration of the world outdoors, when it is not practical to go out in nature, nature's infinite variety can be explored inside, with learning crossing disciplines and domains. In one urban early childhood learning environment, for instance, the students engaged in a "counting adventure" by walking to a common area in small groups accompanied by a teacher. The overarching goal of the activity was to learn the children's proficiency with one-to-one counting:

> *The children began by estimating the number of shells in a clear container, and then surprised us with counting strategies: "Dump them and spread them. Then count them." "Put them in the middle." "We'll each take 10, and count by 10s." "Everyone make a line with your 10." "I was thinking, we should make one row and then count 10, 11, 12, 13, 14, 15."*
>
> *We noticed how the children supported one another. Children who were not so confident in their independent counting ability became fluent counters when counting with their peers. This is the power of co-construction inherent in small group activity! We noticed how much mental math some were doing without prompting ("2 + 2 = 4" "10 + 10 = 20"). We also watched as counting strategies were articulated by one and tried by others. ("You need 10 more." "I need 10 more." "After this, we'll have to count them all together.") Some children could count their shells and recall later*

*how many they'd counted. Others had not reached that stage of conserva-
tion and needed to count the same shells over each time they were asked
how many there were in the row. We watched as children's one-to-one
counting ability improved as they practiced moving a bead on the abacus
for each shell.*

*We watched a group attempt to fill a board with 100 numbered squares
with shells. "Let's use the big shells first." "They fill a lot of space." One
child realized, with excitement, that his estimate of 100 was very close, as
the board filled. "It's hard to find where the shells are not (on the board)."
"There's not 100 shells." "If there's no more shells left, then there aren't
100." "It's not what any of us estimated." "Let's see if we can fill the
board." "It might." "It might not." "It doesn't look like it fills the board.
There are numbers left (uncovered)." "I still have shells." "Is it going to
transform into a visible board?" "There's one more left!" "There are less
shells." "No, there are more shells." "Maybe we could bring shells in?"
Their mathematical vocabulary expanded by the minute.*

*When asked to put the shells away at the end of the activity, one child
broke into a chorus of the song when we put our library books away. It
goes "Put your books on the shelf, on the shelf." He started singing "Put
your shells on the shelf, on the shelf." This is just one example of the many
connections the children make between the hundreds of things we do each
day. Those neurons are always firing!*

THE SOCIAL CONSTRUCTION OF SCIENCE

In his famous essay, "Messing About in Science," Hawkins contends that science should be taught to early learners by allowing sufficient time for them
to engage in "free and unguided exploratory work."[47] They must be allowed
to "mess about": "Children are given materials and equipment—things—and
are allowed to construct, test, probe, and experiment without superimposed
questions or instructions."[48]

Hawkins recognizes that before they enter kindergarten, young children
already have learned more about themselves and their world than they will
learn in the rest of their school years combined. They achieve a staggering
level of "moral, intellectual and aesthetic development" through "messing
about"—exploring, constructing, testing, probing and experimenting.[49]

In light of the success of this early learning environment, Hawkins sees great "folly" in trying to standardize education. If children are given engaging materials and time, they will naturally and joyously evolve their own learning along paths of their own choosing. The teacher therefore should respond to those various paths by supplying the children with "multiple programmed material."[50] These materials make visible what the child has already grasped, but, more importantly, inspire the child to encounter and explore new questions.[51] The materials can be as simple as illustrated cards that present a variety of inquiries or topics or background information.

At some point, the teacher may want to provide direct instruction supporting the common elements of learning that children have pursued or may wish to try to engage small or large groups in a helpful dialogue of questions and answers. The dialogue assists students in representing what they have learned, how they have learned it, and what they want to learn next. In this phase of learning, the teacher and the students will inevitably begin to explore concepts, principles, and theories that may unify and explain what their diverse experiments have revealed.

Even when the teacher is most involved and the discussion is most abstract, however, the students must still be permitted time and freedom to "mess about."

The most sophisticated scientific principles or theories are best learned if children are given freedom to construct their own knowledge in groups. As Hawkins indicates, this social construction of knowledge is the "magical part" of learning and is "most often killed in school."[52] This teacher described to families how and why her students were free to "mess about":

We have the privilege of messing about in boats for not as much time as I'd like, but for more than most of our students will have ever again in their schooled lives. I love that [David Hawkins's] article elevates the value of this work, much of which has no formal "end" to share with families. In our class, our observations of rainbows cast by prisms and colored images cast by sunlight through colored transparencies fall into the messing about category (moving rainbows). Our work with ramps and small-wheeled vehicles falls here, too (weight, speed, distance). As does building tall towers (balance, weight, gravity, congruent angles, etc.). Our work with water, snow and melted and eventually evaporated ice falls here, too. Outside of science, our work with materials traditionally thought of as "art materials" readies the children to express complex ideas across all disciplines in new ways. Until they know how they can mess about with various materials to express original ideas they are hindered in their abilities to express themselves in two and three dimensions.

In addition, the enormous amount of time we spend in class sharing observations of the children's social and emotional development (e.g., "I see you are having trouble keeping your hands to yourself," "Look at his face. Can you tell what he is feeling?") and reflecting on next steps with the children is a kind of "messing about" in the world of social/emotional development. In JK we are limited in the kind of planning we can do around social/emotional curriculum . . . we need to address what arises, when it arises, and in a meaningful way. As a teacher, it often feels like we are messing about, when we'd much rather have and deliver a planned lesson on kind and respectful behavior. But the messing about nature of our time together is necessary and important and not at all a waste of time.

She provided more detail about her classroom's curiosity with rainbows in an earlier blog entry:

One area that seems to have engaged your children's curiosity is light/ shadows and the dancing of rainbows around the classroom. Our location on the east side of the building, and the morning hours of our class, lend themselves to a study of light and reflections in our classroom. We've noticed at various times that the rainbows appear, and vanish. We've noticed that they move or dance. "They shake." "You can not step on them on the rug." "It's on my foot!" "I can't feel the rainbow on my face." "The rainbow on the dark wall is brighter than the rainbow on the white wall." "Some days we do not have rainbows." The children have also noticed rainbows being cast on their hands when they build with translucent colored magnatiles. We have asked ourselves if all of the rainbows we've seen in the classroom look alike or different.

As the year progresses, we hope to build on the children's observations by helping them to formulate questions and hypotheses. As we begin to talk about the weather, we will perhaps look for correlations between the weather and the rainbows. As we begin to talk about time and the seasons, we will perhaps notice whether our rainbows appear in different places in the classroom.

Could I have walked over to the window the first time we saw a rainbow, held a prism, and said, "When the sun shines through this prism it creates a rainbow?" Yes, I could have done this. But I'm fairly sure that this would have reduced every child's sense of wonder about their world. And, I'm not sure that they would ever progress to notice that the same sun and the same prism do not create rainbows in the same places every day. Or to appreciate that there is a difference between the rainbow cast by a clear crystal prism and the colors cast on their hands by the translucent magnatiles. They would, in short, know how to "name" the cause of a phenomenon, without truly beginning to understand its complexity or its promise:

You can know the name of a bird in all the languages of the world, but when you're finished, you'll know absolutely nothing whatever about the bird. . . . So let's look at the bird and see what it's doing—that's what counts. I learned very early the difference between knowing the name of something and knowing something.

—Richard Feynman
U.S. educator & physicist (1918–1988)

How do we, as teachers, decide which phenomena to explore with children in this way? My rule of thumb is to choose phenomena that I as an adult do not fully understand. How does an overhead projector work? How does Skype work? These are the richest areas for exploration—those that we can explore together, and learn more about together in a hands-on experiential way.

NOTES

1. Each of the examples of the social constructivist practices displayed in this chapter comes from the actual interactions between children and their educators that took place in an early childhood program located in a large, diverse urban area.

2. Giacomo Rizzolatti and Corrado Sinigaglia, *Mirrors in the Brain: How Our Minds Share Actions, Emotions and Experience*, trans. Frances Anderson (New York: Oxford University Press, 2006).

3. See generally David Elkind, *The Power of Play: Learning What Comes Naturally* (Philadelphia: Da Capo, 2007). See also Elena Bodrova and Deborah J. Leong, *Tools of the Mind: The Vygotskian Approach to Early Childhood Education* (Pearson 2007), 129.

4. Bodrova and Leong, *Tools of the Mind*, 129.

5. Ibid., 21.

6. Ibid., 132.

7. Ibid.

8. Ibid.

9. Lev Vygotsky, "Play and Its Role in the Mental Development of the Child," *Soviet Psychology* 5 (1933): 10.

10. Bodrova and Leong, *Tools of the Mind*, 133.

11. Ibid.

12. Ibid.

13. Ibid., 134–35.

14. Ibid., 17.

15. Ibid.

16. Ibid., 21.

17. Vygotsky, *Higher Mental Functions*, 106.

18. Ibid., 133.

19. Ibid., 133, citing Vygotsky, "Play and Its Role," 17.

20. Bodrova and Leong, *Tools of the Mind*, 132.

21. Vygotsky, *Mind in Society*, 74.

22. Ibid., 86.

23. Lev Vygotsky, *Thinking and Speech* (New York: Plenum Press, 1987), 211.

24. See Howard Gardner, *Five Minds for the Future* (Boston: Harvard University Press, 2008).

25. Bodrova and Leong, *Tools of the Mind*, 51.

26. Ibid., 67.

27. Ibid., 68.

28. Ibid., 70.

29. Ibid., 82.

30. Lev Vygotsky, *Mind in Society: The Development of Psychological Processes* (Boston: Harvard University Press, 1978), 117–18.

31. Bodrova and Leong, *Tools of the Mind,* 80.

32. Ibid.

33. Ibid.

34. David Hawkins, "Two Essays on Mathematics Teaching: Mathematics—Practical and Impractical," in David Hawkins, *The Informed Vision: Essays on Learning and Human Nature* (New York: Algora, 2002), 101.

35. Ibid., 113.

36. Ibid., 123.

37. Ibid.

38. Ibid., 125–26.

39. David Hawkins, "I, Thou and It," 57.

40. Ibid.

41. Ibid., 59.

42. Ibid.

43. Ibid.

44. Ibid.

45. Ibid., 59–60.

46. Richard Louv, *Last Child in the Woods: Saving Our Children From Nature-Deficit Disorder* (Chapel Hill, NC: Algonquin Books of Chapel Hill, 2005), 2.

47. David Hawkins, *The Informed Vision: Essays on Learning and Human Nature* (New York: Agathon Press, 2002), 68.

48. Ibid.

49. Ibid., 71.

50. Ibid.

51. Ibid.

52. Ibid., 75.

Chapter Ten

Making Learning Visible Through Documentation

Guided by what researchers have learned from observing educators engaged in creating documentation and using it in their work with young children, families, and community, this chapter offers strategies for developing the art of documentation, for practicing documentation to deepen learning, and for using documentation as an authentic method of assessing learning and making it visible to multiple stakeholders.

THE PROCESS OF DOCUMENTATION

Observing

Documentation requires observation of individual and group learning. But observation assumes the involvement of all senses. In particular, the documenter must engage in active listening. In *The Pedagogy of Listening*, Carla Rinaldi explains how listening can be the basis of any learning relationship:

- Listening should be sensitive to the patterns that connect us to others. Our understanding and our own being are a small part of a broader, integrated knowledge that holds the universe together.
- Listening should be open and sensitive to the need to listen and be listened to and the need to listen with all our senses, not just with our ears.
- Listening should recognize the many languages, symbols, and codes that people use to express themselves and communicate.
- Listening to ourselves—"internal listening"—encourages us to listen to others but, in turn, is generated when others listen to us.

- Listening takes time. When you really listen, you get into the time of dialogue and interior reflection, an interior time that is made up of the present but also past and future time and is therefore outside chronological time. It is a time full of silences.
- Listening is generated by curiosity, desire, doubt, and uncertainty. This is not insecurity but the reassurance that every "truth" is so only if we are aware of its limits and its possible falsification.
- Listening produces questions, not answers.
- Listening is emotion. It is generated by emotions; it is influenced by the emotions of others; and it stimulates emotions.
- Listening should welcome and be open to differences, recognizing the value of others' interpretations and points of view.
- Listening is an active verb, which involves giving an interpretation, giving meaning to the message, and valuing those who are listened to by others.
- Listening is not easy. It requires a deep awareness and a suspension of our judgments and prejudices. It requires openness to change. It demands that we value the unknown and overcome the feeling of emptiness and precariousness that we experience when our certainties are questioned.
- Listening removes the individual from anonymity (and children cannot bear to be anonymous). It legitimizes us and gives us visibility. It enriches both those who listen and those who produce the message.
- Listening is the basis for any learning relationship. Through action and reflection, learning takes shape in the mind of the subject and, through representation and exchange, becomes knowledge and skill.
- Listening takes place within a "listening context," where one learns to listen and narrate, and each individual feels legitimized to represent and offer interpretations of her or his theories through action, emotion, expression, and representation, using symbols and images (the "hundred languages"). Understanding and awareness are generated through sharing and dialogue.[1]

Rinaldi concludes "[t]hus, the pedagogy of listening is not only a pedagogy for school but also an attitude for life. It can be a tool, but it can also be something more. It means taking responsibility for what we are sharing. If we need to be listened to then listening is one of the most important attitudes for the identity of the human being, starting from the moment of birth."[2]

Recording

Today, documentation involves recording learning in a variety of media, including note taking, texting, audio-recording, photographs, video, and blogging. Effective communication of children's learning requires the documentarian to consider which media will best convey the learning that he/she wishes to convey. Sometimes a child's words are most important; other times a photo of the child's expression as he/she is engaged in discovery tells more than words could convey. Other times, the process is best captured in audio or video, so as to convey the thinking process over time.

Interpreting

By definition, all documentation is subjective. The listener has a unique perspective. Therefore, documentation is made stronger when it brings together a variety of interpretations. Within a school, educators pool their reflections and share their perspectives on a learning experience. This sharing not only strengthens the documentation but also serves as real-time professional development for educators. The educators' shared reflections invariably cause them to think more deeply about their teaching and to try new approaches within the classroom. The very act of documenting with others is a learning relationship that benefits most everyone with a stake in a classroom.

Sharing

Documentation envisions sharing the records and interpretations of learning beyond the classroom. Once the learning is effectively captured, it needs to be shared. This sharing takes place in many ways:

- Through visually interesting *panels* of photos of children's work displayed in common gathering spaces;
- Through brief descriptions of the day's explorations (often dictated by the children) written on *whiteboards* and displayed for families who may pick up their children without entering the school;
- In *individual student portfolios* that highlight learning moments or explorations that involve a particular child or a group that that child was a member of;
- In *classroom portfolios* that focus on a particular small or whole group project that emerged and evolved over time within the learning community;
- In *newsletters, emails, phone calls, and conferences* between educators and families;
- Through *interactive blogs* that communicate to families small and whole group projects that emerge and evolve over time. Many of the text boxes in previous chapters were shared with families online through a blog platform that invited families to comment on the learning. The following text box includes a communication that was shared electronically with families. It

is a compilation of the families' communications to the teachers about the experience of sharing their child's individual portfolio with their child at the end of the year.

The child's individual portfolio was one means by which we supplemented with child-specific information the information we shared regularly with all of our families in the class blog. The families' comments about the process of sharing these portfolios with their child reflect an increased understanding of their children's thinking. Perhaps even more importantly, the families' comments reflect the children's metacognitive awareness of their own growth.

At its best, for families, documentation acts as both a window and a mirror: a window into experiences that your child had outside of your presence, and a mirror of your engagement with your child's learning. As I've shared before, John Dewey reminded us: "We do not learn from experience . . . we learn from reflecting on experience." So I want to reflect back to you recent communications from your learning community about the (children's individual) portfolios. I think that they show how much each of us, adult and child, learned this year about how children learn and grow, as a direct result of the dialogue that flowed honestly amongst us (all comments have been edited for anonymity):

She was very excited to show me her portfolio. The first thing she wanted to do was show me the two photos on the covers (the front cover photo was taken on the first day, the back cover on the last day). Looking at the front cover prompted her to talk about the start of the year and that everything seemed so new. We then looked through each page. She asked me to read some of the pages but mostly she wanted to look at the artwork and the photos. I was amazed at how she recalled such detail about when and how she created each drawing, painting, etc. She seemed very proud of her work.

"Mommy, see this cover . . . this is me in the beginning of the year, and this is me now (back cover) I am taller . . ."

We saw the (child) on the back cover, a learner, a friend, and taller in every way.

"I feel so special I made all these things! My favorite part is the blueprints we made for our invention."

She really enjoyed explaining what was happening in the photos (some descriptions included stories or feelings that were brought on by looking at the picture but not necessarily directly related to what was happening in the picture, which I found interesting).

He took me through page by page explaining to me what each page was. He was especially excited to show me a picture from his birthday celebration and thought that was a fun surprise for me! He was also very proud of his letter C. For the rest of the day he kept asking aloud who wanted to see his portfolio, so I would raise my hand and got to see it quite a few times! That night he slept with it in his bed. I can tell it is very special to him, and for us too!

We love the menus. Love them. "Meelc" is the best—milk.

He likes looking at his skeleton and colorful lizard.

"It's a one-armed skeleton wearing clothes!"

We also looked at the two photographs of him (front and back) and practiced smiling. This was very fun. He also notices the craziness of how he smiles for the camera!

She said, "I'm so excited to show you my ancient writing!" She was beaming with pride the whole time.

We kind of know what is going on in the classroom, but the pictures and the words that go along with it make it very real, and sometimes it is quite a surprise to see things you had done in the classroom we didn't know about. I have seen the pride with which he came to me to show me the portfolio. He has asked to read it together on a daily basis, and I see he reflects upon the things he did throughout the year. He enjoys revisiting stories and takes great pride in them and the development of his writing skills, asking, "Are you proud of me?" He then demonstrates this pride by saying, "I wanted to make this for you," and then he will start talking about what actually happened that day. You see, when I ask him on a daily basis what he did on any given day, he is quite inexpressive, or has genuinely forgotten. But when he sees the pictures, everything comes back to him.

"I liked all the 'fun-ness' especially the writing center. It is very 'create-able.' There I can create things like 'powers' for the rescue team to use."

"I also like recess because we can run into our ideas that we have like rescuing all the girls."

She pointed to several drawings and said that now she knows she can see into her mind and have that come out onto paper. "School helps you do that." Sometimes her hands can't do what she wants like words, so she can ask other people to write them.

The night he brought his portfolio home, after he was into his pajamas, we sat down on his bedroom floor. He gleefully took me through his portfolio, expounding on each and every page. He was excited and proud to share his work and experiences. As we've reported, he does not typically divulge much to us about what happens at school. I think I gleaned more from him in our time on the floor than I did cumulatively through the year!

"I love looking at my portfolio. When I look at my portfolio, it makes me smile," he said (spontaneously). "And that, it seems to me, was not just a reflection on his portfolio but on the entirety of his JK year!"

When describing his "Cookie Cafe" menu: "I really love the Cookie Cafe menu. We especially need cookies if we call it the Cookie Cafe. Ice cream sandwiches are my favorite on the menu because they have the best unhealthy bread in the world." "I'm going to miss my teachers because they helped me do the Cookie Cafe menu and they love me so much. I will miss my friends too. I might not see them all in the summer." "For my birthday, I want activity books, so I can give them to charity, so people can learn."

Our feedback on the portfolios:

"Can we sit on the couch when we get home and go through all of it?"

"These are things I made so I want to hang all of it up in my room."

We noted all the "water slides" (scribbling) at beginning of the year and then actual drawings of cranes and people at end of the year impressive to us.

His favorite thing is the bead art we made on his birthday with a special note on it.

I asked if he was sad school was ending and he said, "No. I need a break or my head is going to explode, cause I got so many things in my brain." Made us laugh.

He was so excited to display his work, and to go through every page of his portfolio.

He was most excited about the class alphabet. He was proud of his "R," but more proud of "our alphabet," and the picture of all of the letters on the wall. "We finished it!!!!"

There were some drawings in his portfolio that he couldn't remember making, so it was really helpful to have the typed descriptions, and he was so amused and excited when I read them.

What I love about the portfolio is that everything represents an activity that has no "right" or "wrong." Everything relates to a class activity, to an experience that he can remember and appreciate whatever he did. In contrast, he has an early childhood education binder from another school—that has typical worksheets. He loves going through it, but he's lately asking to correct all of his mistakes. It's hard to explain that the binder shouldn't be altered (and that it's not a big deal that he didn't put six stickers next to number 6).

After looking at everything, we talked about summer break. I asked "What do you think your teachers will do during the summer?" "Mr. A is going to Hawaii." After more questions, it turns out "Mr. A, Mr. B, and Mrs. C are going to Hawaii together. They have three, just like us. Mommy, Daddy, and (me)."

One particularly effective way to share documentation and to make learning visible is to invite families into the school to engage with a small group of children and materials around a provocation (e.g., "How do we make lemonade?" or "I wonder if you could use these materials to make something for someone you love?"), to document the dialogue and the learning that the educator sees happening in this group, and then to share the documentation with families. Families involved in the activity see firsthand how capturing the dialogue and photos of the children's learning process and reflection results in a deeper understanding of and appreciation for the learning.

They realize, for example, that they did not simply make lemonade with children. Perhaps through dialogue they inspired the children to think about how and where lemons are grown, how they resemble other citrus fruits and how they are different, how fruit is cut safely, how many lemons are needed, how two halves make a whole. In short, parents involved in such documented learning activities see the literacy, math, and science skills integrated in small group work and begin to see these skills embedded in wider play. Experience has shown that families who begin to think this way create documentation and share with teachers learning observed at home.

All evidence of learning is not equal. Test scores and grades do not necessarily make visible either the depth or breadth of an individual's or a group's learning experience. The learning that takes place in the educational environment must also be made visible to multiple stakeholders.[3] The cornerstone of visible learning is the practice of documentation. As defined by Project Zero and Reggio Children, documentation is the "practice of observing, recording, interpreting, and sharing through a variety of media the process and products of learning . . . "[4]

Documentation is essential to the learning process as it is a deliberate act of reflecting on the process of individual and group growth. The documentation informs all subsequent teaching in and outside the classroom. Even more, documentation provides an authentic assessment of the learning process by giving direct evidence of learning that can be shared with the community surrounding the school.

As Lella Gandini, Reggio Children Liaison in the United States for Dissemination of the Reggio Emilia Approach, has explained, the practice of documentation involves:

- Observing
- Leaving and recording traces of observations
- Interpreting the traces
- Making hypotheses
- Making choices
- Preparing materials and the environment
- Preparing the documentation to share with others
- Revisiting among teachers
- Revisiting with children, and
- Revisiting with parents.[5]

According to Lella Gandini, therefore, documentation begins with skillful observation: "In order to document, one must engage in observation: (1) seeing children and listening to them in an active way; (2) becoming aware of one's own way of interacting with children; and (3) sharing points of view with other educators."[6] But, as Lella Gandini also emphasizes, it is "necessary to leave traces of the observations to examine them. There are many ways of leaving traces, which are documents that should be interpreted to understand children better, to share with colleagues, and to know what to do next."[7]

Although documentation may take many different forms, researchers have observed that the practice of documentation by experienced educators includes five common qualities:

    i. Documentation involves a **specific question** that guides the process.

    ii. Documentation involves collectively **analyzing, interpreting, and evaluating** individual and group observations; it is strengthened by multiple perspectives.

    iii. Documentation **makes use of multiple languages** (different ways of representing and expressing thinking in various media and symbol systems.

    iv. Documentation **makes learning visible** when shared with learners (including children, parents, and teachers).

    v. Documentation is not only summary. It is **prospective**, as it shapes the design of future contexts for learning.[8]

Documentation makes learning visible for teachers, parents, and children. By documenting, teachers are able to see children better, follow their thinking, and understand their learning. They are able to make predictions and to enter into action with the children in ways that can be flexibly adjusted according to observations. In taking documentation, teachers become present in the learning process and are better able to reflect on their practice.

Documentation offers parents a window into how their child thinks and learns. It also provides opportunities for parents to know how their child interacts with materials in the environment. It encourages parents to reflect on their child's ability to form meaningful relationships with others. In short, documentation provides parents opportunities to see their child and other children with "new eyes" or in ways they may not ever have noticed before . . .

Perhaps most important, documentation supports children. It offers them opportunities to revisit, explore further, and become aware of their own learning. It enables children to engage in metacognition, to assess how they learn so that they may replicate their own successful learning strategies.

Documentation also gives children the opportunity to see that their learning is respected and valued.[9]

By capturing a dialogue that included a child's words about her work making "a ticket for our *Frozen* play," the piece of documentation below illustrates just such an opportunity. This piece of documentation enables multiple audiences to see clearly how a four-year-old (enamored with the Disney musical film *Frozen*) has built visual memories from her experience seeing *Frozen* and reading *Frozen* books with family, teachers, and peers and has built motor memories from her experience drawing symbols to represent her ideas. The audience sees the exact moment that those experiences inform her emerging literacy skills—both storytelling and writing.

Teacher: Could you tell me about this?
Teagan: It says "Frozen." It's a ticket for the Frozen play.
Teacher: I can see...I can read it. How did you know how to write that?

"A picture made my eyes...I went back into my eyes from when I saw *Frozen* and it told me how to spell Frozen."
~Teagan (4 years old)

Figure 10.1.

PRACTICING DOCUMENTATION TO DEEPEN LEARNING

In the *Relationship Between Documentation and Assessment*, Brenda Fyfe describes how documentation can be used to support learning. It provides formative assessment, with *formative* meaning that it is usually carried out throughout an educational experience. Fyfe emphasizes that documentation is meant to support "the learner to participate in looking at his or her own learning to construct or reconstruct new and deeper understandings."[10] Quoting Rinaldi, Fyfe says "it is done to make learning visible so that the learners can 'observe themselves from an external viewpoint while they are learning.'"[11]

When children look at documentation of their work on the wall or in their individual student portfolios, they are prompted to develop the skill of self-reflection. They learn to think about thinking, and their meta-cognitive skills are strengthened. Their executive functioning skills also are strengthened as they make plans for the future ("I want to do that again . . . only this time, I'll do it differently."). And the documentation guides them in their search for meaning (Why did we cut open that pumpkin? What did we learn? Do all round fruits have seeds inside? How can I know that?).

In addition, documentation can make visible where children are within their individual zones of proximal development. The zone of proximal development is an authentic assessment tool. It enables educators to determine how close the child is to developing particular mental processes.

The assessment cannot be limited to testing the child's ability to do a task independently. Rather, the teacher must first assess the child's behaviors when the child is being assisted by the teacher or the child's peers. The assessment is designed to determine if the child can engage in a mental process in collaboration with others. If so, then the child and the teacher are within the "zone of proximal development." The teacher can then structure the child's environment to encourage the child to internalize the mental process and to exercise that process independently.[12]

This method of authentic assessment puts the teacher in the role of a researcher. The teacher provides different forms of assistance to the child to determine which ones enable the child to acquire a particular mental tool. In so doing, the teacher analyzes the mental process by which the particular child constructs knowledge. Once the teacher has discovered with the child the way that child learns, the teacher can then provide effective methods of assistance to the child. These methods of assistance will strengthen the tools the child needs to construct knowledge independently.

A truly effective "curriculum" must emerge from the child, in relation to teachers and peers. Only after the teacher acquires an understanding of how the child thinks in collaboration with others, and how the child proceeds toward independent thinking, can the teacher design effective instructional practices. The fundamental purpose of curriculum is to encourage a child to form meaningful relationships with teachers and peers, which will allow the teacher and the child together to create strategies that will enable the child to internalize higher mental functions. Curriculum therefore must emerge from the children.

The true nature of child development also demonstrates the ineffectiveness of static assessments of a child's performance on a standardized test. Authentic assessments produce insight into the way in which the child's mind works, the way in which the child constructs knowledge. That assessment is necessarily "dynamic." It analyzes how a child processes the various types of assistance provided by more knowledgeable peers and teachers. Some forms of assistance are more effective than others in helping a child to internalize particular higher mental functions. In addition, some collaborative settings may be more helpful to the child than others. Authentic assessment, therefore, must be designed to document the process by which children construct knowledge in collaboration with others.

For example, an early childhood education teacher documented the following dialogue that occurred during snack time. This dialogue illustrates the fact that the children are considering concepts and questions about fairness and equality, how our bodies react to the environment, and images versus three-dimensional objects, among others.

Noting that the muffins are not on the list that Adrian can eat (this child has allergies), I pick up the container of Adrian's crackers from home to serve. From across the room, Leo notices and shouts, "I'd like crackers."

Me: These are Adrian's crackers. Adrian is allergic to muffins.

Leo: (loud) I'd like crackers. I'd like crackers. I'd like crackers.

Me: Adrian is allergic to the muffins. Adrian's body is not happy if Adrian eats the muffin, so we have special crackers that Adrian is not allergic to. Sienna is also allergic to the muffin and has a snack that Sienna is not allergic to. Sienna's body is not happy if Sienna eats the muffin.

Emery: I'm allergic, too.

Mary Grace: Me, too.

Annie: I don't like muffins. (after a moment of thought) I'm allergic to food I don't like.

Me: I don't think that being allergic to a food and not liking it are the same. We can dislike foods that we are not allergic to.

Jude: I'm allergic to cats and dogs.

Many children chime in with information about people they know who are allergic to things.

About five minutes later, from across the table, Violet calls Jude's name and says with a twinkle in her eye:

"Jude, you don't eat cats and dogs, do you?"

Jude: No.

Me: I think that he means that he is allergic to their smell, not their taste.

Tommy: (to Jude) Are you allergic to a picture of a cat or a dog?

Jude: No.

Kalista: That's because a picture isn't real.

Liam: A picture is real! It's a real picture!

Me: I think he means that a picture of a cat isn't a real cat.

Liam: Oh. Yeah.

Documentation also models for children listening, research, and literacy skills. When children observe their educators documenting learning they also wish to document their own learning and that of their peers. By modeling the various methods of communicating knowledge, educators inspire children to develop profound literacy skills. As Teagan's documentation of her own process of learning to write *Frozen* indicates, children who are participants with others in the art of documentation can begin to reflect upon their own ways of learning.

USING DOCUMENTATION TO MAKE LEARNING
VISIBLE TO MULTIPLE STAKEHOLDERS

Documentation is an authentic assessment of learning. Beyond providing a tool for deepening learning within a classroom, documentation can also make learning visible to important stakeholders outside of the classroom, including:

- Teachers throughout the school
- School administrators
- Taxpayers and other funding sources
- Community members and potential community members
- Policy makers

As Project Zero has recognized, documentation has the potential to replace, or at least augment, traditional inauthentic forms of assessment through standardized testing. Those researchers also suggest that documentation can be used to mediate the "unprecedented focus on high-stakes testing and accountability."[13] They show that "standards" can be woven into the group learning environment.[14] For example, a teacher who reflects on children's learning using terminology found in the Common Core Standards can create a shared vocabulary that reinforces the validity of documentation as an authentic assessment of the full range and depth of student and community learning.[15]

One teacher documented via photos and text on her blog for families some of the activities the children were involved in during one of the first weeks of school. These activities included:

—*Children have been experimenting with both tempera paint at the easel and with liquid watercolor on watercolor paper. We've used both brushes and pipettes and find that our results differ depending on the materials we use.*

—*We've begun examining patterns among found objects and we've begun creating our own patterns from math manipulatives.*

—*We've shared books:* The Mixed Up Chameleon *by Eric Carle,* The Kissing Hand *by Audrey Penn, and today* Pete the Cat, Rocking in My School Shoes.

—*We had our first P.E. class with the gym teacher last week and will return to P.E. tom'w (Wednesday) and Friday.*

> *—The Spanish teacher joined us in the classroom for Spanish Class yes-*
> *terday. Your children were completely engaged and actively participated.*
> *Asked if he enjoyed Spanish class, one child said "Yes! It was just like a TV*
> *show!" The teacher shares stories and acts out scenarios that allow him*
> *to introduce Spanish words and phrases that are common in everyday life.*
>
> *—(Our assistant teacher) led us up to the library for the first time today*
> *and we introduced ourselves to the librarian. We will return next Tuesday*
> *for a story and to check out a book that we will keep in the classroom.*
>
> *—We've learned our way around the playground, where the bathrooms*
> *are and the water fountains (that we go to with a teacher).*
>
> *—We are finding letters and words in our environment, and creating them*
> *out of tape and play dough as well as in marker and pencil.*
>
> *—(Our assistant teacher) is leading us in physical warm-up exercises and*
> *in a new name game that is helping us learn the names of others in the*
> *class. He is also talking with students and beginning to write stories that*
> *we may eventually act out.*
>
> *—Perhaps most important, the photos show how your children are making*
> *connections with their peers.*

By preserving memories and creating history, documentation makes visible the culture of a school. It also can become an effective advocacy tool for educational opportunities for all children. As Lella Gandini has recognized, documentation "sends powerful messages about the richness and potential of children and childhood."[16]

Finally, as Carlina Rinaldi has insightfully recognized, documentation of the process and products of individual and community learning develops habits of mind and heart that are vital to the flourishing of a democracy.

Documentation can offer children and adults alike real moments of democracy.[17]

Eli wrote "I love Eli. I love Mom. I love my classmates." On the second page he wrote "I love my teachers." By documenting his reflections on his identity and his relationships with his family, teachers, and his peers, Eli (age 4) makes visible his construction of knowledge and meaning through those relationships. What was also documented in myriad ways throughout the year is the goal shared between school and family to strengthen Eli's finger muscles so that he could improve his grip on the writing instrument. The

Figure 10.2.

many opportunities he had to write symbols in meaningful contexts within the classroom and at home were fully documented as well. Underlying his ability to focus on his message was the documented healthy separation from his family and his attachment to educators and peers at school.

Eli recognizes the power of his ideas and shares them with those who listen, those he loves. By constructing knowledge through meaningful relationships in a supportive learning community, Eli and his peers become empowered to make their own meaning. The skills of collaboration and self-governance that children develop through learning relationships are vital not only to their individual success and well-being, but also to the health of the American democracy. Moreover, through these same relationships, children learn to love learning.

With wonder in his eyes and a smile that enveloped his world, Eli joined his friends in the classroom and shared with his teacher:

> Every day you get something new in your brain when you go to school. I'm going to get something new in my brain today.

NOTES

1. Carla Rinaldi, "The Pedagogy of Listening: The Listening Perspective from Reggio Emilia," in *The Hundred Languages of Children*, ed. C. Edwards, L. Gandini, and G. Foreman (Santa Barbara: Praeger, 2012), 234, 235.

2. Ibid.

3. M. Krechevsky, B. Mardell, M. Rivard, and D. Wilson, *Visible Learners* (San Francisco: Jossey Bass, 2013), xv.

4. Project Zero and Reggio Children, *Making Learning Visible: Children as Individual and Group Learners* (Reggio Emilia, Italy: Reggio Children, 2001).

5. Lella Gandini, "Reflections on Documentation," transcription by Lynn White on file with authors at Loyola University Chicago School of Law, Chicago, IL (1996).

6. Ibid.

7. Ibid.

8. Project Zero: *Making Learning Visible*, Harvard Graduate School of Education (2005), see http://www.pz.gse.harvard.edu/making_learning_visible.php.

9. Gandini, "Reflections on Documentation."

10. Brenda Fyfe, "The Relationship Between Documentation and Assessment," in *The Hundred Languages of Children*, eds. Carolyn Edwards, Lella Gandini, and George Forman (Santa Barbara: Praeger, 2012), 275.

11. Ibid.

12. See generally Lev Vygotsky, *Tool and Sign in the Development of the Child* (New York: Plenum Press, 1999). See also Bodrova and Leong, *Tools of the Mind*, 43.

13. Ibid., xv.

14. Ibid.

15. Ibid. See also Project Zero and Reggio Children, *Making Learning Visible: Children as Individual and Group Learners* (Reggio Emilia, Italy: Reggio Children, 2001).

16. Gandini, "Reflections on Documentation."

17. Carlina Rinaldi, "Observation and Documentation," paper presented at Research Conference in Reggio Emilia, Italy (June, 1995), cited in Gunilla Dahlberg, "Pedagogical Documentation: A Practice for Negotiation and Democracy," in *The Hundred Languages of Children*, ed. C. Edwards, L. Gandini, and G. Foreman (Santa Barbara: Praeger, 2012), 230.

Conclusion

This book began with a provocation. We wondered how educators, policy makers, and jurists might respond to the overwhelming evidence demonstrating that an investment in early childhood education programs would produce significant educational, social, and economic benefits for children and for the country. The book began by providing legal, political, pedagogical, and economic support for expanding access to those programs for three- and four-year-olds in America.

But the book also demonstrated that early childhood education programs dedicated to developing in children the capacity to construct knowledge through meaningful relationships have achieved particularly robust investment returns. The economic and neuro-scientific evidence indicates that these programs, which are exemplified by the early learning centers in Reggio Emilia, have obtained those robust returns for two interdependent reasons. First, learning itself takes place only through meaningful relationships. Second, children who develop the habit of building meaningful relationships achieve remarkable personal success and well-being and are unlikely to exhibit the kind of behavior that would increase the social costs of crime, healthcare, and remedial education.

We hope that educators, policy makers, and jurists will be provoked by this compelling evidence from multiple disciplines to pursue the various implementation strategies provided in the book's final section. If they did so, America would also move closer to realizing the Framers' vision of a democracy in which all children develop the habits of mind and heart that enable them to lead, to govern, to express themselves, to contribute to their communities, to form associations, to construct meaning, and to disseminate knowledge. America also would move closer to treating all of its children as capable, curious, creative, caring, and connected members of the community.

And we would all move closer to honoring a true image of the child.

APPENDIX A

A Model Complaint

_____ , Plaintiffs,

v.

State of _____ and _____ Board of Education, Defendants.

VERIFIED COMPLAINT

Plaintiffs, _____ and _____ (collectively "Plaintiffs"), by their attorneys _____, state as follows for their complaint against Defendants State of _____ ("State") and _____ State Board of Education ("State Board") (collectively "Defendants"):

NATURE OF ACTION

a. This action arises from the State's failed school funding scheme, the discriminatory impact that scheme has on minority students, especially African Americans and Latinos, and the unconstitutional denial of adequate and equitable educational opportunities for hundreds of thousands of public school children. The lawsuit challenges the State's method for raising and distributing education funds to local school districts and the State Board's implementation of that fatally flawed system. The State has established a funding scheme that generates a _____ funding gap between low and high income schools. The State's public school funding scheme (1) disparately impacts racial and ethnic minority students who attend school districts with a high concentration of minority students by distributing an unequal level of funding to those school districts in violation of the State Civil Rights Act;

(2) violates the [taxation provision] of the State Constitution; (3) violates students' right to attend [insert relevant state constitutional language: (i.e. *high-quality, efficient, thorough, adequate, basic*)] educational institutions guaranteed by the [Education Article] under the State Constitution; and (4) violates students' rights to equal protection under the State Constitution.

b. Under the State Constitution, the State has the primary responsibility for financing public schools and is obligated to provide for the establishment of schools that deliver [insert relevant state constitutional language: (i.e. *high-quality, efficient, thorough, adequate, basic*)] education to the _____ students enrolled in elementary and secondary public schools in the State.

c. Since at least _____, however, [the State] has ranked _____ in state contributions to school funding. The State's share of the revenue raised for public schools in [the State] has decreased steadily.

d. In strong contrast to its place on the list for state level of funding of public education, [the State] has _____ personal income and currently operates the _____ largest public school system in the United States. [more facts about the State here]

e. Despite its capacity to raise revenue, for the last several years, the State has fallen woefully short of satisfying its mandate to provide a "high-quality" education to its public school students.

f. Among those most substantially and negatively impacted by the State's unconstitutional funding scheme are students who attend school in majority-minority districts. At schools in these districts, students score lower on state-wide performance assessments, drop out of school more often, and do not attend college at the same rates as their peers in majority white school districts.

g. These marks of poor academic performance are a direct result of the lack of resources available to students in these school districts. Many of these schools lack the basic critical resources needed to provide all of their students with a "constitutionally guaranteed high-quality" education. Class sizes are at historic highs and capital spending on school facilities is at an historic low, often forcing students to learn in crowded or dilapidated school buildings and using technologically outdated facilities. Recent reports put the cost of unmet capital needs among school districts at _____. Many basic programs have been reduced or cut altogether.

h. The school funding system is fundamentally flawed. Although the State Constitution mandates that the State shall have the "primary responsibility" for financing public schools, it is actually local property taxpayers who bear the brunt of the cost for the State's constitutional obligation. For ____ years, the State has enforced and implemented a funding scheme that requires over _____ percent of the funds to be raised through non-state levied taxes.

i. At the core of the State's school funding system is an over-reliance on local property taxes. This over-reliance on locally raised revenues reinforces past discrimination and virtually ensures that in communities where property wealth has been negatively impacted by patters of residential segregation, the school districts have no capacity to raise the revenues they desperately need to close the funding gap. Compared to other states, [the State's] property taxpayers contribute _____ and pay _____ towards school funding.

j. The effects of inadequate and disparate funding across the State on public school districts are significant. Almost _____ of the State's _____ school districts are facing serious financial difficulties and have received a negative rating from the State Board on financial management. About _____ percent of the State's school districts operate with budget deficits.

k. The adoption of the No Child Left Behind Act, 20 U.S.C. Section 6301, which has the stated purpose of "ensur[ing] that all children have a fair, equal, and significant opportunity to obtain a high-quality education" and the concomitant enforcement of statewide learning and achievement goals by the State Board, now establish standards for determining whether the State's funding scheme enables school districts or provide for a system of schools that provide all students with a [insert relevant state constitutional language: (i.e. *high-quality, efficient, thorough, adequate, basic*)] education.

l. The State's failed school funding scheme has left many school districts, particularly those who serve a high concentration of low income and minority students, with a mounting educational crisis. As the federal and statewide standards for learning are raised higher and higher each year, these school districts find themselves with fewer and fewer resources. The persistent, substantial disparity in school funding across the State has left thousands of Illinois school children, particularly African American and Latino students, without an educational opportunity and the [insert relevant state constitutional language: (i.e. *high-quality, efficient, thorough, adequate, basic*)] education guaranteed to them under this State's Constitution.

m. The continuous and unmitigated harm that results each year from the State's persistent failure to meet its constitutional obligation to treat all students equally, regardless of race or ethnicity, to provide all _____ students with access to equal educational opportunity and to provide a system of schools offering a [insert relevant state constitutional language: (i.e. *high-quality, efficient, thorough, adequate, basic*)] education, is irreparable and unconscionable. Plaintiffs therefore seek preliminary and permanent injunctive relief on the grounds that the State's school funding scheme, as presently enforced and applied across the State, violates the State Civil Rights Act and the basic rights guaranteed to all State citizens under the State Constitution.

SUMMARY OF CLAIMS
PARTIES
JURISDICTION AND VENUE
FACTS
COUNT I – VIOLATION OF THE STATE CIVIL RIGHTS ACT
COUNT II – VIOLATION OF THE STATE CONSTITUTION

n. WHEREFORE, Plaintiffs respectfully request that the Court enter an order:

    a. Declaring that Defendants have failed to appropriate sufficient funds to permit school districts, including those attended by children of Plaintiffs and similarly situated students across the State of _____, necessary to enable those districts to provide the critical basic resources necessary to ensure students have the opportunity to meet or exceed the _____ Learning Standards;

    b. Declaring that Defendants have failed to appropriate sufficient funds to enable low property wealth and Majority-Minority Districts, including those attended by children of Plaintiffs' members and similarly situated students across the State of _____, to provide the critical basic resources necessary to ensure all students have the opportunity to meet or exceed the State's Learning Standards;

    c. Declaring that Defendants' enactment, adoption and implementation of the existing state funding scheme under deprives children of Plaintiffs and similarly situated students equal protection under the laws in violation of the Education Article of the State Constitution;

    d. Preliminarily and permanently enjoining Defendants from implementing the existing state funding formula and appropriations adopted for Calendar Year _____ and any year thereafter until such time as Defendants can demonstrate that the state funding scheme complies with the requirements of the Equal Protection Clause of the State Constitution;

e. Preliminarily and permanently enjoining Defendants from implementing the existing state funding formula and appropriations adopted for Calendar Year _____ and any year thereafter until such time as Defendants can demonstrate that the state funding scheme provides all school districts with sufficient funding to provide students a reasonable opportunity to attend a [insert relevant state constitutional language: (i.e. *high-quality, efficient, thorough, adequate, basic*)] high-quality public educational institution;

f. Requiring Defendants to ascertain the actual cost of providing all students throughout the State with an opportunity to receive a "high-quality" education;

g. Requiring Defendants to reform the current system of school funding to ensure that every school in the State of _____ has the critical basic resources necessary to provide all students the opportunity to receive a "[insert relevant state constitutional language: (i.e. *high-quality, efficient, thorough, adequate, basic*)] education.

h. Ordering Defendants to submit within 6 months a detailed plan for establishing, funding, and implementing a state-wide system of early childhood education centers that are available and accessible to all three- and four-year-old children in the state regardless of their race, ethnicity, and socio-economic status, and that provide learning environments that are consistent with social constructivist best practices and therefore produce educational, social, and economic benefits to children and the State.

i. Awarding Plaintiffs their costs of suit incurred herein;

j. Granting such other relief as the Court deems just and equitable.

Respectfully Submitted,
[Plaintiffs]

By:_____
One of Plaintiffs' Attorneys

APPENDIX B

An Example of a Community Use Policy

Community Use of School Facilities

The School District's buildings and grounds shall be made available to the people within the School District for activities if their use will benefit the students or residents of the District and will not interfere with the regular School District programs or activities.

Buildings and grounds are available, in the following priority, for the following usages. No other outside usages may be approved under this policy.

1. *Government-sponsored activities, through lease, intergovernmental agreement, or otherwise, by another governmental entity.*
2. *Early childhood education programs that primarily serve residents of the District and which are deemed by district administrators to be sufficiently designed and staffed to enable children to construct knowledge through meaningful relationships.*
3. *Recreational or social programs that primarily serve residents of the District.*

This policy effectively gives to other governmental entities such as a park district the right of first refusal on the use of school district facilities. It then prioritizes specific kinds of early childhood programs.

The policy should also provide a process by which the organization goes about applying to use the school's facilities. For example:

260

Persons who desire to use school facilities shall make application, in writing, to the Superintendent, and provide copies to the individual school Principal and Director of Buildings and Director of Buildings and Grounds. Usage shall be subject to payment of a rental rate. Rates for such charges shall be determined by the Board of Education and shall be on file at the Principal's office at each school. Rental charges may be waived when the user is an Early Childhood Education Provider, District Resident or Governmental Entity.

APPENDIX C

An Example of an Intergovernmental Agreement

The following is a template for an intergovernmental agreement between a school district and a park district in which the park district is willing to allow the school district to use park facilities to provide an early childhood education program in exchange for maintenance services:

A. Recitals

WHEREAS, the School and the Park are units of local government authorized to enter into this Intergovernmental Agreement; and

WHEREAS, the Park does currently own, and may acquire in the future, certain real property within the limits of and/or within two miles of its district boundaries; and

WHEREAS, the Park owns certain buildings on said real property within the boundaries of the District; and

WHEREAS, the School and the Park desire to enter into an Intergovernmental Agreement pursuant to which the School will fulfill certain responsibilities with respect to maintenance of the Park's property that is within the boundaries of the District; and

WHEREAS, the School and the Park further desire to enter into an Intergovernmental Agreement pursuant to which the School will provide to the Park certain maintenance services and pursuant to which the School will have permission to utilize the Park's buildings and grounds that are within the boundaries of the District for early childhood programs and activities, subject to certain restrictions and limitations; and

NOW, THEREFORE, for consideration set out below in this Agreement and other valuable consideration the receipt and sufficiency of which is hereby acknowledged and in the spirit of good faith and intergovernmental cooperation, the School and the Park agree as follows. . . .

B. The Term and Termination Clause

Typically, the term of such an agreement would be five years. The term clause often is related to the extension and termination provisions.

C. The Exchange of Consideration

The exchange of consideration clause is the core of the deal. When all is said and done, the park simply wants to allow the school to use its facilities in return for the school's maintenance services. The maintenance services are usually defined in exhibits incorporated by reference in the agreement. For instance, the park may be willing to give the school and its defined list of permittees the right to use its facilities for "supervised early childhood education programs and activities," but only when the park's facilities are not being used for other "recreational purposes." The agreement's language should clearly indicate that (1) the park gives the school the right to use its facilities whenever the park is not using those facilities for other recreational purposes; and (2) the park gives the school priority over all other users of its facilities.

D. Risk Allocation

As with most agreements that involve the use of property, an intergovernmental agreement typically contains provisions regarding indemnification and insurance for liability associated with the use of the property.

E. Incorporation and/or Preservation of Prior Agreements

This incorporation and/or preservation of prior agreements clause is a common term typically makes clear that the Agreement supersedes all prior agreements between the parties. This provision also preserves all other contracts entered by the school with other parties.

F. Discrimination

The discrimination clause is also important in intergovernmental agreements. It makes clear that any non-district user may not discriminate in violation of federal and state law. Such a clause is one way in which the school and the park district can try to insulate itself from any unlawful, discriminatory use of its facilities

APPENDIX D

A License Agreement

LICENSE AGREEMENT

THIS LICENSE AGREEMENT (hereinafter "License") made this ___ day of _____ ____, ___, between School District No. 100 (hereinafter "Licensor") and _____

Early Childhood Education Provider, a Nonprofit Corporation (hereinafter "Licensee") states the terms pursuant to which Licensor agrees to grant a License to Licensee to use the property (hereinafter defined as "Premises") described below for the purposes set forth below.

WHEREAS, Licensor is the owner of certain real property; and **WHEREAS,** Licensee desires to use certain real property of Licensor for a fee; and

WHEREAS, Licensor has the authority pursuant to the *School Code* and other implied authority to grant a license for the use of school property to suitable licensees for educational purposes and for any other purpose which serves the interests of the community when such property is declared to be temporarily unnecessary or unsuitable or inconvenient for a school or the uses of the Licensor and when the best interests of the residents of the Licensor will be enhanced by entering into such license; and

WHEREAS, Licensor has determined pursuant to the *School Code* that the aforementioned property is temporarily unnecessary, unsuitable, and inconvenient for school purposes for the term of this License and that the best interests of the residents of the Licensor will be enhanced by granting such License; and

WHEREAS, Licensee desires to use said Premises of Licensor, and Licensor desires to allow Licensee to use said Premises, for the purpose of operating a summer day camp; and

WHEREAS, Licensor has determined that the use of said property by Licensee will not interfere with or impede the normal operations of Licensor; and

WHEREAS, the parties mutually desire to enter into a written agreement defining their rights, duties and liabilities with respect to said Premises; and

WHEREAS, Licensor agrees to permit Licensee to use certain real property of Licensor subject to this License, Board Policy (Attachment Exhibit A) and the School Facilities Rental Form (Attachment Exhibit B), as such Policy and Form may be amended from time to time.

NOW, THEREFORE, in consideration of the mutual covenants and conditions set forth herein, it is agreed by the parties hereto as follows:

1. INCORPORATION OF PREAMBLES: The preambles are hereby incorporated into and made a part of this License.

2. PARTIES: Licensor's principal offices are located at 1000 Main St. Licensee's principal offices are located at 500 Camp Rd.

3. PREMISES: Licensor hereby grants to Licensee and Licensee hereby accepts from Licensor the non-exclusive right to use designated classrooms, the multipurpose room and portions of the fields and playgrounds at the School (the "Premises") as more specifically described in the School Facilities Rental Form attached hereto and incorporated herein, as Exhibit B, during the times set forth in Paragraph 5. Licensee shall also be permitted to use, on a non-exclusive basis, the restroom facilities indicated on Exhibit B. Licensee shall not have the exclusive right to use the Premises during the term of this License, except at the times stated herein, and Licensee's rights under this License are in the nature of a license to use the Premises. Further, Licensee shall have the non-exclusive right to use the parking lot for parking purposes, along with the refrigerators, art room and teachers' lounge located on or about the Premises and designated hallways and pathways for access to the Premises (the "Additional Facilities"). Use of the Additional Facilities and the Premises by Licensee, its employees, agents, participants, invitees, licensees or other persons for Licensee's business purposes shall be subject to reasonable regulation by the Licensor. This Licensor shall not confer upon Licensee the right to use any other areas or facilities other than those set forth in this License or on the attached Exhibit B, as incorporated herein. Throughout the remainder of this License, the Additional Facilities and the Premises are collectively referred to as the "Premises."

4. PROGRAM: Licensee agrees to provide an early childhood education program (hereinafter "Program") to serve the children of the District and the surrounding communities, electing to participate therein (hereinafter "Participants"). Licensee shall provide all necessary staffing, materials and management to effectively operate the Program. Licensor shall have the exclusive authority to determine whether the Licensee's program meets any and all of Licensor's standards, policies, requirements, and obligations.

5. PROGRAM SCHEDULE: Licensee will operate its Program from 7:00 a.m. to 8:00 p.m. Monday through Friday. Licensee may request thirty (30) days in advance, to use the Premises for evening parent meetings and conferences, subject to Licensor's approval. Licensee shall either remove or shall store in a cabinet provided on the Premises, promptly at the conclusion of the Program each day all personal property belonging to Licensee, its employees and Participants. Licensee may remain on the Premises no later than 8:30 p.m. for each day of the Program for the express purpose of straightening up, removing or storing materials.

6. EMPLOYMENT RELATIONSHIP: All staff members and volunteers of Licensee involved in the operation of the Program are the employees of Licensee for all purposes under this License and otherwise. Licensee is responsible for all compensation, employment and other taxes and filings. Nothing in this License or otherwise makes the Licensor the employer of the Licensee, its agents or staff.

7. SUPERVISION: Licensee shall be fully responsible for the implementation of its Program, and supervision and safety of all employees, Participants and invitees and licensees of the Program. Licensor shall not in any way be responsible for Licensee's Program or the supervision or safety of the employees, Participants, invitees or licensees of the Program.

8. PAYMENT OF FEE: Licensee agrees to pay a license fee (the "License Fee") for the term hereof, payable in equal installments on the first day of each month. In the event that this License Agreement is renewed, such License Fee shall be increased on an annual basis at a rate agreed by the parties. The parties acknowledge that the fee charged hereunder is solely to cover the costs incurred by Licensor and that Licensor is not letting the Premises for a profit.

9. UTILITIES: It is agreed that all utilities, including electricity, gas, sewer and disposal services are included in the License Fee, except as otherwise provided in Paragraph 13. Water will be provided to Licensee, at no additional charge, as long as Licensee does not exceed Licensee's consumption level for the same period of time as covered by this License (the "Level"). In the event that Licensee's consumption of water exceeds the Level, Licensee shall be responsible for the cost of providing such excess water.

10. CUSTODIAL SERVICES: Licensee shall be responsible for removing from the Premises, or storing in the provided cabinets, after each and every use, all Licensee's items, materials and equipment associated with the Program. Licensee is not otherwise permitted to leave on the Premises any of its belongings associated with the Program or otherwise. Licensee shall return the Premises to their original condition after each day's use. Licensee agrees to pay the charges for Licensor's custodial time if needed to clean the Premises as a result of Licensee's use, as determined by Licensor, in accordance with the fees set forth in attached Exhibit B.

11. NO ALTERATION OF PREMISES: Licensee shall not make any alterations to the Premises or any other of Licensor's property, except as specifically approved in advance in writing by Licensor.

12. RESTORATION OF DAMAGE: During the term of this License, Licensee shall repair and restore any damage to the Premises, or any other property of Licensor, including, but not limited to, walls, glass, frames and hardware in the doors and windows on the Premises, fixtures, plumbing, and flooring, which replacement or restoration shall be of a like kind and quality, to the extent such damage is caused by Licensee, its agents, employees, Participants, invitees, or licensees. Licensee shall not be obligated to repair or restore damage constituting ordinary wear and tear on the Premises. Licensor, at its own cost and expense, shall keep the heating, electrical, plumbing and all other mechanical equipment in good repair, condition and working order and shall furnish any and all parts, mechanisms and devices required therefore. Any major repairs or replacements to said mechanical equipment, to the roof, exterior walls and structural portions of the building, shall be made by the Licensor, subject to indemnification by Licensee as required by this License.

13. NO WASTE OR MISUSE: Licensee, its employees, agents, and/or Participants shall not allow waste, misuse or neglect of water or electricity on the Premises in excess of that required for the operation of the Program. Licensee will pay all costs caused by such waste or misuse, to be determined by the Licensor based on the documented written reports of usage generated by the utility companies.

14. PHONE: Licensee may use the telephone in the classroom on the Premises as well as public pay telephones on Licensor's property. Licensee shall reimburse Licensor for any charges incurred by the use of such phones, as reasonably determined by Licensor.

15. PERMITS: Licensee shall secure at its sole cost and expense appropriate accreditation or permits authorizing operation of the Program pending accreditation, prior to commencing the Program, and operate at all times under all other required licenses and permits. Failure to secure accreditation or to operate absent a valid license of permit will automatically terminate this License. Licensee shall provide proof of said accreditation to Licensor's Assistant Superintendent for Business and Operations before the commencement of the Program and from time to time as requested by Licensor. Additionally, Licensee shall abide by all applicable statutory requirements, and other applicable laws, rules and regulations and failure to do so will automatically terminate this License. Licensee also shall be responsible for conforming with all local building codes, ordinances and any other applicable legal requirements as well as securing any necessary permits, certificates and licenses in addition to any required accreditation. Licensor shall have no responsibility whatsoever for maintaining said licensure or for operating the Program in compliance therewith. Licensee shall ensure that all its employees undergo a criminal background investigation pursuant to statute, or as otherwise required by law, and shall provide copies of such criminal background investigations to Licensor.

16. REGULATION OF LICENSEE'S EMPLOYEES, PARTICIPANTS AND CLASSROOM: Licensor shall have the right to establish reasonable rules and regulations:

a. For the conduct of Licensee, its agents, employees, Participants, or persons entering or on Licensor's property, including the Premises.
b. For the reasonable use of the Premises. Licensor also shall have the right to prohibit certain of Licensee's agents, employees, Participants, invitees, licensees or others from entering on Licensor's Premises upon reasonable grounds.

17. SUBLETTING: Licensee shall neither sublet the Premises or any part thereof nor assign this License nor permit by any act or default any transfer of Licensee's interest by operation of law or contract, including, but not limited to, the granting of any mortgage on or security interest in Licensee's rights under this License, or other the Premises or any part thereof for lease or sublease, nor permit the use thereof for lease or sublease, nor permit the use thereof for any purpose other than as above mentioned, without, in each case, the written consent of Licensor.

18. INSURANCE: Licensee assumes full responsibility for providing at its expense any insurance to protect its property on the Premises. The Licensor shall not be liable for any defects in the building or on the Premises, or any loss or damages to the person or property of the Licensee or any of its agents, employees, Participants, invitees or licensees in or about the Premises, the building or other of Licensor's property, unless such loss or damage is caused by the negligent or wrongful act of Licensor or any of its employees. The Licensor further shall not be responsible for damages caused by any acts of Licensee, its employees, agents, Participants, invitees or licensees. Notwithstanding the foregoing, or any other provision in this License, nothing in this License shall be construed as a waiver by Licensor of its right to assert immunities under state or federal common law or statutes. Licensee shall maintain in full force and effect Commercial General Liability Insurance covering the operation of the Program, with One Million Dollars ($1,000,000) per occurrence coverage, a general aggregate limit of no less than Three Million Dollars ($3,000,000) and Two Million Dollars ($2,000,000) umbrella coverage. Licensee agrees to obtain and maintain in full force and effect Commercial Automobile Liability Insurance with limits of not less than One Million Dollars ($1,000,000) combined single limit for bodily injury and property damage, on all vehicles owned by Licensee or operated for purposes of the Program. Licensee's general liability and auto liability policies shall name Licensor, its individual Board of Education members, its employees, agents and volunteers as additional insureds. Licensee also agrees to obtain and maintain in full force and effect statutory Workers' Compensation Insurance. All policies must be on an occurrence basis and not a claims made basis. Prior to the commencement of the term of this License or any extensions thereof, and upon request, the Licensee shall provide the Licensor Certificates of Insurance evidencing proof of all insurance required, in a form satisfactory to Licensor, including but not limited to, a copy of the policy endorsement. All Certificates of Insurance shall state that the insurer shall provide Licensor a 30-day notice prior to cancellation, modification, material change or non-renewal of the policies.

19. COMPLIANCE WITH LAWS: Licensee shall comply with all applicable laws, including, but not limited to: local, state and federal tax laws; state and federal non-discrimination laws applicable to employees, Participants, invitees and licensees; workers' compensation laws and state and federal wage and hour laws. The rights and duties of Licensee and Licensor shall be controlled by all applicable State and Federal Laws.

20. GOVERNING LAW: This License and the rights and responsibilities of the parties hereto shall be interpreted and enforced in accordance with the laws of this State.

21. NONDISCRIMINATION: The Licensee agrees to fully comply with the requirements of the *State Human Rights Act,* including, but not limited to, the provision of sexual harassment policies and procedures. The Licensee further agrees to comply with all federal Equal Employment Opportunity Laws, including, but not limited to, the *Americans With Disabilities Act,* 42 U.S.C. Section 12101 et seq., and rules and regulations promulgated thereunder to the extent applicable to Licensee. Furthermore, Licensee agrees that it is responsible for ensuring that all programs, activities and Premises are accessible in accordance with the requirements of the *Americans With Disabilities Act* and other nondiscrimination laws, and shall ensure that the building, structure, or facilities used for the Program comply with such requirements. Licensor represents to Licensee as of the time of execution of this License that it has not received any notice that it is in violation of any local, state or federal law, including the requirements of *Americans With Disabilities Act,* with respect to the Premises.

22. INDEMNIFICATION FROM SUIT: Licensee agrees to indemnify, protect, release and hold harmless, and, at the option of the Licensor, defend, the Licensor, its agents, Board of Education members, administrative staff, employee, volunteer personnel and student teachers, and the Regional Board of School Trustees from any and all liability, claims, demands, actions and causes of action, of any kind, arising out of the operation of Licensee's

Program, including, but not limited to, administrative actions, civil rights damage claims and suits, constitutional rights damage claims and suits, and death and bodily injury and property damage claims and suits, including defense thereof and all legal expenses and attorneys' fees associated therewith, when damages, fees, fines or costs are sought for negligent or wrongful acts alleged to 1) have been committed by Licensee, its agents, administrative staff, employees, participants or invitees or licensees, or 2) otherwise arise from operation of the Program, participation in the Program or the nature or use of the Premises under this License. Licensee shall assume all such losses, damages, injuries, claims, demands and expenses of the investigation, litigation, settlement or the defense of any suit or other legal or administrative proceedings brought and shall satisfy judgments entered in any such suit or suits or other legal proceedings. The indemnities and assumptions of liabilities or obligations herein provided for shall continue in full force and effect notwithstanding the termination of this License.

23. TERM: The term of this License shall commence on June 1 of this year attendance and shall extend through August 20 of next year. If this License is not extended during its term and thereafter Licensee wishes to use the Premises on terms and conditions similar to those contained herein, Licensee shall notify the Licensor by February 1st the next year of Licensee's desire to re-enter into a similar License Agreement. The Licensor shall notify the Licensee by May 31 of that year, whether it will agree to such renewal.

24. TERMINATION: If Licensee defaults in the payment of the License Fee, or any part thereof, or breaches any other covenant herein contained to be kept by Licensee, then Licensor shall have the right to declare this License terminated if such default is not cured within fourteen (14) days following written notice from Licensor to Licensee; provided, however, that if such default cannot reasonably be cured within said fourteen (14) day period, Licensee shall have such other time as may be reasonably necessary to cure so long as Licensee has promptly and diligently undertaken to cure such default within the required fourteen (14) day period. Licensee may also terminate the License, upon fourteen (14) days prior written notice if the Premises are determined not to meet the facility requirements of the State Department of Children and Family Services, to the extent applicable to this Program, or those required by licensure. Licensee shall, upon termination of the License, by lapse of time or otherwise, return the Premises, and all keys thereto, and any school equipment provided by Licensor, to Licensor in the same condition as received by Licensee at the commencement of the term of this License, ordinary wear and tear and acts of God excepted. Any repairs or replacements made necessary by the waste or misuse of the Premises by Licensee, its agents, employees, Participants or invitees and licensees, shall be made promptly by the Licensee, at its own expense and in a manner to prevent liens from attaching to the property or Licensor's funds, as a result thereof. At the termination of the License, by lapse of time or otherwise, Licensee agrees to yield up immediate and peaceable possession to Licensor.

25. RIGHT OF REMOVAL: The Licensor shall have the right to temporarily remove Licensee, under emergency situations, as determined by Licensor, or to honor other priority lease or license agreements or responsibilities as referred to in Paragraph 5 of this License, with as much notice as is possible. In such event, Licensor shall endeavor to move Licensee to another comparable Licensor building and Licensee shall have exclusive use, if possible, of that building and adjacent field, in accordance with the terms of this License. If Licensor is unable to secure another location for the Licensee that is comparable to the Premises, then Licensee shall be entitled to the remedies set forth in Paragraph 26.

26. LIMITATION OF RECOVERY: In the event Licensee is prohibited from using the Premises by Licensor for any reason and Licensor is unable to find a comparable site for Licensee's use, Licensee's relief is limited to a refund of any pre-paid License fee for the number of days for which use is prohibited.

27. INFORMATIONAL SIGNS: Licensee shall have the right to place informational signs in or about the Premises. Licensor reserves the right to approve the placement, size, and content of the exterior signs only.

28. USE OF LICENSOR'S NAME: Licensee shall not use the name of the Board of Education of School District No. 100, or any references to the Board, the District, or its employees, in any advertising, signage, promotional or informational material or other communications without the express, written permission of the Licensor.

29. PLURALS, SUCCESSORS: The words "Licensor" and "Licensee" wherever used in this License shall be construed to mean Licensors or Licensees in all cases where there is more than one Licensor or Licensee, and to apply to individuals, male or female, or to firms or corporations. This Licensee shall be binding upon, apply and inure to the benefit of Licensor and Licensee and their respective heirs, legal representatives, successors and assigns.

30. AMENDMENTS: No modifications or amendments or waiver of any provision hereto shall be valid and binding unless in writing and signed by both parties.

31. COMPLETE UNDERSTANDING: This License, Board Policy (Exhibit A), as it may be amended from time to time, and the School Facilities Rental Form (Exhibit B), as it may be amended from time to time, set forth all the terms and conditions, and agreements and understandings between Licensor and Licensee relative to the subject matter hereof, and there are not agreements or conditions, either oral or written, expressed or implied, between them other than as herein set forth. In the event of conflict between the provisions of this License and any other documents referenced in this paragraph, the provisions of this Licensee shall control.

About the Authors

Each one of the authors of this book has experience as a practicing lawyer, a teacher, and an administrator.

Michael J. Kaufman, J.D., M.A., is the Dean for Academic Affairs and Professor of Law at Loyola University Chicago School of Law. He founded and directs Loyola University Chicago's Education Law and Policy Institute. Dean Kaufman has written more than fifty books and countless articles in the areas of his expertise, including education law and policy. With his co-author Sherelyn R. Kaufman, he has published the education law and policy textbook that is used in Law School and Education School classes throughout the world. Dean Kaufman also was elected to the Board of Education of a large, diverse public school district in the Chicago area, where he served for 12 years as the board's president and vice president.

Sherelyn R. Kaufman, J.D., M.A.T., is a professor on the adjunct faculty at the Erikson Institute Graduate School of Child Development. She practiced education law in private law firms for many years before joining the United States Department of Education, Office for Civil Rights. After her tenure at the Department of Education, Professor Kaufman pursued and received advanced degrees and certifications in teaching and early childhood administration. She has taught at virtually every grade level, from early childhood education through graduate school. She served as the director of a not-for-profit early childhood education program for six years and is frequently asked to provide expert consulting to early childhood programs.

Elizabeth C. Nelson, J.D. M.A.T., is a professor on the adjunct faculty at Loyola University Chicago School of Law, specializing in education law and policy, as well as professional skills development. She has practiced law in the Office of the Attorney General for the State of Illinois and worked on complex matters involving the education and welfare of children in private law firms and at the Office of the Public Guardian. Professor Nelson also taught third grade in the city of Chicago and has created and directed research conferences and academic programs dedicated to issues involving education law and policy.